Elizabethan World

Biographies

Elizabethan World

Biographies

Elizabeth Shostak

Sonia G. Benson, Contributing Writer

Jennifer York Stock, Project Editor

U·X·L

An imprint of Thomson Gale,
a part of The Thomson Corporation

Detroit • New York • San Francisco • New Haven, Conn. • Waterville, Maine • London

Elizabethan World: Biographies

Elizabeth Shostak and Sonia G. Benson

Project Editor
Jennifer York Stock

Editorial
Kate Potthoff

Rights and Acquisitions
Margaret Chamberlain-Gaston,
Lisa Kincade

Imaging and Multimedia
Lezlie Light, Michael Logusz, Kelly Quin

Product Design
Pamela Galbreath, Jennifer Wahi

Composition
Evi Seoud

Manufacturing
Rita Wimberley

LIBRARY OF CONGRESS CATALOGING-IN-PUBLICATION DATA

Shostak, Elizabeth, 1951–
   Elizabethan world--biographies / Elizabeth Shostak; Sonia G. Benson, contributing writer.
     p. cm. — (Elizabethan world reference library)
   Includes bibliographical references and index.
   ISBN-13: 978-1-4144-0190-4 (hardcover : alk. paper)
   ISBN-10: 1-4144-0190-6 (hardcover : alk. paper)
   ISBN-13: 978-1-4144-0188-1 (reference library set : alk. paper)
   ISBN-10: 1-4144-0188-4 (reference library set : alk. paper)
   1. Great Britain–History–Elizabeth, 1558-1603–Biography–Juvenile literature. I. Benson,
Sonia. II. Title.
   DA358.A1S56 2006
   942.05'50922–dc22
                                                                      2006019438

This title is also available as an e-book.
ISBN-13: 978-1-4144-1038-8 (set), ISBN-10: 1-4144-1038-7 (set)
Contact your Thomson Gale sales representative for ordering information.
Printed in the United States of America

10 9 8 7 6 5 4 3 2 1

Table of Contents

Reader's Guide

When Elizabeth I (1533–1603) was crowned queen in 1558, England was, compared to other European nations, a poor and backward country. At this time England was deeply divided by religious strife. It was too weak to protect itself from its enemies, lacking a strong military. Furthermore, England had been too beleaguered by its conflicts to participate in the Renaissance, the great artistic and intellectual movement that had swept Europe beginning in the fourteenth century. The people of England must have wondered what the inexperienced twenty-five-year-old queen could possibly do to strengthen her nation.

Nonetheless, when people today think of the Elizabethan Era most envision the dazzling, red-headed queen skillfully reigning over a vibrant court lively with music and dance, splendid costumes, and dashing young statesmen, explorers, and artists. Soon after she took the throne, Elizabeth's moderate religious settlement eased some of the divisions between Protestants and Catholics that had been tearing the nation apart, providing England with a stability that allowed it to grow in many directions. During Elizabeth's reign commerce flourished. London became one of Europe's largest and greatest cities. The era produced unparalleled advances drama, and not surprisingly, the Elizabethan Era has become known as the age of Shakespeare in honor of its leading dramatist and poet. There was growth in other spheres as well. As the new middle class developed, public education advanced, and England experienced a higher level of literacy than ever before. This made it possible for people who were not born into the nobility to rise in position. Elizabeth's reign also marked the beginning of English exploration of the New World. Militarily, Elizabethans restored England to its place as a major European power. When the Spanish Armada arrived in the English Channel in 1588 hoping to invade England, Elizabeth's small but highly skilled navy was up to the task of defending the small island from the world's largest power. The English people celebrated the victory with a new sense of pride in their nationality.

Historians differ greatly over how much credit to give Elizabeth for all the advances that occurred during her reign. Many elements of change were clearly already in process. Although we will probably never determine the extent of her contribution, her story has nevertheless fascinated historians worldwide for centuries after her death. The story of Elizabethan England provides valuable insight not only into English history, but also into the transition of Western society into modern times.

Coverage and features

Elizabethan World: Biographies profiles twenty-six significant figures who participated in the transformation of England during the Elizabethan Era. Included are some of Elizabeth's favorites, the statesmen to whom she gave great powers and advantages and who helped her run her country, such as Robert Dudley and Robert Devereux; the sea traders and explorers who opened up the New World and other trade routes, including John Hawkins, Francis Drake, and Walter Raleigh; the scientists, philosophers, and educators who brought England's medieval thinking to new, non-religious inquiry, such as Francis Bacon, Richard Hakluyt, and John Dee. Also featured are the royal opponents of the queen, such as Mary Stuart, Queen of Scots, and King Philip II of Spain; Catholic and Protestant leaders like William Allen and John Knox; and the great writers of the day, including Christopher Marlowe, Philip Sidney, and William Shakespeare. The volume includes fifty photographs and illustrations, a timeline, and sources for further reading.

U•X•L Elizabethan World Reference Library

Elizabethan World: Almanac presents an overview of this golden age of English history and the remarkable cultural, political, religious, and economic developments that occurred during the era. The volume's twelve chapters briefly examine the Tudor monarchy prior to Elizabeth, especially the difficult path from Catholicism to Protestantism beginning in the reign of Elizabeth's father, Henry VIII, and the tumultuous short reigns of her half brother, the Protestant Edward VI, and half-sister, the Catholic Mary Tudor. The achievements of Queen Elizabeth and her talented group of statesmen, such as William Cecil, Robert Dudley, and Francis Walsingham, are presented, including the religious settlement of 1559 and the conflicts with Scotland, Ireland, and Spain. Elizabeth's conflict with Catholics of England and Europe, and some of the conspiracies to overthrow her rule, are also featured. In addition, the *Almanac* places significant emphasis on the culture of the times, from Elizabeth's court to the rural pageants, and from the New World explorations to the remarkable flowering of literature and drama for which the era is renowned. Finally, the volume presents a look at Elizabethan daily life, social structures, holidays, and much more. The volume includes nearly sixty photographs and illustrations, a timeline, a glossary, research and activity ideas, and sources for further reading.

Elizabethan World: Primary Sources presents eighteen full or excerpted written works, speeches, and other documents that were influential during the Elizabethan Era. Included are speeches and a poem by Elizabeth I; the Catholic pope's bull of 1570 directed against the English queen; and an excerpt from the sensational and highly influential *Book of Martyrs* by John Foxe. Several examples of the literature and journals of the times are featured, including memoirs from the ill-fated settlement in Roanoke, Virginia; an excerpt from Edmund Spenser's *Faerie Queene*, a Shakespeare play and two of his sonnets, and much more. Nearly fifty photographs and illustrations, sources for further reading, a timeline, and a list of and sources for further reading supplement the volume.

A cumulative index of all three volumes in the U•X•L Elizabethan World Reference Library is also available.

Comments and suggestions

We welcome your comments on *Elizabethan World: Biographies* and suggestions for other topics to consider. Please write: Editors, *Elizabethan World: Biographies,* U•X•L, 27500 Drake Rd. Farmington Hills, Michigan 48331-3535; call toll free: 1-800-877-4253; fax to 248-699-8097; or send e-mail via http://www.gale.com.

Timeline of Events

1494 The Treaty of Tordesillas divides the New World between Spain and Portugal.

1509 Henry VIII takes the English throne.

1512 Nicholaus Copernicus explains his heliocentric theory.

October 31, 1517 German monk Martin Luther nails to a church door his list of ninety-five statements attacking certain Roman Catholic practices.

1520s The Protestant Reformation movement sweeps through major parts of Europe.

1530s The Catholic Church refuses to grant Henry VIII a divorce from his first wife. Henry breaks with the church, declares himself head of the church in England, and marries Anne Bolelyn.

1536 John Calvin sets up his Protestant government in Geneva, Switzerland.

1536–40 Henry VIII closes England's monasteries.

1545–63 The Catholic Council of Trent holds numerous meetings.

1547 Henry VIII dies and Edward VI takes the English throne, establishing a Protestant kingdom.

1547 Catherine de Medici becomes queen of France.

1553 Edward VI dies; the Catholic **Mary I** takes the throne after the ill-fated nine-day reign of the Protestant Jane Grey.

1554 Mary I marries **Philip II**, heir to the Spanish throne.

February 1555 Mary I orders the burning at the stake of English subjects who refuse to accept Catholicism as their religion; in all three hundred Protestants are burned for their beliefs.

1558 Mary I dies; **Elizabeth I** takes the throne.

January 14, 1559 Elizabeth I makes her royal entry into the city of London on the eve of her coronation.

1559 Elizabeth establishes the Anglican Church, or the Church of England, with Parliament's approval.

1559 Scotish Protestant **John Knox** delivers his famous sermon at Perth.

Late-1550s–early-1560s A romance is rumored between Elizabeth and her Master of Horse, **Robert Dudley**.

1561 The Catholic **Mary Stuart** returns from France to take her place as the queen of a now-Protestant Scotland.

1562 English seaman **John Hawkins** begins a slave trade between Africa and the New World.

1562–89 The French Wars of Religion.

1564 Playwright **William Shakespeare** is born in Stratford-upon-Avon.

1567 The Scottish lords rise up against Mary Stuart for her scandalous behavior; she gives up the Scottish throne to her infant son and flees to England.

1568 Mary Stuart is placed under the watchful guardianship of George Talbot and his wife, **Bess of Hardwick**.

1568–1648 Eighty Years' War between Spain and the Netherlands.

1569 In the Northern Rising, Catholic rebels attempt to place Mary Stuart on the English throne.

1570 The Catholic pope issues a bull proclaiming that Elizabeth is not the rightful queen of England. He encourages English Catholics to rise up against her and to help Mary Stuart take the throne.

1570 The Church of England orders all major churches to obtain a copy of Foxe's *Book of Martyrs*.

1571 Elizabeth's government foils the Ridolfi scheme, in which English Catholics backed by the Roman Catholic church and Spain attempt to rise up against Elizabeth.

1572 Nicholas Hilliard paints his first portrait miniature of Queen Elizabeth, establishing a popular English art form.

1572 St. Batholomew's Day Massacre.

1575 Elizabeth grants a monopoly on printing music to royal musicians William Byrd and Thomas Tallis.

1576 Actor James Burbage erects England's first permanent structure designed specifically for staging plays, calling it simply The Theater.

1577 Explorer **Francis Drake** sets out on his historic round-the-world voyage.

1580 The Catholic pope calls for the murder of Elizabeth I.

1580 Philip II of Spain begins to assemble a large naval fleet, the Spanish Armada.

1581 Catholic missionary **Edmund Campion** is executed for treason.

1582 Astologer **John Dee**, with the help of Edward Kelley, studies the supernatural quality of crystals.

1583 Spymaster **Francis Walsingham** uncovers the Throckmorton Plot against Elizabeth.

1584 **William Allen** writes a pamplet defending English Catholics charged with treason.

1584–94 A small group of top professional playwrights arises in London; they are known as the University Wits.

1585 The ill-fated Roanoke, Virginia, colony is directed and financed by **Walter Raleigh** under a patent by Queen Elizabeth I to colonize America.

1586 Elizabeth sends English troops to support the Dutch uprising against Spain.

1587 Playwright **Christopher Marlowe** writes *Tamburlaine,* the first English tragedy to effectively use blank verse.

1588 The Spanish Armada sails into the English channel with a mission to invade England. After major sea fighting between the English and

Spanish, storms end the confrontation with heavy losses for the Spanish.

August 18, 1588 Elizabeth I gives her famous victory speech at Tilbury.

1588 Thomas Harriot, who was with the expedition to Roanoke, publishes *A Briefe and True Report,* the first book in English to describe the Americas.

1589 Richard Hakluyt publishes *The Principal Navigations, Voyages, and Discoveries of the English Nation.*

1590 Edmund Spenser publishes the first three books of his epic poem *The Faerie Queene.*

1591 Philip Sydney's sonnet sequence *Astrophil and Stella* is published after the poet's death.

1593 Irish pirate **Grace O'Malley** petitions Queen Elizabeth to be allowed to continue her seafaring activities.

1594–97 England's crops fail due to three seasons in a row of bad weather; a famine sets in.

1594–1603 England and Ireland fight the Nine Years War.

1598 Willliam Cecil, Elizabeth's long-time advisor, dies.

1599 Elizabeth sends her favorite companion, **Robert Devereux**, to Ireland to command England's forces in the war against the Irish rebels. Devereux badly botches the mission.

1600–01 Shakespeare writes *Hamlet,* which will become the most frequently performed, read, and discussed play in the English language.

1601 England enacts a stronger version of its poor laws in an attempt to combat growing poverty.

March 24, 1603 Elizabeth I dies after ruling England for forty-five years. James VI of Scotland takes the throne as **James I** of England.

1620 Francis Bacon publishes *Novum organum (New Instrument),* which presents the Baconian method.

Words to Know

alchemy: A science of medieval times that attempted to transform base metals into gold and find a potion for eternal life.

allegory: A story or painting that represents abstract ideas or principles as characters, figures, or events.

alliteration: Repetition of the same consonant at the beginning of words or syllables.

amphitheater: A large, semi-circular outdoor theater with seats rising in tiers from a central acting area.

angel: A spiritual being ranking superior to humans, but at the lowest level of heavenly beings.

ambassador: A high-ranking official who represents his or her own country to the government of another country.

archangel: A spiritual being ranked above the angels.

archbishop: The head bishop of a province or district.

armada: The Spanish word for a fleet of ships.

astrology: The study of the position of stars and planets in the belief that they influence human affairs and events on Earth.

astronomy: The scientific study of the stars, planets, and other celestial bodies.

B

bishop: A clergyman with a rank higher than a priest, who has the power to ordain priests and usually presides over a diocese.

blank verse: A type of poetry with regular meter (the pattern of stressed and unstressed syllables) but no rhyme.

bull: A written communication from the pope to all Catholics worldwide.

bureaucracy: Staff of administrative officials.

C

capitalism: An economic system in which private individuals or companies own and invest in the country's businesses and industries with little government control.

cardinal: A top official in the Roman Catholic Church, ranking just below the pope.

cartography: Mapmaking.

chiaroscuro: In drawing or painting, a method of depicting depth and space by contrasting light and dark and creating shadows.

civic: Relating to the rights and duties of citizens.

classical: Of or relating to the art, literature, architecture, and way of life of ancient Greece or Rome, roughly between 500 BCE and 500 CE.

clergy: Authorized religious leaders, such as priests and ministers.

colony: A group of people who settle far from home but remain at least partially under the rule of their homeland.

comedy: Plays written in a light and amusing manner that present the struggles and eventual successes of everyday heroes as they overcome non-life-threatening problems.

coronation: The crowning ceremony in which a monarch officially becomes king or queen.

courtier: A person who serves or participates in the royal court or household as the king's or queen's advisor, officer, or attendant.

D

dignitary: A person of high rank or importance.

diocese: A large church district made up of many parishes that falls under the administration of a bishop.

doctrine: A principle (or set of principles) held by a religious or philosophical group.

Elizabethan Era: The period associated with the reign of Queen Elizabeth I (1558–1603) that is often considered to be a golden age in English history.

empirical scientist: A scientific researcher who relies on observation and experiments rather than theory.

epic: A long poem that relates the deeds of a hero and is of particular importance to a culture or nation.

episcopal: Governed by bishops.

etiquette: The conduct expected to be followed in a social or official environment.

evangelical: A member of a Protestant group that believes salvation can be attained only through faith in Christ's sacrifice and God's mercy; that the Bible, particularly the first four books of the New Testament, is the supreme authority; and that people can achieve faith only through personal experience and preaching rather than through ceremonies and rituals.

famine: The scarcity of food causing widespread hunger and starvation.

farce: Comedy that presents absurd characters and scenes in order to make the audience laugh.

feudal lord: The landowner and ruler of a district during the Middle Ages (c. 500–c. 1500) to whom the villagers owed loyalty, military service, and labor.

fresco: A painting done on wet plaster.

gentry: Landowners who did not hold titles but were from influential families.

heliocentric: Relating to the principle that the sun is the center of the solar system, with the planets rotating around it.

heresy: A religious opinion that conflicts with the church's doctrines.

heretic: Someone who expresses an opinion that opposes established church doctrines.

hierarchy: Ranking, or classification, of beings according to some standard, such as ability, importance, or social standing.

history chronicle: A play based on historic people or events.

Holy Roman Empire: A loose confederation of states and territories, including the German states and most of central Europe, that existed from 962 to 1806 and was considered the supreme political body of the Christian people.

humanism: A cultural and intellectual movement during the Renaissance, following the rediscovery of the art and literature of ancient Greece and Rome, that focused on human values, interests, and welfare.

hypothesis: An explanation of natural phenomenon that has not yet been tested; a theory.

iambic foot: A unit of poetic meter that consists of one unstressed syllable followed by one stressed syllable, as in the sound of da-DUM.

iambic pentameter: A poetic line that contains five iambic units.

iconoclasm: The deliberate destruction of religious icons (sacred images, statues, objects, and monuments) usually for religious or political reasons.

idolatry: The worship of religious icons (sacred images, statues, objects, and monuments).

knight: A man granted a rank of honor by the monarch for his personal merit or service to the country.

lady-in-waiting: A woman in the queen's household who attends the queen.

latitude: Imaginary lines that run from east to west on the globe measuring the angular distance north or south from the Earth's equator, measured in degrees.

lay person: A person who is not a member of the clergy.

longitude: Imaginary lines drawn on globes or maps that run from north to south, measuring angular distance east or west of the prime meridian, measured in degrees.

lute: A plucked string instrument similar to a guitar but shaped like a pear, with six to thirteen strings and a deep round back.

madrigal: A polyphonic love song for four to six voices without musical accompaniment.

malnutrition: Ill health caused by not eating enough food or not eating the proper balance of nutrients.

martyr: A person who chooses to be punished or put to death rather than to abandon his or her religious beliefs.

masque: A short drama, usually full of music and dance, that presents an allegory.

meter: The pattern of stressed and unstressed syllables in poetry.

Middle Ages: The period of European history between ancient times and the Renaissance (c. 500–c. 1500).

missionary: A person sent by his or her church to help people of other countries and to convert nonbelievers to the church's doctrines.

monopoly: The exclusive right to trade with a particular market or group of markets.

mortality rate: The frequency of deaths in proportion to a specific population.

mystery play: A play enacting a scene or scenes from the Bible.

nationalism: Patriotism and loyalty to a person's own country.

navigation: The science of setting the course or direction of a ship to get it from one location to another.

nobles: Elite men and women who held social titles.

pageant: A dramatic presentation, such as a play, that often depicts a historical, biblical, or traditional event.

papal legate: A representative of the pope within a particular nation.

parish: The community served by one local church.

patron: Someone who financially sponsors, or supports, an artist, entertainer, or explorer.

patronage system: A system in which a person with a lot of power or wealth grants favors to, financially supports, enters into contracts with, or appoints to office people who in return must promise to give their political support or access to their artistic achievements.

peasant: A class of farmers who worked in the fields owned by wealthy lords. Part of the crop was paid to the lord as rent.

peer: A noble holding the title of duke, marquis, earl, viscount, or baron.

perspective: An artistic technique used to make a two-dimensional (flat) representation appear to be three-dimensional by considering how the objects within the picture relate to one another.

pious: Highly devoted to one's religion.

polyphony: Music with many voices; or the mixing together of several melodic lines at the same time in a musical composition.

presbyterian: Governed by presbyters, or church elders.

progress: A royal procession, or trip, made by a monarch and a large number of his or her attendants.

privateers: Seafarers who own and operate their own ships independently but are authorized by their government to raid the ships of enemy nations, often capturing the entire ship with all its cargo.

Privy Council: The board of advisors that carried out the administrative function of the government in matters of economy, defense, foreign policy, and law and order, and its members served as the king's or queen's chief advisors.

prose: Ordinary speech or writing; not poetry.

Protestant: A member of one of the western Christian churches that, following reform doctrines, broke away from the Roman Catholic Church in the sixteenth century.

Protestant Reformation: Also known as the Reformation; a sixteenth-century religious movement that aimed to reform the Roman Catholic Church and resulted in the establishment of Protestant churches.

Puritans: A group of Protestants who follow strict religious standards.

rational: Based on reason rather than on spiritual belief or church authority.

Reformation: A sixteenth-century religious movement that aimed to reform the Roman Catholic Church and resulted in the establishment of Protestant churches.

regent: Someone who rules for a king or queen when the monarch is absent, too young, or unable to rule.

Renaissance: The era beginning around 1350 in Europe, in which scholars turned their attention to classical Greek and Latin learning and shifted to a more rational (based on reason rather than spiritual belief or church authority) approach to philosophy, religion, and science.

retinue: Group of attendants.

revenge tragedy: A play concerned the theme of vengeance for a past wrong—usually murder.

rhyme scheme: The pattern of rhymes in a poem.

ritual: An established ceremony performed in precise ways according to the rules of the church.

romance: A literary work about improbable events involving characters that are quite different from ordinary people.

S

saint: A deceased person who, due to his or her exceptionally good behavior during life, receives the official blessing of the church and is believed to be capable of interceding with God to protect people on earth.

salvation: In Christianity, deliverance from sin and punishment.

scholasticism: An effort to reconcile the teachings of the ancient classical philosophers with medieval Christian theology.

secular: Non-religious.

seminary: A school similar to a university that trains students in religion, usually to prepare them to become members of the clergy.

seraphim: The top level of angels, ranking closest to God.

shire: County.

simile: A comparison between unlike things usually using the words "like" or "as".

soliloquy: A speech in which a character, alone on stage, expresses his or her thoughts aloud.

stanza: A group of lines that form a section of a poem.

sumptuary laws: Statutes regulating how extravagantly people of the various social classes could dress.

symmetrical: Balanced, with the same-sized parts on each side.

T

theocracy: A state governed by religious, rather than political, principles.

Tower of London: A fortress on the Thames River in London that was used as a royal residence, treasury, and, most famously, as a prison for the upper class.

tragedy: Drama of a serious nature, usually featuring an admirable but flawed hero who undergoes a serious struggle ending in a devastating downfall.

transubstantiation: In Roman Catholic doctrine, the miraculous change that occurs when a priest blesses the Eucharist (bread and wine) and it changes into the body and blood of Christ, while maintaining the appearance of bread and wine.

vagrant: A person who wanders from town to town without a home or steady employment.

virginal: A small, legless, and rectangular keyboard instrument related to the harpsichord.

Elizabethan World

Biographies

William Allen

BORN: 1532 • Rossall, Lancashire England

DIED: October 16, 1594 • Rome, Italy

English cardinal; scholar

"[My students] not only hold the heretics in perfect detestation, but they also marvel and feel sorrow of heart that there should be any found so wicked, simple and reckless of their salvation."

William Allen. © ANN RONAN PICTURE LIBRARY/HIP/THE IMAGE WORKS.

William Allen was the head of the Roman Catholic Church in England during the years when Catholics were harshly persecuted under the rule of **Queen Elizabeth I** (1533–1603; see entry). Because Catholics were not allowed to practice their religion legally in England, Allen left the country. In exile in Europe, he became the leader of England's Catholics and worked to restore Catholicism in England. He established training schools for English Catholic priests in Europe, and he arranged for them to return to England and minister to Catholics there in secret. Many of these priests were captured by the English government and put to death as traitors. Though Allen did not succeed in his plan to restore Catholicism to legal status in England, his work did ensure that the religion did not die out as English government authorities hoped it would.

Studied for the priesthood

William Allen, the third son of John Allen, was born in Rossall, Lancashire, in 1532. When he was fifteen Allen was sent to Oriel College at Oxford University. An outstanding student, he completed his bachelor's degree in 1550 and was elected a fellow, or senior member, of Oriel College. In 1554 he earned his master's degree, and in 1556 he became principal of St. Mary's Hall at the university. He also served as a canon, or member, of York Cathedral.

Allen planned to pursue a career in the church, as was customary among those who received a university education during this period. But just as he was completing his studies and preparing to become a priest, the question of religious loyalty became a matter of great political importance. **King Henry VIII** (1491–1547; see entry) had broken away from the Catholic Church in the 1530s, refusing to acknowledge the authority of the pope. (The pope is the head of the Catholic Church.) Instead, Henry declared himself the head of the church in England. Those who wished to continue practicing their religion under the traditional leadership of the pope were often suspected of disloyalty to the king, and they were subjected to fines and imprisonment.

Henry's daughter, **Mary I** (1516–1558; see entry), was a devout Catholic, and when she became queen in 1553 she made Catholicism legal once again. But many government advisors disapproved of this move because they believed it made England vulnerable to the influence of Spain, a rival country that was strongly Catholic. When Mary died and Elizabeth ascended to the throne in 1558, Elizabeth declared Protestantism the official religion of the nation. She established the Anglican Church (also known as the Church of England) as the official church of the country. Anyone who wanted a career in politics or the church had to sign the Oath of Supremacy, a document stating that they accepted the queen as the head of the church.

Allen, a committed Catholic, refused to sign this oath. Realizing that he would not be able to continue his career in England, he went to Louvain (also spelled Leuven), Belgium, in 1561. Many English Catholic students had fled to this university town after Elizabeth outlawed the practice of their religion in England. Allen joined them and continued his studies in theology. He also began to write religious essays. By 1562 he had returned to England to help reestablish Catholicism there. He had not yet been made a priest, but he wanted to support people who wished to remain loyal Catholics. He encountered many people who told him that they had become Protestants against their will. They had sworn the Oath of Supremacy only to keep the government from seizing their homes and possessions, not because they truly wished to become members of this new church. This experience convinced Allen that the majority of English people would prefer to go back to the Catholic Church, and that Protestant rule would be a temporary thing.

The queen's advisors soon discovered that Allen was in the country. Since any attempt to bring people back to Catholicism was against the law, Allen risked serious danger to himself by continuing his work. He went back to Oxford, where he had the opportunity to speak with students who were interested in his ideas about religion. Later he was forced to seek protection from the Duke of Norfolk's family in Norfolk. In 1565, fearing arrest, he returned to Belgium.

Establishes seminary at Douai

Allen was ordained a priest in Belgium, and he began to teach theology in the Catholic college in Malines (now Mechlin). In 1560 he was appointed a professor of divinity at the University of Douai, a Catholic institution that had been founded by **King Philip II** (1527–1598; see entry) of Spain in 1559. As was the case in Louvain, many English Catholics had found their way to this university in order to continue studying for the priesthood. Seeing a need to unite these English students in their own particular college, Allen traveled to Rome in 1567. He hoped to persuade the pope to allow him to establish a seminary, a type of college that trained men for the priesthood, specifically for English students in Europe. The priests who graduated from this seminary could then return to England once Catholicism was restored there. The pope agreed, and Allen returned to Douai, a city that is now part of northern France but was then under Spanish rule, to open his new seminary.

Within just a few years, more than 150 students were enrolled at Allen's seminary. In addition to Latin, they studied Greek and Hebrew, the original languages in which the Bible was written. Allen instituted this course of study to make sure that students would not be influenced by Anglican ideas about the scriptures, some of which might be found in the Latin translations of the Bible. Seminary students read through the Old Testament, the first half of the Bible, at least twelve times. They read through the entire New Testament, the second portion of the Bible, at least sixteen times. Allen believed that this rigorous course of study would, as quoted in Alice Hogge's *God's Secret Agents: Queen Elizabeth's Forbidden Priests and the Hatching of the Gunpowder Plot*, ensure that his priests would "all know better how to prove our doctrines by argument and to refute the contrary opinion."

Allen and the other professors wrote and published numerous articles about theology. One of the most important scholarly works to come from the seminary at Douai was an English translation of the Bible. The New Testament portion was published in 1582, and the Old Testament translation was completed in 1609. The Douai Bible, based on the Latin translation of original Hebrew texts, became the Catholic Church's official English version of the Bible.

In 1576 the pope asked Allen to help establish a second English seminary, this one to be located in Rome. Allen accepted this assignment and then returned to Douai. But the situation there was no longer safe. The English government had reportedly sent spies to Europe to assassinate Allen. In addition, Spain was growing increasingly distrustful of England, and Belgian authorities began to believe rumors that students at the Douai seminary were undercover agents of the queen. In 1578 the students were expelled from Douai, and Allen was forced to move the seminary to Rheims, in France.

Sends missionaries to England

The two schools trained hundreds of priests, many of whom eventually returned to England to work as missionaries. (Missionaries are people sent by the church to help people of other countries and convert non-believers to the church's doctrines.) This had not been Allen's original goal. At first he had planned only to train priests who would be ready to return to England when it became legal to do so. But Allen realized that Catholics in England could not wait, and that they needed priests to support them immediately. So he developed plans to send priests back to England in violation of the law. In 1580 the first two priests, Robert Persons (1546–1610) and **Edmund Campion** (1540–1581; see entry), who were both members of the Jesuit order, crossed the English Channel and began their missionary work. By late 1581 Campion had been captured and condemned to death. His execution made Allen and his students even more determined to restore Catholicism to England. During the 1580s, 438 priests who had studied at the English College at Douai were sent to England. Ninety-eight of them were executed, and many others were imprisoned.

Robert Persons

Robert Persons often worked closely with William Allen on plans to restore the legality of the Roman Catholic religion in England. Born in Somerset, England, in 1546, Persons began a promising career at Oxford University but, partly because he was a Catholic, was forced to resign. He was known to be stubborn, argumentative, and willing to take risks. He traveled to Italy, where he began studying medicine. After two years, however, he changed his mind and joined the Jesuit order of priests in 1575. Persons soon began trying to persuade Jesuit leaders to begin missionary work in England. In 1580 Persons led a secret mission there with his fellow Jesuit Edmund Campion. They were ordered to minister to English people who wished to remain Catholics, despite the law banning practice of the religion. When Campion was captured, Persons returned to Europe. He spent the rest of his life in exile there.

Persons founded several seminaries in Spain, as well as a school for English Catholic boys in France. He established another English Catholic school at St. Omers, France in 1594; this institution later moved to Stonyhurst Hall in Lancashire, England. Stonyhurst became one of the largest Catholic colleges in the country. Persons published many books, the best-known of which was

Robert Persons. PUBLIC DOMAIN.

The Book of Resolution. When Allen died in 1594 Persons hoped that the pope would appoint him the new head of the Catholic Church in England. But Persons did not receive this honor. He died in 1610 in Rome.

In 1584 Allen wrote a pamphlet defending English Catholics from the charge of treason brought against them by the queen's advisor, **William Cecil** (Lord Burghley; 1520–1598; see entry). In 1585 Allen went to Rome once more with Robert Persons. War between England and Spain now seemed inevitable, and Persons hoped that English Catholic missionaries could ally themselves with Spain and work to overthrow Elizabeth. He convinced Allen to support this plan. Allen had given up hope that Catholicism could be restored in England by peaceful means, and he published works that urged rebellion against the queen. In 1587 he wrote a book defending Sir William Stanley (1548–1630), an English military leader who had captured the city of Deventer, Netherlands, for the English but then surrendered to Spain and pledged allegiance to the Spanish king. Allen wrote that this action was justified because Elizabeth was a heretic, a person whose religious opinions conflict with the doctrines of the Catholic Church.

Conspires with Spain

After Elizabeth's Catholic cousin, **Mary Stuart** (Queen of Scots; 1542–1587; see entry), was executed in 1587 for her part in an assassination plot against Elizabeth, Allen saw his chance. He wrote to King Philip II, urging him to attack England and reestablish the Catholic Church there. Allen also wrote a book, *An Admonition to the Nobility and People of England and Ireland Concerning the Present Warres [Wars] made for the execution of his Holines Sentence, by the highe and mightie Kinge Catholike of Spaine.* It described Queen Elizabeth as an "incestuous bastard, begotten and born in sin of an infamous courtesan" (quoted by J. P. Sommerville). It also urged the English to rise up against the queen and surrender to the Spanish army. This book, known simply as *Allen's Admonition*, had been prepared in hopes that Spain's planned invasion of England in 1588 would succeed. With a much larger navy, Spain had every reason to believe it would easily conquer England.

Allen, who led the English Catholic Church even though he lived in exile, helped to plan this invasion and hoped that it would advance his career. The pope had made him a cardinal, the highest position in the church except for pope, in 1587. After Spain conquered England, Allen hoped to become Archbishop of Canterbury and Lord Chancellor of England—positions that would have made him one of the most powerful men in the country. But the invasion failed. Several battles were fought in the English Channel, with neither side winning a clear advantage. Then the weather intervened. First, strong winds blew the Spanish Armada, or navy, off course. Retreating to Spain by sailing around Ireland, the Armada was caught in a severe hurricane—a type of storm unusual in those northern seas. Many ships were destroyed. The English considered the defeat of the Armada as a sign that God approved of Elizabeth's reign. Little hope remained that Catholicism could be restored as England's official religion.

In 1589 Allen helped establish a new English seminary in Valladolid, Spain. He spent his remaining years in Rome, but he continued to keep in touch with Catholics in England. He was named Librarian of the Holy Roman Church by Pope Gregory XIV (1535–1591). Allen participated in four church conclaves, meetings in which cardinals discuss and vote on important church matters such as the election of a new pope. But after the defeat of the Armada, Allen's influence among church leaders decreased. He lived the rest of his life in poverty and debt. He died on October 16, 1594, and he was buried in Holy Trinity Chapel at the English College in Rome.

Late in his life Allen expressed some doubts about his decision to send Jesuit missionaries to England. This mission, he realized, had given the English government a reason to suspect his seminary students of treason. This suspicion increased the danger to his priests. When Allen died English Catholics found themselves without effective leadership.

For More Information

BOOKS

Hogge, Alice. *God's Secret Agents: Queen Elizabeth's Forbidden Priests and the Hatching of the Gunpowder Plot.* New York: HarperCollins, 2005.

WEB SITES

"History of the Douay Rheims Bible." http://www.speakingbible.com/ douay_rheims/about.htm#history (accessed on July 11, 2006).

Sommerville, J. P. "History 123 Lecture Notes." *University of Wisconsin Madison.* http://history.wisc.edu/sommerville/123/123%20263% 201580s%20%2090s.htm (accessed on July 11, 2006).

"William Allen." *Catholic Encyclopedia.* http://www.newadvent.org/cathen/ 01322b.htm (accessed on July 11, 2006).

Francis Bacon

BORN: January 22, 1561 • London, England

DIED: April 9, 1626 • London, England

English philosopher; statesman

"Knowledge is power."

Francis Bacon is considered the most important English thinker of the Elizabethan Era, the period associated with the reign of Queen Elizabeth I (1558–1603) that is often considered to be a golden age in English history. He believed that knowledge should come from direct observation of the world. He rejected traditional ways of teaching because they were not founded on scientific methods, and he argued that education should be based on active observation and experimentation. His theories deeply influenced other thinkers of the time and helped to introduce modern methods of learning. Bacon also held various government posts in the courts of **Elizabeth I** (1533–1603; see entry) and her successor, **James I** (1566–1625; see entry).

Though Bacon enjoyed great prestige, wealth, and power, he spent the last few years of his life in social disgrace after being convicted of political corruption. Nevertheless, he continued to write and publish works that provoked intense debate among leading scholars. He is remembered today for his contributions both

Francis Bacon. PUBLIC DOMAIN.

9

to English literature and to the development of modern scientific thinking.

Born into influential family

Francis Bacon was born in London, in 1561. Bacon's family was extremely powerful and influential. His father, Sir Nicholas Bacon (1510–1579), was lord keeper of the great seal of England. His mother, Anne Cooke (1533–1610) was the daughter of Sir Anthony Cooke (1505–1576), who had served as tutor to Edward VI (1537–1553). The Cooke household valued education and maintained close connections with the royal court. Anne's sister, for example, was married to Queen Elizabeth's principal advisor, **William Cecil** (Lord Burghley; 1520–1598; see entry). Francis and his older brother, Anthony (1558–1601), grew up surrounded by some of the most important political figures of the time.

Bacon and his brother spent most of their childhood at their father's big country house in Gorhambury, Hertfordshire. When Anthony was fourteen, he entered Trinity College at Cambridge University. Though Francis was only twelve, he went with his brother and also enrolled as a student. Francis finished his studies at Cambridge in 1575 without completing a degree. He then began his training as a lawyer at Gray's Inn, London. While still a student Bacon went to France for two and a half years to serve the English ambassador. He returned to England after his father's death in 1579 and resumed studying at Gray's Inn. He became a lawyer in 1584.

That same year Bacon was elected to his first term in Parliament, the English legislature. One of his most notable actions as a member of Parliament was to speak in favor of the execution of **Mary Stuart** (Queen of Scots; 1542–1587; see entry). A Roman Catholic cousin of Elizabeth, Mary had been involved in a plot to assassinate the queen. Though Mary was found guilty of treason, the question of her sentence was controversial. If the English government put her to death, this action would threaten the authority of the monarchy. Mary was a legitimate queen. By authorizing Mary's execution, Elizabeth would be establishing the legal right of a head of state to execute another sovereign monarch. This precedent, she feared, would weaken the principle that monarchs could not be subjected to the death sentence for treason. Bacon sided with those who insisted that Mary be executed.

Gains support from queen's favorite

Bacon also served on various parliamentary committees and as a legal consultant. In 1589 he was named Clerk of Star Chamber, a law court at Westminster Palace. Historians think it is likely that his uncle, William Cecil, helped him get this job. Bacon also served as Queen's Counsel (attorney), but Elizabeth never made this a formal appointment. Though these were respectable jobs, they did not pay very much. Bacon, who had expensive tastes and wished to live in luxury, wanted more income. He tried to persuade one of the queen's favorite advisors, **Robert Devereux** (Earl of Essex; 1566–1601; see entry), to help him get a higher appointment in the government. Although Devereux recommended Bacon very highly to the queen, she chose not to appoint him to any additional positions.

Devereux continued to be one of Bacon's most powerful supporters. From 1592 to 1601 Bacon worked in Devereux's service. One of his tasks was to compose masques to entertain Devereux's friends. (Masques are staged performances featuring music, poetry, song, and dance.) In 1592 Bacon composed such a masque, "In Praise of Knowledge," for Elizabeth in honor of the anniversary of her coronation, or crowing as queen. This masque contained flattering language about the queen, honoring her deep respect for learning. Bacon had also flattered the queen by dedicating an earlier composition, "Maxims of the Law," to her. Bacon received many favors from Devereux during his service. However, when Devereux was arrested for treason in 1601, Bacon joined the government in prosecuting him. Elizabeth asked Bacon to be her lawyer in the case against Devereux, and Bacon agreed. Devereux was found guilty and was sentenced to death. Though many people considered Bacon's actions a betrayal of his friend and supporter, Bacon argued that he was obeying his duty to his queen.

Bacon's career and finances improved dramatically after Elizabeth's death. When James I took the throne in 1603, he made Bacon a knight. (A knight is a man granted a rank of honor by the monarch for his personal merit or service to the country.) Four years later the king named him solicitor general. In 1613 the king made Bacon attorney general, and in 1616 he appointed Bacon a member of the Privy Council, the board of advisors that carried out the administrative function of the government in matters of economy, defense, foreign policy, and law and order, and its members served as the king's chief advisors. In 1617 Bacon was given the position his father had once held, lord keeper of the great seal. He became

Was Bacon the Real Shakespeare?

William Shakespeare (1564–1616; see entry) is the most famous playwright of the Elizabethan Era. Because few records remain of Shakespeare's life, some scholars began to question whether it was actually Shakespeare or someone else who wrote his famous plays. Starting in the mid-1800s, some scholars began to suggest that Francis Bacon was the real author of Shakespeare's plays. Shakespeare, they reasoned, did not have enough education to have written so brilliantly about so many complex ideas and characters. But Bacon did. And Bacon's works showed exceptional literary talent; his language, they believed, was as brilliant and stylish as that attributed to Shakespeare. In addition Bacon sometimes liked to use ciphers, a type of code, in his writing. Some scholars argued that he wrote the plays and used this system of ciphers to disguise his identity as their true author. This theory that Bacon was the true author of Shakespeare's plays caused intense controversy for decades and still inspires debate. But it has become less respected over the years, as many scholars have concluded that the evidence for this theory is not convincing.

lord chancellor in 1618. Also that year he was given a title, Lord Verulam. In 1621 the king made Bacon the Viscount St. Alban.

Marriage had also improved Bacon's financial situation. In 1607 he wed Alice Barnham (1592–1650), a member of a rich family. She brought a large income with her as part of her dowry. (It was traditional at that time for a woman's family to provide a gift of money or property, called a dowry, to her new husband.) Alice was only fourteen when the wedding took place; Bacon was a middle-aged man of almost forty-five. The couple spent much of their time apart and did not have any children. It appears that they may not have been happy together. Just a few months before he died, Bacon removed his wife from his will so that she would not be able to inherit anything from him.

Major publications

Bacon published his first book, a collection of essays, in 1597. He had been working on these writings since at least 1592, when he wrote to his uncle that he intended to devote his mind to writing books that would revolutionize human learning. Bacon's essays became quite popular. They differed significantly from an earlier tradition of essays that emphasized abstract, or theoretical, thinking. Instead, Bacon's essays focused on concrete observations and ideas. For example, when he wrote about friendship he did not talk about various theories of friendship. He wrote about such practical subjects as how friendships could enrich a person's life and what qualities were ideal in a friend. A second edition of his *Essays* was published in 1612 and a third edition in 1625. Bacon wrote about a wide range of topics in his essays, from architecture and gardening to love and death.

The Advancement of Learning, which Bacon wrote in 1605, explained his belief in the importance of scientific education. He dedicated it to King James in hopes that it would persuade the king to support this kind of learning. In 1609 he published *De sapientia veterum (On the Wisdom of the Ancients),* in which he wrote about ancient myths.

Bacon's most important work, *Novum organum (New Instrument),* was published in 1620. This book detailed his new system of scientific study. As Bacon explained in the dedication, quoted in *Hostage to Fortune: The Troubled Life of Francis Bacon* by Lisa Jardine and Alan Stewart, he intended his book to describe "a new logic, teaching to invent and judge by induction [reaching a conclusion by testing facts] … and thereby to make philosophy and sciences both more true and more active." This new method, which came to be known as the Baconian Method, involved the study of natural phenomena through the careful observation of facts. Most English philosophers before Bacon used the *a priori* method of argument. They simply assumed a point was true and then explained their reasoning, considering this sufficient proof of their idea. Bacon believed that *a priori* argument was flawed because it was not based on observable facts. Instead of starting with an abstract idea and devising an argument that made that idea compatible with concrete information, Bacon began with the observation of facts. From these he could develop theories that he went on to test in a scientific way. He believed that this method was the only way to obtain knowledge that was truly accurate. *New Instrument* was only part of a huge work that Bacon planned to publish as *The Great Instauration.* This work would present his entire philosophy. Though Bacon did work on this gigantic project for the rest of his life, he never completed it.

Though Bacon's writings focused most often on his ideas about obtaining knowledge, he also wrote some works that dealt more specifically with scientific matters. These he compiled in *Abecedarium naturae (Alphabet of Nature).* Bacon intended this project to be read by specialists in the sciences, and it received much less attention than his other works. But he did arrange to have Italian astronomer and mathematician Galileo Galilei (1564–1642) read the section on the ocean tides. Galileo is believed to have sent Bacon a letter in response.

Luxury and scandal

By the early 1620s Bacon had achieved wealth and professional respect. He lived in luxury, throwing elaborate parties and spending huge sums of money on entertainments. He employed almost three hundred personal servants, including twenty-six gentlemen waiters, as well as pages, cooks, wardrobe masters, tailors, secretaries, a sergeant-at-arms, a seal bearer, and numerous others. Many people in London considered Bacon a show-off, and they laughed at his fancy dress and behavior. They even joked about his bad breath, which was the subject of a humorous poem called "On the Lord Chancellor Bacon's stinking breath."

In addition to making jokes about him, people began to challenge some of Bacon's legal decisions. They had evidence that made it appear that Bacon was letting wealthy people influence him to rule in their favor when they were taken to court. In 1621 Bacon was charged with accepting bribes. He eventually pleaded guilty, and the High Court of Parliament sentenced him to prison and ordered him to pay an enormous fine. In addition he was banned from holding public office again and from entering Parliament. The man who had enjoyed such tremendous fame and power had been cast into disgrace.

After being forced to retire from public service, Bacon spent the rest of his life doing research and writing books. He was often ill with gout, a painful disease of the joints, and he was constantly in debt. But his mind was too active for him to rest. In 1622 he published *History of the Reign of Henry VII,* which he dedicated to King James. The following year he published *De augmentis,* a book that expanded on the theories that he had introduced earlier in *The Advancement of Learning.* Bacon wrote *The New Atlantis,* a work that described a utopia, or ideal society, in 1624 but it was not published until after his death in 1627. Unlike most of Bacon's other works, this book was written for all people, not just scholars. In *The New Atlantis,* Bacon suggested that a perfect society could be achieved through science. Though other philosophers before him had written about ideal societies, they had imagined that such utopias would be created by means of legislation or other reforms. Bacon was the first utopian writer to argue that science could be used for the improvement of society. Scholars have continued to admire *The New Atlantis* for its original ideas and its amazing ability to imagine new technologies. Among the future inventions that Bacon imagined in the book were airplanes, telephones, and submarines.

Death and influence

Even Bacon's death, in 1626, was connected with his interest in observation and experimentation. On a very cold day that March, he was riding in a carriage near the outskirts of London and decided to stop and make some scientific tests on the effects of refrigeration. He wondered whether packing meat in snow could keep it fresh. To test this idea, he bought a slaughtered chicken from a woman in the area and started stuffing its body cavity with snow. In the process, he caught a chill. He stopped for shelter at the nearby home of Thomas Howard (Earl of Arundel; 1586–1646), but was put to bed in an unheated room. Bacon developed bronchitis, an inflammation of the lungs, and died on April 9. He was buried at St. Michael's Church in the Hertfordshire town of St. Albans.

Bacon's writings directly influenced many generations of philosophers and intellectuals, including the English poet John Milton (1608–1674); English philosophers Thomas Hobbes (1588–1679) and John Stuart Mill (1806–1873); and English scientist Charles Darwin (1809–1882). The German philosopher Immanuel Kant (1724–1804) dedicated the second edition of his most important work, *Critique of Pure Reason,* to Bacon. Indeed, students still read Bacon's work and debate his ideas.

Many of Bacon's aphorisms, or brief sayings, remain well known. For example, he wrote such famous words as "The remedy is worse than the disease," and "Knowledge is power." About children he wrote, "Children sweeten labours, but they make misfortunes more bitter." The statement that might be considered among the best descriptions of Bacon himself reads simply: "Chiefly the mould [shape] of a man's fortune is in his own hands."

For More Information

BOOKS

Jardine, Lisa and Alan Stewart. *Hostage to Fortune: The Troubled Life of Francis Bacon.* New York: Hill and Wang, 1998.

Pitcher, John, ed. *Francis Bacon: The Essays.* London and New York: Penguin Books, 1986.

Vickers, Brian, ed. *Francis Bacon: The Major Works.* New York: Oxford University Press, 2002.

WEB SITES

"Francis Bacon." *The Internet Encyclopedia of Philosophy.* http://www.iep.utm.edu/b/bacon.htm#H2 (accessed on July 11, 2006).

"Francis Bacon." *Stanford Encyclopedia of Philosophy.* http://plato.stanford.edu/entries/francis-bacon/ (accessed on July 11, 2006).

Modern History Sourcebook: Francis Bacon, The New Atlantis. http://www.fordham.edu/halsall/mod/1627bacon-atlantis.html (accessed on July 11, 2006).

"The Utopian Tradition." http://www2.kenyon.edu/Depts/IPHS/Projects/Stella/Bacon.htm (accessed on July 11, 2006).

Westfall, Richard. "Francis Bacon." *The Galileo Project.* http://galileo.rice.edu/Catalog/NewFiles/bacon.html (accessed on July 11, 2006).

Edmund Campion

BORN: January 25, 1540 • London, England

DIED: December 1, 1581 • London, England

English priest; scholar

"My charge is, of free cost to preach the Gospel, to minister the Sacraments, to instruct the simple, to reforme sinners, to confute errors—in brief, to crie alarme spiritual against foul vice and proud ignorance."

Edmund Campion. ©
HULTON-DEUTSCH
COLLECTION/CORBIS.

Edmund Campion, a brilliant scholar at Oxford University, abandoned the chance to have a powerful career as an Anglican priest under the protection of **Elizabeth I** (1533–1603; see entry) because he believed in the supremacy of the Roman Catholic Church. He fled England and became a Jesuit priest, later returning to England to minister to Catholics there who were strictly forbidden to practice their religion. After publishing a pamphlet denouncing the Anglican Church, Campion was arrested as a traitor. He was imprisoned and tortured before being put to death in 1581. Recognizing him as a martyr, or someone who died for his faith, the Catholic Church made him a saint in 1970. (A saint is a deceased person who, due to his or her exceptionally good behavior during life, receives the official blessing of the church and is believed to be capable of interceding with God to protect people on earth.)

Early life and education

Edmund Campion was born in London, on January 25, 1540, into a Catholic merchant family. He had two brothers and one sister. His father, also named Edmund, was a bookseller. From a very early age, young Campion showed exceptional intelligence, and an organization of merchants in the city arranged for him to attend a grammar school and to study at Christ Church Hospital. According to the *Catholic Encyclopedia,* Campion was the schoolboy chosen to give a formal Latin greeting to **Mary I** (1516–1558; see entry) when she first entered London as queen in 1553. Later he attended St. John's College at Oxford University, becoming one of the first students admitted there under the college's founder, Sir Thomas White (1492–1567). Campion became a junior fellow at St. John's when he was only seventeen. By 1560 he was well-known as a public speaker, and he went on to excel as a professor.

During the years before Campion's birth and throughout his youth, England underwent numerous political and religious changes. In the 1530s **King Henry VIII** (1491–1547; see entry) broke with the Roman Catholic Church and declared himself head of the church in England. He tried to eliminate Catholic influence in the universities. At that time the universities educated students to become priests, and for centuries they had been under the control of Catholic monks and scholars. Henry fired many professors and pressured others to accept his religious authority. Instead, however, many high-ranking clergy members resigned from their positions as church leaders. As a result the church faced a great shortage of priests who could serve as its bishops and teachers. Henry's oldest daughter, Mary, was a devoted Catholic and when she became queen she reinstituted Roman Catholicism as the official religion of the nation. By this time the Reformation, a sixteenth-century religious movement that aimed to reform the Roman Catholic Church and resulted in the establishment of Protestant churches, had gained considerable support in England. During her five-year reign, Mary had many Protestants burned at the stake as heretics, or people whose opinions oppose established church doctrines (principles).

Elizabeth, a Protestant, took the throne in 1558. She established the Anglican Church, also called the Church of England, as the country's official church. The practice of Catholicism was outlawed. In 1566 the queen visited Oxford with her advisors, **Robert Dudley** (Earl of Leicester; 1532–1588; see entry) and **William Cecil** (Lord Burghley; 1520–1598; see entry). Elizabeth hoped to strengthen some of the scholastic traditions that had suffered under her father's reign. During her trip to Oxford, she also hoped to find talented scholars who would agree to be ordained as Anglican priests and lead the new church.

Impresses Queen Elizabeth

The university welcomed the queen with many days of speeches and ceremonies. Since Campion's college at Oxford, St. John's, was known as a place that was still predominantly Catholic, Cecil ordered that professors giving speeches to the queen should choose nonreligious subjects so that the visit would not be spoiled by controversy. Campion was assigned to explain how the tides are influenced by the moon, and how the planets are influenced by the higher bodies of the universe. Speaking in Latin, he first praised the queen at great length for her learning and her support of scholarship. He then spoke briefly about the tides. So eloquent was his speech that Elizabeth was thoroughly charmed. She recommended Campion to Dudley, who offered to become Campion's political patron and help him build a powerful career.

Campion continued his studies at Oxford and was ordained a deacon, or helper, of the Anglican Church in 1568. In order to be ordained, he was required to sign the Oath of Supremacy, which proclaimed that the queen was the supreme head of the church in England. But Campion had strong doubts about Protestantism and the validity of the Anglican Church, and he did not hesitate to express these doubts in public. Since it was against the law to worship as a Catholic, Campion's friends worried that he was placing himself in political danger. In 1569 he left his post at Oxford and soon afterward made his way to Dublin, Ireland.

In Ireland, where the people still practiced Catholicism without much interference, Campion was able to resume his scholarly work. He lived with the Stanihurst family in Dublin and hoped to obtain a position at Dublin University, which had been temporarily closed. He also wrote a book, *The History of Ireland.* Since Campion did not read Gaelic, the Irish language, he based his book on sources from English writers, who often held negative stereotypes of Irish people. Not surprisingly, his book presented an inaccurate and insulting picture, and it was not popular in Ireland.

By 1572 the political situation had worsened for Catholics in Dublin, and Campion returned to England. He remained there for a brief time, and he was among the crowd who witnessed the trial at Westminster Hall of the Catholic scholar John Storey (1504–1571), who had supported Mary I's persecution of Protestants. Campion was deeply impressed with Storey's courage during his trial, and this experience strengthened his desire to remain a Catholic. In danger of being arrested himself, Campion arranged to go to France. While crossing the English Channel, however, his boat was stopped and he was taken into custody and returned to Dover. Reportedly bribing the officer in charge of his arrest, Campion was able to escape. Staying with friends nearby, he raised enough money to sail to France again, this time successfully. According to Evelyn Waugh, author of the biography *Edmund Campion*, when Cecil learned that Campion had fled the country, he stated, "It is a great pity to see so notable a man leave his country, for indeed he was one of the diamonds of England."

Joins the Jesuit order

Campion made his way to the town of Douai, in northern France, where **William Allen** (1532–1594; see entry) had established a Catholic seminary for English students. (A seminary is a school similar to a university that trains students in religion, usually to prepare them to become members of the clergy.) This seminary preserved Catholic teachings and trained priests in the hope that, once Catholicism was restored in England, educated clergy would be ready to return. Campion studied divinity there and taught rhetoric, the art of debate. He finished his degree in 1573 and then traveled to Rome, Italy, where he planned to enter the Society of Jesus, a Roman Catholic order of priests more commonly known as the Jesuits.

After having been accepted as a novice, or new member, in the Jesuit order, Campion was sent to study in Brunn, then part of Austria, and later in Prague, which is now the capital of the Czech Republic. Campion spent six years in Prague, advancing his studies and teaching at the university. He was ordained a priest in 1587. In Brunn, according to the *Catholic Encyclopedia*, Campion experienced a vision in which the Virgin Mary told him that he would be put to death for his faith. In 1580 the pope called Campion to Rome. There the Jesuit received the assignment that would make this prophecy come true.

On Allen's recommendation, Campion, along with his fellow Jesuit Robert Persons (1546–1610), was chosen to return to England and work

Missionary Priests in England

The first missionary priest in England to be executed was Cuthbert Mayne (1544–1577), who had been raised as an Anglican and was ordained an Anglican priest. But when he went to Oxford University to pursue further studies, he was inspired by influential Catholic teachers there, especially Edmund Campion. Mayne decided to convert to Catholicism. He fled England and studied at the Catholic seminary at Douai, returning to England as a missionary priest in 1576. Soon after, he was arrested as a traitor. He was executed in 1577.

In 1584 and 1585 Parliament strengthened laws against Catholics. Before this, it had been illegal for priests to say Mass or try to persuade Anglicans to return to Catholicism. The new law, though, stated that any Englishman proved to have been ordained a Roman Catholic priest could be put to death. But this did not stop the work of the missionary priests. During the 1580s, Douai College sent 438 priests to England. Of these, 98 were put to death. The people who helped to hide priests were also in danger. Between 1581 and 1588, eighteen men and two women were put to death for hiding priests.

An estimated three hundred English Catholics, many of them priests, were executed between 1535 and 1679. In 1970 the Catholic Church canonized forty of these martyrs as saints. They are known as the Forty Martyrs of England and Wales. Mayne and Campion were among the Forty Martyrs.

to strengthen Catholicism there. The two men would have to operate in disguise and hide their behavior from the political authorities. Although their orders strictly forbade them to get involved in political matters, they knew that their mission would place them in grave danger. Indeed, English law stated that it was high treason—punishable by death—to engage in any activities that would bring people back to the Catholic Church. Knowing he faced the prospect of eventual capture, trial, and execution, Campion sailed back to England disguised as a jeweler and made his way to London.

A life in hiding

English Catholics were overjoyed at Campion's return, and many prominent Catholic families helped give him shelter while he traveled through the countryside saying Mass, hearing confessions, and preaching. At the suggestion of friends who worried that he and Persons would be captured and killed without having a chance to defend themselves, Campion wrote a pamphlet describing the purpose of their work. Published as *Decem Rationes (Ten Reasons)*, but more popularly known as *Campion's Brag,* the document stated that Campion's mission was to minister to Catholic souls. As quoted by Waugh, the document added that Campion was "strictly forbidden by our Father that sent me [the pope], to deal in any respect with matter of State or Policy of this realm, as things which appertain [relate] not to my vocation." But the pamphlet also presented a complete argument rejecting the Anglican Church in favor of Catholicism. Its publication outraged the queen's advisors, and they intensified their efforts to find Campion and arrest him.

In July 1581 Campion left Persons and was staying with a Catholic family in Lyford, Norfolk. There an informer, George Eliot, discovered him and two local priests saying Mass for a group of people in the house. Eliot alerted the magistrate, who brought a band of soldiers with him to the house to arrest the Jesuit. Hoping to save the others from being arrested as well, Campion wished to surrender himself, but the family insisted on hiding him. The house had several secret rooms, and Campion and the other priests were hidden in a tiny room behind a bedroom on the top floor. The soldiers searched the house, but despite discovering several hiding places, they could not find Campion. They searched all day without success. The next morning, July 17, they were ready to give up. They thought that Campion must have somehow escaped before their arrival. Just then, however, Eliot's partner noticed a chink of light in the wall above the stairs. Tearing at it with a crowbar, he exposed the secret room. Campion and his companions were caught at last.

Campion did not resist arrest. With his companions, and a fourth priest who had been arrested when he came to visit the house at Lyford, he was brought to London as Eliot's prisoner. The Jesuit was thrown into a dungeon in the Tower of London, and he was held in solitary confinement until the queen sent for him a few days later. (The Tower of London was a fortress on the Thames River in London that was used as a royal residence, treasury, and, most famously, as a prison for the upper class.) Dudley, Campion's old patron, sat beside the queen at this meeting and questioned the priest about his activities. Campion replied that his work was purely religious, and that he would obey the queen in all matters not relating to the Church. Then they posed the most important question. Would he publicly renounce Catholicism and become a priest in the Anglican Church? They hoped that Campion would take this chance to avoid execution for treason. But he refused, and Elizabeth sent him back to the Tower.

Refuses to betray his faith

Cecil and Dudley ordered Campion to be tortured on the rack. He was tied by his wrists and ankles to a frame that was then stretched until his limbs were dislocated. In intense pain, Campion blurted out the names of a few people who had sheltered him. But he did not disclose any information that could implicate them in any deliberate plot against the Elizabeth. Campion was then required to participate in four formal conferences in which Anglican officials demanded answers to questions about his pamphlet. Without any opportunity to prepare for these debates, and despite being severely weakened by his brutal torture, Campion presented arguments that the officials could not refute.

The queen's council was frustrated. Its members wanted to condemn Campion to death and they had the legal authority to do so, but they preferred to have evidence of political treason first. Campion still had many supporters, and the council did not wish to provoke their anger by executing him on religious grounds. So the council invented charges that Campion was part of a plot initiated in Rome to assassinate Elizabeth and to persuade foreign armies to invade England. Though these charges were completely false, Campion was put on trial at Westminster Hall on November 20.

Campion was so weak after months of imprisonment and torture that he could not even raise his right arm to swear his oath at his trial. A fellow prisoner kissed Campion's arm and helped him hold it up. Campion pleaded innocent and presented a defense that many witnesses considered brilliant, but the council pronounced him guilty and sentenced him to death. According to Waugh's biography Campion responded: "If our religion do make us traitors, we are worthy to be condemned; but otherwise are, and have been, as good subjects as ever the Queen had. In condemning us you condemn all your own ancestors—all the ancient priests, bishops and kings—all that was once the glory of England, the island of saints, and the most devoted child of the See of Peter."

Execution

During the eleven days he lay chained in his Tower cell between his trial and his day of execution, Campion rejected one last chance, brought to him by his sister, to reject Catholicism and thus spare his life. He spent his last days in fasting and prayer. Finally on December 1, 1581, he and two fellow prisoners were driven through the muddy streets of London to the gallows at Tyburn.

Executions in Elizabethan England were gruesome affairs that attracted large crowds of spectators. Those convicted of high treason were sentenced to be hanged, drawn, and quartered. They were first hanged on the gallows until almost dead, then cut down—preferably while still conscious—and disemboweled. After that, their limbs and head were hacked off. Addressing the crowd at Tyburn just before his death, Campion forgave the council for condemning him. He also asked forgiveness for any harm he might have caused by giving names under torture. With his last words he prayed for the queen and wished her a long and prosperous reign.

Though Elizabeth and her advisors hoped Campion's death would lead to the end of Catholicism in England, it had the opposite effect. Many were so inspired by Campion's eloquence and courage that they were strengthened in their determination to remain Catholics. Others decided to convert. Campion's example also inspired other Jesuits to carry on his work; many of them, in turn, were executed as martyrs. Historians consider Campion one of the most brilliant scholars and writers of his age. A building at Oxford University, Campion Hall, was named after him. In 1970 the Catholic Church canonized Campion as a saint.

For More Information

BOOKS

Hogge, Alice. *God's Secret Agents: Queen Elizabeth's Forbidden Priests and the Hatching of the Gunpowder Plot.* New York: HarperCollins, 2005.

Waugh, Evelyn. *Edmund Campion.* Garden City, NY: Image Books, 1946; reprinted, 1956.

WEB SITES

Brennan, Malcolm. "English Martyrs: Saint Cuthbert Mayne." *The Angelus.* http://www.sspx.ca/Angelus/1978_July/Saint_Cuthbert_Mayne.htm (accessed on July 11, 2006).

"Edmund Campion." *Catholic Encyclopedia.* http://www.newadvent.org/cathen/05293c.htm (accessed on July 11, 2006).

"Edmund Campion." *Tudor Place.* http://www.tudorplace.com.ar/Bios/EdmundCampion.htm (accessed on July 11, 2006).

"Forty Martyrs of England and Wales." http://www.catholic-forum.com/Saints/martyr02.htm (accessed on July 11, 2006).

"Saint Edmund Campion." *SJ Web.* http://www.sjweb.info/history/saint_show.cfm?SaintID=50 (accessed on July 11, 2006).

William Cecil

BORN: September 13, 1520 • Bourne, Lincolnshire, England

DIED: August 4, 1598 • London, England

English statesman

"No prince in Europe hath such a counsellor as I have in mine."

— Queen Elizabeth I. Quoted by Hugh Bibbs in "William Cecil: An Elizabethan Man."

The most trusted and influential advisor to **Queen Elizabeth I** (1533–1603; see entry), William Cecil is considered one of the greatest statesmen in English history. He was largely responsible for shaping Elizabeth's foreign policy in an age of exploration, expansion, and political danger. Cecil's counsel helped Elizabeth's government defend itself against Roman Catholic rebellions and to follow policies that increased the country's wealth and power.

Born into a tradition of government service

William Cecil was born into an old and wealthy family. His father, Richard Cecil, owned the vast Burghley estate in Northamptonshire (now in Cambridgeshire) and his mother was Jane Heckington. Cecil's grandfather, David, had been King Henry VII's (1457–1509) yeoman of the guard, and he had served under **Henry VIII** (1491–1547; see entry)

William Cecil. © MICHAEL NICHOLSON/CORBIS.

25

as sergeant-of-arms and as sheriff of Northamptonshire. Richard Cecil continued this tradition of service to the king, becoming a groom of the wardrobe at the royal court. During his childhood William accompanied his father to court to serve as a page of the robes. The only son in the family—he had three sisters—Cecil was sent to school at Grantham and then at Stamford.

At age fourteen Cecil enrolled in St. John's College, Cambridge University. He studied Greek under John Cheke (1514–1557), one of England's leading classical scholars and a loyal Protestant. Near the end of his studies, Cecil fell in love with Cheke's sister, Mary. He married her in 1541, the same year he left Cambridge without having earned a degree. Mary died two years later, leaving Cecil with an infant son named Thomas.

In 1542 Henry VIII gave Cecil a position in the Court of Common Pleas, a royal court that ruled on disputes according to the tradition of English common law. A year later Cecil was first elected to Parliament, England's legislative body. When he married Mildred Cooke in 1545, he formed important political ties through her family. Mildred's father, Sir Anthony Cooke (1505–1576), served in Henry VIII's court and was appointed tutor to Henry's son, Edward VI (1537–1553). Mildred's sister, Anne, married Henry's lord keeper of the great seal, Sir Nicholas Bacon (1510–1579), and was the mother of the philosopher and states-man **Francis Bacon** (1561–1626; see entry).

Serves the Duke of Somerset

Through these family connections, Cecil was introduced to powerful Protestants at the royal court. In addition to his father-in-law, Cecil also met Edward Seymour (1506–1552), the Duke of Somerset and brother of Henry VIII's third wife, Jane Seymour (1509–1537). The Duke became Edward VI's protector, or guardian, when the nine-year-old boy became king after Henry's death. This position gave Seymour almost as much power as the king himself.

Seymour supported King Henry VIII's strategy to create an alliance between England and Scotland by arranging a marriage between Edward and the infant queen of Scotland, **Mary Stuart** (1542–1587; see entry). However, the Scots rejected Henry's proposal, and Henry launched a war against Scotland. When Seymour led a large military force to Scotland in 1547, Cecil accompanied him. On September 10, the English troops faced Scottish royal troops at the Battle of Pinkie Cleugh. It was a disaster for the Scots.

In 1548 Cecil became Seymour's secretary. He was also responsible for registering legal requests brought by residents of the area to Seymour's estate at Somerset House. Seymour had many enemies. As royal protector, he acted with almost unchecked power. He made decisions that King Edward VI, still a child, was not capable of making. Some rival lords resented this authority. In 1549 these lords, led by John Dudley (1502–1443), Earl of Warwick and first Duke of Northumberland, arrested Seymour and threw him into prison. Because he was so close to Seymour, Cecil faced serious danger as well. In fact, Cecil was imprisoned himself for a brief time in the Tower of London, a fortress on the Thames River in London that was used as a royal residence, treasury, and, most famously, as a prison for the upper class.

Seymour was released, but in 1551 he was arrested again. This time he was found guilty of treason; he was beheaded in 1552. But Cecil, meanwhile, had managed to win Dudley's favor, and this alliance assured Cecil's safety and the advancement of his career. On September 15, 1550, Cecil became one of King Edward VI's two secretaries. In 1551 he was made a knight. (A knight is a man granted a rank of honor by the monarch for his personal merit or service to the country.)

Cecil avoided political danger once again when disagreement arose regarding who would inherit the throne after Edward died. Edward was seriously ill and, an unmarried teenager, he had no children. Dudley wanted Edward to sign a document preventing his half-sisters, **Mary I** (1516–1558; see entry) and Elizabeth, from becoming queen. Dudley wanted Lady Jane Grey (1537–1554), who was married to his son, to take the throne after Edward. Edward took Dudley's advice, but Cecil disagreed with this change. Fearing the anger of both the king and Dudley if he refused to cooperate, however, Cecil reluctantly signed the document.

As it turned out, Lady Jane Grey did become queen after Edward died in 1553, but only for nine days. Mary's supporters then forced her out of power, and she was beheaded. Cecil now faced grave danger as a politician who had signed Edward's document. But he was able to persuade Queen Mary that he would be her loyal servant. She was so impressed with his honesty that she offered him a position in her court, but he declined.

Secretary of state

When Elizabeth became queen in 1558 Cecil became her secretary of state. This was the most powerful position in government, after the queen herself. Elizabeth needed expert advice on how to handle England's economy, trade, and relations with foreign powers. When Elizabeth first took the throne, England faced many dangers. It was a small country with many financial difficulties. It was vulnerable to France and Spain, bigger and stronger countries that plotted to overthrow the Protestant Elizabeth and replace her with a Catholic ruler. In order to keep her throne and help England become a prosperous and powerful country, Elizabeth had to act with great care. Cecil's advice helped her to make choices that strengthened England's power and allowed the country to triumph over its rivals.

One of Cecil's early concerns was the situation in Scotland. Its queen, Mary Stuart, had inherited the throne when she was just an infant. She had been sent to live in France and had married the heir to the French throne, Francis II (1544–1560). Through this marriage, Scotland fell under French Catholic rule. Since Mary was a cousin to Elizabeth and a Catholic, Cecil feared that French influence in Scotland could be dangerous for England. If Catholics in Scotland obtained enough power, they might try to overthrow Elizabeth and make Mary queen of England as well as Scotland. So when Scottish Protestants rebelled against the French, Cecil saw an opportunity to eliminate the French danger. He persuaded Elizabeth to send military support to the rebels. At first she was reluctant to interfere, but she took Cecil's advice. English troops fought with the Scottish rebels and defeated the French in Scotland, leading to the Treaty of Edinburgh in 1560. This treaty ended Scotland's alliance with France and made Scotland an ally of Protestant England.

The queen always valued Cecil's advice, but he did have rivals among the Privy Council, the board of advisors that carried out the administrative function of the government in matters of economy, defense, foreign policy, and law and order, and whose members served as the queen's chief advisors. **Robert Dudley** (Earl of Leicester; 1532–1588; see entry) became a strong opponent of Cecil. Dudley sometimes recommended foreign policy actions that Cecil considered too extreme. To help weaken Dudley's influence, Cecil introduced the Duke of Norfolk, Thomas Howard (1538–1572), to the council. Howard, more conservative than Dudley, generally took Cecil's side in foreign policy recommendations.

Though the immediate French threat had been eliminated, Cecil remained concerned about potential dangers to the queen. He kept in close contact with people who could provide information about secret Catholic plots to remove Elizabeth from power. He was particularly

Burghley House

Cecil's most splendid home, Burghley House, is still the residence of one of Cecil's descendants. But the house, which stands on ten thousand acres in Lincolnshire, is now open to the public. Cecil designed most of the original house himself, and it took more than thirty years to build. The original part of the house was laid out in the shape of a capital E, in honor of Queen Elizabeth. The main part of the house has thirty-five major rooms on the ground floor and first floor. There are also more than eighty smaller rooms. The roof over the original part of the building covers three-quarters of an acre. The house also includes gardens that were supervised by the botanist John Gerard (1545–1612), the first person in England to publish a scientific listing of herbs and other plants and their folklore. Burghley House was famous in Cecil's time as a beautiful and luxurious estate.

Since the late 1500s the house has been modernized, but its historic features and furnishings have been maintained. In the early twenty-first century two major movies, *Pride and Prejudice* (2005) and *The Da Vinci Code* (2006) were filmed, in part, at Burghley House.

Burghley House. © MICHAEL FREEMAN/CORBIS.

suspicious of Spain, and in 1568 he grew alarmed by the presence of Spanish troops in the Netherlands, under the command of the Duke of Alva (1507–1582). Cecil arranged the seizure of ships that were carrying gold and silver to Alva. Furious, Alva retaliated by closing the busy port city of Antwerp to English trade. The incident almost provoked open war between England and Spain. Howard, usually Cecil's ally on the council, joined with Dudley after this incident to urge Cecil's dismissal as secretary of state. But the queen refused to allow this, and Cecil kept his position of power.

Elizabeth rewarded Cecil for his service by making him the first Baron Burghley in 1571. In 1572 he became a knight of the garter and was made lord treasurer. This position increased his power at court and weakened Dudley's influence. Cecil was also a patron of the arts. He built three magnificent homes that he designed himself and furnished with expensive objects. In 1559 he became chancellor of Cambridge University. He often invited scholars to his home, and he supported advances in learning and teaching.

The Northern Rising and the Ridolfi plot

In the late 1560s and early 1570s Cecil dealt with several plots to assassinate Elizabeth and place the Catholic Mary Stuart on the throne. By this time Mary had been forced to give up her throne in Scotland. She fled to England where she was held under house arrest in the homes of noblemen loyal to Elizabeth. Mary now plotted to take the English throne. She sought help from others, promising to restore Catholicism to England when she became queen. She charmed Thomas Howard, and the two began planning their marriage. (Mary was now a widow.)

Another of Mary's supporters was Roberto Ridolfi (1531–1612), a wealthy Italian merchant and banker. Ridolfi came to London around 1555, during the rule of the Catholic Mary I. He also later earned the trust of members of Elizabeth's government. But he was a devoted Catholic and sympathized with Catholics in England who hoped to restore the country to Catholic rule. He conspired with rebels in northern England who, in 1569 and 1570, attempted an uprising to overthrow Elizabeth and place Mary on the English throne. The Northern Rising, as the rebellion was called, failed. Elizabeth's spies learned of plans for the rebellion. Howard was imprisoned in the Tower of London and Mary was moved so that the rebels could not get to her.

Ridolfi next sought foreign military support. In 1571 he went to Europe to persuade **King Philip II of Spain** (1527–1598; see entry) and the Duke of Alva to provide soldiers to invade England. Spanish forces would free Mary, who would immediately marry Howard and take the throne. (Howard had been released from prison after promising to stay away from Mary—a promise he did not keep.) Philip and Alva agreed to Ridolfi's plan. But in April Cecil's agents discovered the Ridolfi plot when Ridolfi's messenger, Charles Baillie, entered the English port city of Dover. Baillie was carrying letters that incriminated Spain and that named Howard as the leader of this attempted revolution.

The conspirators were arrested and thrown in prison. Howard was executed as a traitor in 1572. The incident greatly worsened relations between England and Spain, leading Cecil to recommend that England pursue closer ties with France. With the Treaty of Blois, signed in 1572, the historic hostility between England and France came to an end. Spain was now seen as England's primary rival.

Conflict with Spain

By the early 1570s Protestants in the Netherlands, under William of Orange (1533–1584), were resisting Spanish Catholic rule there. When William was assassinated in 1584, England was in an extremely vulnerable position. Some of the queen's counselors, including Dudley, urged her to authorize military action to support the Protestant rebels. Cecil, however, believed that a more cautious approach was necessary. War with Spain, he believed, would not be in England's best interest.

Cecil used his diplomatic skills to try to ease tensions between England and Spain. But by 1585 he had given up hope that war could be avoided. He supported Dudley's plan to lead a military expedition to the Netherlands, an action that Queen Elizabeth authorized. This decision was one of the factors leading to open war between England and Spain three years later.

The Babington plot

Cecil continued to suspect Mary Stuart of involvement in Catholic plots to remove Elizabeth from power. After exposing the Ridolfi plot, he realized that the dangers to the queen were so extensive that England needed a more advanced system of espionage. But his new duties as lord treasurer prevented him from concentrating on this crucial task. He gave **Francis Walsingham** (1530–1590; see entry) the job of organizing a well-trained group of spies capable of conducting undercover operations. Walsingham's spy network operated in England and in foreign countries as well. It was the largest and most professional secret service of its time, and it provided Cecil with valuable intelligence about the intentions of England's rivals.

With information from Walsingham's spies, Cecil learned that Mary Stuart was conspiring with a group of English Catholics led by Anthony Babington (1561–1586). One of Walsingham's secret agents, Gilbert Gifford, arranged to get written proof of this conspiracy. Acting undercover, he pretended to join the plot and offered to carry messages between Mary and the conspirators. But the letters were intercepted and decoded before being passed on to the recipients. Mary eventually wrote a letter that clearly stated her support for Elizabeth's assassination and her intention to become queen of England after Elizabeth's death. Cecil finally had proof of what he had suspected for so many years. He urged Elizabeth to execute Mary.

But Mary was of royal blood, and Elizabeth was reluctant to sign the death warrant of a fellow queen. Pressure from her advisors and from Parliament finally prompted Elizabeth to sign the warrant of execution. Cecil and Walsingham had the warrant immediately delivered to Mary in prison and the Scottish queen was executed on February 8, 1587. Elizabeth regretted her decision and blamed Cecil, who found himself temporarily in disgrace.

The Spanish Armada

Before long, though, the queen realized that Mary's execution had been necessary. And another threat loomed: a massive invasion by Spain. King Philip II, provoked by England's interference in the Netherlands and by raids on Spanish ships by English seamen such as **Francis Drake** (1540–1596; see entry), planned a naval assault that he hoped would enable Spanish troops to occupy England. He would then remove Elizabeth from power and restore the country to Catholic rule. He spent two years drawing up plans for the attack. Finally, in 1588 the mighty Spanish Armada (navy) sailed for England.

Cecil devoted all his energies to preparing for this assault. He worked closely with Walsingham to monitor reports from English spies in Europe, who conveyed crucial details about Spain's military buildup. He also sought support from **James I** (1566–1625; see entry), then King James VI of Scotland. As royal treasurer, Cecil took steps to ensure that the nation had enough money for ships and supplies that the English fleet needed for its defense. He also watched carefully for any sign of Catholic uprisings that might deflect attention from the crisis.

After several skirmishes in the English Channel, the Armada was chased into northern waters. It planned to sail back to Spain via that route, but encountered a severe storm that blew most of its ships off course and destroyed many of them. The defeat of the Armada saved England from invasion by Spain, and, although luck and weather played a huge role in this outcome, Cecil took much of the credit for England's victory.

Final years

Cecil's favored position at court was further strengthened when rival Dudley died in 1588. Walsingham died two years later, and Cecil's son, Robert, took over as secretary of state. In declining health by this time, Cecil nevertheless remained active in government. He supported anti-Spanish military campaigns in France and the Netherlands and naval expeditions that attacked Spanish ships in the Atlantic and Caribbean. Near the end of his life, however, Cecil urged the queen to make peace with Spain. He died in 1598, before peace negotiations were concluded.

Cecil is remembered as the top advisor among Elizabeth's Privy Council. He recommended foreign policies that helped to weaken England's enemies and build England into a world power. He also worked to limit widespread corruption in government and to ensure efficient rule. But he has also been criticized for harsh policies against those he considered enemies of the English state. He approved the use of torture to extract confessions from suspects, and some historians believe he used any means necessary—even cruel or illegal methods—to achieve his goals. But Cecil lived during an era when England faced many serious dangers. With the queen threatened by assassination plots and military invasions, Cecil took the steps he believed necessary to protect his country.

For More Information

BOOKS

Alford, Stephen. *The Early Elizabethan Polity: William Cecil and the British Succession Crisis, 1558–1569.* Cambridge, England and New York: Cambridge University Press, 1998.

Croft, Pauline, ed. *Patronage, Culture, and Power: The Early Cecils.* New Haven, CT: Yale University Press, 2002.

Graves, Michael A. R. *Burghley: William Cecil, Lord Burghley.* London and New York: Longman; New York: Addison-Wesley 1998.

WEB SITES

Bibbs, Hugh. "William Cecil: An Elizabethan Man." *Medieval History.* http://www.medievalhistory.net/page0012.htm (accessed on July 11, 2006).

"Burghley House." http://www.burghley.co.uk/ (accessed on July 11, 2006).

"William Cecil." *Tudor Place.* http://www.tudorplace.com.ar/Bios/WilliamCecil(1BBurghley).htm (accessed on July 11, 2006).

John Dee

BORN: July 13, 1527 • London, England

DIED: March 26, 1609 • London, England

English mathematician; astrologer

"There is (gentle reader) nothing (the works of God only set apart) which so much beautifies and adorns the soul and mind of man as does knowledge of the good arts and sciences. . . . "

John Dee was a mathematician and astrologer who was eager to learn as much as possible about the universe. (An astrologer is someone who studies the position of stars and planets in the belief that they influence human affairs and events on Earth.) He studied geometry and arithmetic as well as less scientific subjects such as magic and crystals. He traveled throughout Europe to study with some of the best scientists of the time, and he helped to introduce their new theories in England. He gained considerable fame as a scholar and teacher, and he was appointed to serve as the astrological advisor to **Queen Elizabeth I** (1533–1603; see entry). But he was also suspected of practicing black magic because some of his experiments dealt with the supernatural. Though some of Dee's ideas were not scientifically correct, his work helped to advance exciting new ways of thinking in many scientific fields.

John Dee. © MICHAEL NICHOLSON/CORBIS.

An eager student

The only child of Roland Dee and Jane Wild, John Dee was born in London in 1527. His father was in the textile (cloth) business and had been appointed to sew materials for the court of **King Henry VIII** (1491–1547; see entry). Records show that the family had probably originally come from Wales. The Dees were relatively wealthy, and they could afford to give their son a good education. As a boy Dee attended Chelmsford school in Essex. He was sent to St. John's College at Cambridge University at the age of fifteen.

Dee excelled in school, where he took courses in several difficult subjects, including Greek, Latin, philosophy, geometry, arithmetic, and astronomy. (Astronomy is the scientific study of the stars, planets, and other celestial bodies.) He loved to study. In fact, he was so excited about learning that he studied for eighteen hours a day. He slept only four hours each night so that he could have more time to devote to his schoolwork.

Dee completed his bachelor's degree in only two years and then became a lecturer at the university. In 1546 he became a founding fellow of Trinity College, a new school at Cambridge University established by Henry VIII. Dee was particularly interested in mathematics. Government authorities were often suspicious of mathematics at this time, because they associated it with magic. For example, universities taught the theories of the ancient Greek philosopher Pythagoras (569–475 BCE), who had developed a way to determine the measurements of right triangles. But Pythagoras also believed that numbers had special powers, and some scholars in Elizabethan times tried to use his numerical theories to explain various mysteries of the universe, such as the number of planets in the solar system. This way of thinking made mathematics seem closely related to magic.

Numbers and stars

Fascinated by such numerical theories, Dee devised a way to demonstrate the special power of number combinations. As Benjamin Woolley explained in his book *The Queen's Conjurer: The Science and Magic of Dr. John Dee, Adviser to Queen Elizabeth I,* while he was at Trinity College Dee put on a play by the Greek writer Aristophanes. In this play, *Peace,* a character rides up to the heavens on a giant dung beetle to ask the god Zeus to help mortals achieve peace on earth. Dee wanted to make it look like the dung beetle was really flying, but the theater had no way to produce such special effects. So Dee decided to use numerical relationships to achieve this. No one knew exactly how he did it, but he made the dung beetle appear to fly on stage.

According to Woolley, Dee may have used pneumatics (compressed air), mirrors, springs, and pulleys to execute this feat.

This production gained Dee much attention. But he soon realized that he could not hope to deepen his studies of mathematics and related subjects if he remained in England. The best scholars in these fields taught in Europe, and that is where the best students went to complete their education. In 1547 Dee arrived in Louvain (also spelled Leuven), Belgium, to study at its acclaimed university. There he met many of the finest mathematicians and scientists in Europe. Among his close friends was Gerhard Mercator (1512–1594), the famous mapmaker who devised a mathematical method to project geographical information about the spherical earth onto a flat map. Mercator's Projection, as this was called, created a map that was far more accurate than earlier ones and was especially helpful to ocean navigators. Dee also admired the work of Polish astronomer Nicolaus Copernicus (1473–1543), who in 1543 published a book that argued that the sun was the center of the solar system. This was a revolutionary theory because it challenged the previously held belief that the center of the universe was the planet Earth.

Dee became so well respected in Louvain that Charles V (1500–1558), the Holy Roman Emperor, offered him a job in his court. (The Holy Roman Emperor was the head of the Holy Roman Empire, a loose confederation of states and territories, including the German states and most of central Europe, that existed from 962 to 1806 and was considered the supreme political body of the Christian people.) But Dee turned down this offer. In 1551 he went to Paris, where he presented a series of public lectures on Euclid (325–265 BCE), the Greek mathematician whose studies in geometry influenced many scholars. These were the first such lectures ever given in a Christian country. They were an immense success. According to an account quoted in Woolley's book, so many students wanted to attend that latecomers had to lean in through the windows to catch Dee's words. Dee was offered a teaching position at the Sorbonne (the University of Paris), but he chose instead to return to England later that year. He brought with him a brass astronomer's staff and two globes made by Mercator.

In England Dee was given a job in charge of the parish of Upton-upon-Severn in Worcestershire. Soon afterward he began receiving financial support from the Earl of Pembroke and from the Duke of Northumberland. He tutored the Northumberland children, including **Robert Dudley** (Earl of Leicester; 1532–1588; see entry). As a favorite advisor of Queen Elizabeth, Dudley was later able to promote Dee's career in Elizabeth's court.

Dee's lectures on Greek mathematician Euclid (pictured) were extremely popular. © BETTMANN/ CORBIS.

Faced religious change

In 1553 Henry VIII's son, King Edward VI (1537–1553), died and **Mary I** (1516–1558; see entry) became queen. Mary soon took steps to restore Roman Catholicism in England. Her father, Henry, had rejected the authority of the pope in the 1530s and declared himself the head of the church in England. He had done this in order to declare his marriage to Mary's mother, Catherine of Aragon (1485–1536), invalid—an action that the pope had refused to allow. This break with the church caused great turmoil in England. Many people wished to remain loyal to the Catholic religion, but Henry began to outlaw Catholic practices and to punish Catholics by taking away their property or putting them in prison. Many Catholics lived in fear. When Mary took the throne, she began to persecute the Protestants, those who had broken away from the Roman Catholic Church. Many who refused to go back to the Catholic church were burned to death as heretics, people who express an opinion that opposes established church doctrines.

It was a dangerous time to be a Protestant. Dee's father was put in prison briefly and lost all his property. Dee himself was arrested in 1555 and accused of practicing black magic in order to destroy the queen. This was a serious charge, and Dee was lucky to escape a guilty verdict. After three months in prison, he was released. Though Dee did not agree to become a Catholic, records show that he later helped Mary's government interrogate Protestants who were in prison and who were eventually put to death.

Not much is known about Dee's religion. Historians believe that he was ordained in the Anglican church, the official Protestant church of England, but there is no record of when or where. He felt comfortable among both Catholics and Protestants, and he never made any public statement condemning either religion.

The Queen's royal astrologer

When Elizabeth became queen in 1558, Dee attracted her interest. She admired his learning, and she even asked him to draw up a horoscope—a chart of the stars and planets that, people believed, could forecast the future—to determine the most favorable day for her coronation. Elizabeth made Dee her scientific advisor, sometimes sending him on missions overseas. In fact, some historians believe he may have worked for her as a spy.

Dee continued his extensive studies of mathematics, astrology, and other subjects that attempted to explain the mysteries of the universe. During his travels he collected as many scholarly books as he could, building up one of the most impressive personal libraries of the time. He also published his own works, including *Propaedeumata Aphoristica* in 1568. He presented this book, a blend of physics, mathematics, astrology, and magic, to Queen Elizabeth. In 1570 he edited an edition of the works of Euclid. When a new star appeared in the sky in 1572, experts asked Dee for information about it. He used the principles of trigonometry, a branch of mathematics based on triangles, to calculate the distance of this star and published his findings in the book *Parallacticae commentationis praxosque.* The queen continued to admire his work and support his research. According to *The Galileo Project,* Elizabeth was so interested in Dee that, when he developed a serious illness in 1571, she sent two doctors to treat him.

Dee married for the third time in 1578. Though there was a big difference in age between Dee, who was fifty at the time of the wedding, and his bride, Jane Fromands, who was twenty-two, the marriage was a relatively happy one. The couple had eight children.

In 1582 Dee proposed that England join the rest of Europe in adopting the Gregorian calendar, which the pope had commanded the Catholic world to use. This new calendar would replace the ancient one introduced by Roman emperor Julius Caesar (100–44 BCE), which had been based on incorrect astronomical measurements. The Gregorian calendar would remove ten days from that year's calendar in order to reset the new one to the correct measurements. Though Dee agreed that the new calendar should be used, he calculated that eleven days needed to be removed instead of ten. Though many of the queen's advisors approved of Dee's proposal, the Archbishop of Canterbury prevented it from being adopted. As a result England continued to use the outdated and inaccurate calendar until 1752.

In addition to his work as an astronomer and mathematician, Dee supported advances in geography. In 1555 he became a consultant to the Muscovy Company, an association formed by explorer Sebastian Cabot (1474–1557) and several London businessmen. This company, which obtained the exclusive right to trade with Russia, was interested in finding shorter routes to Russia through Arctic waters. Dee created nautical charts for the company, and he also tutored sailors in geometry so that they could navigate routes more accurately.

Dee's interest in exploration extended to foreign policy as well. In 1577 he met with the queen to outline his belief that England should challenge an order that the pope had made in 1494. This order divided the territories of North and South America between Spain and Portugal, leaving England out. Dee argued that, because English explorers had already reached many of the regions claimed by Spain and Portugal, England had the right to play a much more active role in exploring and colonizing the Western Hemisphere. He explained this belief in a huge four-volume book, *General and Rare Memorials Pertayning to the Perfect Arte of Navigation.* The first volume detailed a plan to build and pay for an English navy. The second volume, a collection of navigational tables and charts created with a compass that Dee had invented, was never published because it was too large and complicated to print. In manuscript form, it was bigger than the English Bible. The third volume, according to Dee's letters, contained information that was so secret that it should be burned. Historians do not know whether it was ever published;

Edward Kelley assisted Dee in his work with crystals. HULTON ARCHIVE/GETTY IMAGES.

no copy of it has survived. The fourth volume, which was published, described several famous and successful voyages.

Spirits, crystals, and magic

As he continued his scholarly work, Dee was drawn deeper and deeper into subjects that were more like magic than science. For example, he studied alchemy, a science of medieval times that attempted to transform base metals into gold and find a potion for eternal life. He also experimented with something he called "crystallomancy." This was his name for a method of communication with supernatural beings through the use of crystals. The idea came to him, he said, in a vision in which the angel Uriel appeared. Uriel gave Dee a crystal and told him that if he stared into it, angels would appear and foretell the future. Dee was eager to try this, but because he wanted to be able to write down what the angels said, he needed someone to look into the crystal for him while he wrote. In 1582 he found a helper, Edward Kelley.

Kelley was not a very trustworthy character. He had been convicted of forgery, and as punishment for this crime his ears had been clipped. He dabbled in alchemy, and he was reported to be able to communicate with the dead. He agreed to look into Dee's crystals and report what he saw. Kelley claimed that the angel Uriel as well as several other mystical beings appeared. They spoke to him in an angelic language, Enochic, and told him how to make various alchemical formulas such as the elixir of life, a substance that would make humans live forever. The angels also predicted the future. Dee, however, saw nothing at all. Nevertheless, he wrote down everything that Kelley reported. His account was published in *A True and Faithful Relation of What Passed between Dr. Dee and Some Spirits; Tending, Had it Succeeded, to a General Alteration of Most States and Kingdoms in the World* by Meric Casaubon in 1659.

Dee had been fooled. The visions Kelley described were nothing but lies. But Dee was so fascinated by the mysteries of these crystals that he kept conducting his experiments. Soon he announced that he had discovered the elixir of life. Curious people flocked to see him, and he became famous. From 1583 to 1589 he traveled throughout Europe with his wife and Kelley, giving demonstrations of mystical knowledge and magic at royal courts in Poland and Bohemia (now the Czech Republic). By 1589, however, Dee and Kelley had quarreled, and Dee returned with his wife to his home in the village of Mortlake, near London.

To his horror, he discovered that several books from his valuable library had been stolen. Many of his scientific instruments had been taken as well. Facing financial problems, he tried to earn money as a fortune-teller, a decision that damaged his reputation as a serious scholar. Dee spent his remaining years struggling to support himself and his family. He tried many times without success to persuade the queen to appoint him to a government position. In 1591 Dee asked to be made master of St. John's Cross, an institution for the poor in Winchester. He wanted to create a school for science there that would allow leading scholars to pursue their research under the protection of the queen. Elizabeth approved this plan, but the Archbishop of Canterbury objected to it and Dee never got the appointment. He did, however, find a modest job as chancellor of St. Paul's Cathedral in London.

In 1596 Dee finally obtained a relatively secure job as warden of the Collegiate Chapter in Manchester. He moved there with his family. But plague struck the city in 1605, killing Dee's wife and several of his children. He moved back to London and died in 1609 at the age of seventy-nine. He was buried in Mortlake.

Though Dee's interest in magic tarnished his reputation in his own time, he is remembered today for his exceptional intellect and his keen desire to understand the mysteries of the universe. At a time when the study of science received little serious support in England, Dee made important contributions to astronomy, mathematics, and physics.

For More Information

BOOKS

Clulee, Nicholas H. *John Dee's Natural Philosophy: Between Science and Religion.* London and New York: Routledge, 1988.

Harkness, Deborah E. *John Dee's Conversations with Angels: Cabala, Alchemy, and the End of Nature.* Cambridge, England and New York: Cambridge University Press, 1999.

Woolley, Benjamin. *The Queen's Conjurer: The Science and Magic of Dr. John Dee, Adviser to Queen Elizabeth I.* New York: Henry Holt and Company, 2001.

WEB SITES

"A Bond for All the Ages: Sir Francis Bacon and John Dee; The Original 007." *Sir Francis Bacon's New Advancement of Learning.* http://www.sirbacon.org/links/dblohseven.html (accessed on July 11, 2006).

"About Dr. John Dee." *The John Dee Society.* http://www.johndee.org/ (accessed on July 11, 2006).

Heisler, Ron. "John Dee and the Secret Societies." *The Alchemy Web Site.* http://www.levity.com/alchemy/h_dee.html (accessed on July 11, 2006).

"John Dee." *Tudor Place.* http://www.tudorplace.com.ar/Bios/JohnDee.htm (accessed on July 11, 2006).

The John Dee Publication Project. http://www.john-dee.org/ (accessed on July 11, 2006).

O'Connor, J. J. and E. F. Robertson. "John Dee." http://www-groups.dcs.st-and.ac.uk/~history/Mathematicians/Dee.html (accessed on July 11, 2006).

Westfall, Richard S. "John Dee." *The Galileo Project.* http://galileo.rice.edu/Catalog/NewFiles/dee.html (accessed on July 11, 2006).

"Writings of John Dee." *Esoteric Archives.* http://www.esotericarchives.com/dee/ (accessed on July 11, 2006).

Catherine de Medici

BORN: 1519 • Florence, Italy

DIED: 1589 • Blois, Department Loir-et-Cher, France

French queen; regent

"God has taken [my husband] from me and still, not content with that, He has taken [my son] ... now I am left with three small children and a kingdom divided into factions."

A s the Queen of France from 1547 to 1559 and then as the mother of three French kings, Catherine de Medici played a significant role in the complex struggles for power among European kingdoms during the Elizabethan Era, the period associated with the reign of Queen Elizabeth I (1558–1603) that is often considered to be a golden age in English history. She exerted great influence on her sons' rule of France during a period of bitter religious conflict. Her efforts to maintain control despite the intense rivalries between Roman Catholic and Protestant factions resulted in years of civil war that deepened religious hatreds in France and helped to destabilize other kingdoms in western Europe. Violence against French Protestants played a major role in England's determination to suppress Catholic dissent at home and to guard against foreign conspiracies to overthrow **Elizabeth I** (1533–1603; see entry) and replace her with a Catholic monarch.

Catherine de Medici. © BETTMANN/CORBIS.

Early life and education

Catherine de Medici was born into a rich and powerful family that had ruled the Italian city state of Florence since the early 1400s. Under her great-great-grandfather, Cosimo (1389–1464), Florence had become a wealthy and cultured city famous throughout the world for its art and learning. The city flourished even more dazzlingly during the rule of his son, Lorenzo the Magnificent (1449–1492), though Lorenzo's brutal political policies contributed to growing resentment of Medici wealth and power. Catherine's father, Lorenzo (1492–1519), ruled from only 1516 to his death in 1519. Other prominent members of the Medici family included Giovanni (1475–1521), who became Pope Leo X; and Giulio (1478–1534), who became Pope Clement VII.

Catherine's mother, Madeleine de la Tour (c. 1500–1519), was a princess of French Bourbon ancestry. Madeleine died a few days after Catherine was born and Lorenzo died a week later, leaving the orphaned infant in the care of her father's relatives. Catherine's uncles, including Pope Clement VII, saw to her education and brought her up with the expectation that she would marry royalty. But religious conflict broke out in Italy during Catherine's childhood. An army hired by Charles V (1500–1558), Holy Roman Emperor and King of Spain, attacked Rome in 1527 and forced the pope to flee. The people of Florence, who resented the power and alleged corruption of the Medici family, captured Catherine and held her hostage. The pope hired an army to rescue her and drive Charles's army out of Florence.

Realizing that Italy remained vulnerable to Charles V's armies, Pope Clement VII arranged a marriage between Catherine and Henry (Duke of Orleans; later Henry II; 1519–1559) the younger son of King Francis I (1494–1547) of the Valois dynasty in France. This marriage, he hoped, would make France a strong military ally of Italy. The wedding took place in 1533, when Catherine and Henry were only fourteen. The pope himself conducted the ceremony at Marseilles Cathedral. Legend has it that Catherine, who was very short and plain, asked her fashion designers to create special heels for her to wear at the wedding—the first reference in European history to women's high-heeled shoes.

Becomes Queen of France

For several years Catherine was forced to play a secondary role with her husband, who remained in love with his mistress, Diane de Poitiers

(1499–1566). He met Diane when he was sixteen, and remained her lover until his death. Henry gave Diane much power and influence, while Catherine played the role of quiet observer. For the first ten years of her marriage, Catherine remained childless—a condition that did little to reduce the suspicion with which the French regarded her as a foreigner. Greatly worried by her infertility, she consulted astrologers who, she believed, could help her conceive. In time, Catherine gave birth to ten children, seven of whom survived.

In 1536 Henry's older brother, heir to the French throne, died. Rumors quickly circulated that one of Catherine's servants, acting on her behalf, had poisoned him in order to clear the way for Henry to become king. When Francis I died in 1547, Henry was crowned king and Catherine became queen. As before, however, Catherine lived quietly while Diane de Poitiers influenced the king in matters of governance. Henry even allowed Diane to oversee the education of his and Catherine's children. Diane and the king made arrangements in 1548 for Henry's and Catherine's oldest son, the future Francis II (1544–1560), to become engaged to marry **Mary Stuart** (Queen of Scots; 1542–1587; see entry), thus strengthening a French Catholic alliance with Scotland. The marriage, which took place in 1558, caused great concern to England during the reign of Elizabeth I. Because her rule was not considered legitimate according to Catholic law, Elizabeth was vulnerable to plots by Catholic leaders to remove her from power and replace her with a Catholic monarch. France's ties with Scotland, therefore, caused considerable worry, especially since many Catholics believed that Mary Stuart, great-granddaughter of King Henry VII (1457–1509) of England, had a more legitimate claim to the English throne than did Elizabeth.

Rise of Huguenot minority

Though France was a strongly Catholic country, it experienced a rise in religious conflict in the 1500s. As in other parts of Europe and in England, dissenters were beginning to reject Catholic leadership and policies that they considered corrupt. These Protestants, known in France as Huguenots, wished to worship in reformed churches under Protestant clergy. But in traditionally Catholic countries, Protestants were considered heretics, or holders of false religious beliefs. They risked losing their jobs, lands, and other political rights, and in many cases even risked execution for treason.

Patron of Arts and Architecture

Like her Florentine relatives, Catherine de Medici was an avid supporter of the arts. She often invited Italian musicians to her court, and she introduced the ballet to France. She also brought Italian master chefs with her to France, and their rich dishes and exotic ingredients influenced fine French cuisine. In addition to fine arts, Catherine was curious about the occult. She regularly consulted astrologers, who claimed to be able to predict the future according to the position of the stars. She became an admirer of Nostradamus (1503–1566), who wrote several works of prophecy that, he claimed, predicted events such as assassinations and revolutions.

Particularly interested in architecture, Catherine built or extended many royal palaces. Among these was the Chateau of Fontainebleau, the largest of the royal palaces, which dated from the late twelfth century. Catherine and Henry II ordered extensive additions to this palace and its grounds. But Catherine's favorite chateau was Chenonceau, which her husband had given to Diane de Poitiers as a gift. This chateau, built along the River Cher, included beautiful views and gardens that Diane de Poitiers had designed. Catherine wanted Chenonceau for herself, and after Henry II's death, forced Diane de Poitiers to move out. Catherine then made Chenonceau her favorite residence, redecorating, adding her own gardens, and hosting lavish parties. The first fireworks display in France occurred there in 1560 to celebrate Catherine's son, Francis II's, inheritance of the throne.

Another of Catherine's major building projects was the Tuileries palace in Paris, which she began planning after Henry II's death in 1559. This huge palace now adjoins the Louvre Museum. Catherine died at the Chateau de Blois, where the cabinets in which she allegedly kept her poisons can still be seen.

The number of Huguenots in France increased dramatically in the early 1500s, and their influence spread. The noble Navarre family became allied with the Huguenot cause, while the powerful Guise family, to whom Mary Stuart was related, led the Catholic struggle against them. Rulers in other parts of Europe and in England, which had become a Protestant country under Elizabeth, watched the situation in France with caution. They feared that violence against Protestants there could rapidly spread to their own countries.

In July 1559 Henry II was killed in a jousting accident when his helmet was shattered by the lance of a Huguenot nobleman. The lance pierced Henry through the eye and entered his brain, killing him a few days later. His and Catherine's son, Francis II, became king at age sixteen. With a teenager now ruling the kingdom, the Huguenots decided to launch a rebellion. They hoped to overthrow the king or at least force him to let them control his royal court, which was dominated by the Guise family. But the uprising failed, and the Huguenot leaders, associated with the Navarre family, were arrested. Fifty-seven of them were executed for treason. This incident worsened the longstanding political rivalry between the Navarre and the Guise families.

Wars of religion

When Francis II died in 1560 after only about one year on the throne, his younger brother, Charles IX (1550–1574), became king at age ten. Since the boy was too young to govern on his own, Catherine was appointed regent for him, meaning that she would rule in his name until he became an adult. For most of Charles's reign, France was plagued by civil war between Huguenots and Catholic extremists. The Guise family, which had dominated at Francis II's court, hoped to retain control of the government, but influential Huguenots challenged them. Catherine, who remembered the trauma of the civil war that she had lived through as a child, struggled to find a way toward peace while keeping the crown independent of either faction. She made alliances with both Protestants and Catholics, hoping to keep either faction from seizing too much power. As was customary in the Medici family, she wielded power with ruthlessness and skill. She was particularly talented at manipulating her enemies against each other, and she became famous for her alleged knowledge of poisons as a weapon of assassination.

In 1562, during the first of several civil wars known as the French Wars of Religion, the Huguenots appealed to Elizabeth, a Protestant, for help. She agreed to support their cause, but only in exchange for the cities of Dieppe and Le Havre in northern France, which she demanded as pledges for the eventual return of Calais, which the English had lost to France during the reign of **Mary I** (1516–1558; see entry). Alarmed that England was gaining a foothold into French territory, Catherine made a deal with the Huguenot leader, promising to give basic rights to French Protestants if they would drive the English out of the country. By the terms of the Peace of Amboise (March 1563), French Catholics and Protestants agreed to work together to recover Dieppe and Le Havre. Because of England's failure to gain control of French territory, Elizabeth was reluctant to consider supporting the Huguenots in their further struggles against the Catholic majority. At the same time, she remained wary of Catholic power in France, where support for Mary Stuart remained strong.

In 1563 Catherine declared that Charles was of age to rule. Continued plotting by the Guises, however, led to a second civil war from 1567 to 1568 and a third from 1568 to 1570. Catherine did her best to keep the kingdom intact and was able to put down the second rebellion fairly quickly, but she could not prevent the third war from escalating into a major conflict. During this war the cardinal of Lorraine, Mary Stuart's uncle and brother of the Duke of Guise, began promoting Mary's cause. She had been forced out of power in Scotland and had taken refuge in England, where Elizabeth allowed her to live under guard. But the cardinal's schemes went well beyond a plan to return Mary to the Scottish throne. Alarmed that French Catholics might be plotting to overthrow Elizabeth and replace her with the Queen of Scots, Elizabeth's ambassador to France at that time, Sir Henry Norris, strongly urged her to send aid to the Huguenots. Though she had refused to become involved during the second war, the circumstances were now more threatening. Elizabeth agreed to send aid to the French Protestants, who also received support from Germany. With this foreign support the Huguenots were able to hold out against the Catholic majority for two years. As the war dragged on, both sides committed atrocities, burning towns and killing the inhabitants.

To help put an end to these devastating wars of religion, Catherine arranged for her daughter, Marguerite de Valois (1553–1615), to marry Henry of Navarre (later Henry IV of France; 1553–1610), a Huguenot noble of the Bourbon dynasty. Catherine also tried to persuade Elizabeth, a Protestant, to agree to marry her son Henry (Duc d'Anjou; later Henry III; 1551–1589). When Elizabeth rejected this proposal, Catherine suggested her youngest son, François (Duke of Alençon; 1555–1584), instead. Though Elizabeth demonstrated what some thought was real affection for the young man, she had no intention of marrying.

St. Bartholomew's Day Massacre

The civil wars came to an end in 1570 with the Peace of St. Germain, which allowed Admiral Coligny, the Huguenot leader, to return to the royal court. At first Catherine believed Coligny would be a moderate influence, but he soon exerted so much power over the king that Catherine considered him dangerous. With the help of the Guise family, Catherine arranged to have Coligny assassinated in Paris in 1572 when the city would be filled with Huguenots attending the wedding of her daughter to Henry of Navarre. But the assassin only wounded the admiral, and the king—who had had no prior knowledge of Catherine's scheme—vowed to

Catherine de Medici inspects victims of the St. Bartholomew's Day Massacre. © BETTMANN/CORBIS.

punish the attempted murderers. Determined to prevent this, Catherine was able to persuade Charles that Coligny had been plotting to overthrow the Catholic court. Many historians believe that Catherine exerted relentless pressure on her son to order Coligny's death, but her exact role in these events remains in some dispute. Charles finally relented, exclaiming that all the Huguenots would have to be killed so that none of Coligny's supporters would remain alive to reproach him.

What followed was a massacre. Before dawn on St. Bartholomew's Day, August 24, 1572, Catholic troops began their attack. Soon all order broke down, and Catholics ransacked Protestant areas of the city, destroying property and slaughtering thousands of Huguenot men, women, and children. The violence spread to other regions of France and took several days to be subdued. In Paris alone, according to one estimate, almost three thousand people were killed. Thousands more were slaughtered in outlying areas.

After some hesitation, Charles assumed responsibility for ordering the massacre. But many people assumed that Catherine had been behind it. Civil war broke out again immediately, and the massacre dramatically increased tensions between France and England, where many Huguenot survivors had fled for safety. Indeed, Elizabeth's newly appointed Protestant ambassador to France, **Francis Walsingham** (1530–1590; see entry), was in Paris during the massacre and believed his own life to be in danger during the riots. The savagery of the anti-Protestant attacks contributed to his intense distrust of France and his resolve to defeat the Catholic cause in England. He made this a central theme of his later career as Elizabeth's secretary of state.

End of Valois dynasty

When Charles IX died in 1574 Catherine's favorite son, Henry, who had been elected king of Poland in 1573, became King Henry III of France. As Catherine waited for him to return to France to assume his royal duties, she worried about continuing civil strife. Her son, François, she had discovered, had joined a moderate Catholic faction intent on destroying the power of the Guise family, and this faction had promised to put him on the throne after Charles died. Alarmed by this plot, Catherine threw François in prison. After Henry III returned to France, escaped and joined a revolt against the king. He continued to oppose Henry III for many years until finally begging his forgiveness in 1583. Though Henry did pardon his brother and promise that the crown would go to him on Henry's death, François himself died soon afterward. Catherine now had only one son, Henry, who remained childless.

Unlike Charles, Henry did not allow his mother to exert much influence over him. In 1567 he signed the Edict of Beaulieu, which gave minor concessions to French Protestants. In response the Duke of Guise formed the Catholic League, which pressured Henry to invalidate many of the edict's terms. Once in favor of tolerating some basic Huguenot demands, Catherine now supported the Catholic extremist Guise. Religious conflict continued; King Henry III joined Henry of Navarre against the Catholic League. In 1589 Henry III's bodyguards murdered Guise, causing Catherine to despair that the balances she had worked so hard to promote between the religious factions in France had no hope of success. She died that year, only eight months before Henry III was assassinated by a Catholic friar. Since he died without an heir, the Valois dynasty came to an end and the French throne went to Henry of Navarre.

Catherine had failed to make France the strong and unified kingdom that she had envisioned, but she did succeed in keeping neither the Guise family nor the Huguenot faction from completely usurping the power of the throne. France was a seriously weakened country by the time of her death. Once one of the most formidable kingdoms in Europe, France now played a lesser role in world affairs as Spain emerged to become England's primary rival for power.

For More Information

BOOKS

Fridea, Leonie. *Catherine de Medici*. New York: Weidenfeld & Nicholson, 2003; Harper Perennial, 2006.

Somerville, Barbara. *Catherine De Medici: The Power Behind the French Throne*. Minneapolis, MN: Compass Point Books, 2006.

Whitelaw, Nancy. *Catherine De'Medici: And the Protestant Reformation*. Greensboro, NC: Morgan Reynolds Publishing, 2004.

WEB SITES

"Catherine de' Medici." *Andros on Ballet*. http://michaelminn.net/andros/ biographies/de_medici_catherine.htm (accessed on July 11, 2006).

"Catherine de Medici." *History Learning Site*. http://www.historylearningsite. co.uk/catherine_de_medici.htm (accessed on July 11, 2006).

"The French Wars of Religion." *History Learning Site*. http:// www.historylearningsite.co.uk/FWR3.htm (accessed on July 11, 2006).

"The Medici Family." *The Galileo Project*. http://galileo.rice.edu/gal/ medici.html (accessed on July 11, 2006).

"The Medici Queens." *The Open Door Web Site*. http://www.saburchill.com/ history/biblio/020.html (accessed on July 11, 2006).

"The Wars of Religion." *World Civilizations*. http://www.wsu.edu/~dee/ REFORM/WARS.HTM (accessed on July 11, 2006).

Robert Devereux

BORN: November 10, 1566 • Netherwood, Herefordshire, England

DIED: February 25, 1601 • London, England

English courtier

"I was never proud till you sought to make me too base [lowly]."

— Robert Devereux, in a letter to Queen Elizabeth I.

A favorite courtier, or court attendant, of **Elizabeth I** (1533–1603; see entry) during her later years, Robert Devereux (sometimes spelled Devereaux) was charming, handsome, and ambitious. He was also arrogant, and he abused his position of favor with the queen. Intent on winning fame and fortune, he was capable of bravery in battle but often made unwise decisions and even disregarded orders. After failing to subdue a rebellion in Ireland and abandoning his military post without permission, he fell out of favor with the queen. Frustrated by his failure to improve his career after these events, he launched a rebellion against the queen that resulted in his execution for treason.

Early life

Robert Devereux was born into a high-ranking family closely associated with Elizabeth I. His mother, Lettice Knollys (1540–1634), was a cousin of the queen. His father, Walter Devereux (1541–1576), was made earl of

Robert Devereux.
© BETTMANN/CORBIS.

55

Essex as a reward for distinguished service to the crown. Walter Devereux died when Robert was nine years old; at the time, some suspected that he had been poisoned by **Robert Dudley** (Earl of Leicester; 1532–1588; see entry), who was rumored to be romantically involved with Lettice. In fact, some speculated that Robert was really Dudley's son, not Devereux's. There is no evidence to support the poison claim, however. Furthermore, historians have pointed out that Dudley had many enemies, and their wish to damage his reputation may have led to this gossip. After Walter Devereux's death, Robert was placed in the care of the queen's most trusted advisor, **William Cecil** (Lord Burghley; 1520–1598; see entry). In 1578 Dudley married Lettice and became Robert's stepfather.

Robert spent much of his boyhood at his father's estate in Wales. At age twelve he entered Cambridge University, and in 1581 he received a master of arts degree. From 1584 Dudley, the queen's closest friend, began to promote his stepson's career at court. Devereux, a handsome and courteous young man, quickly made important friends and contacts. In 1585 he accompanied Dudley on a military expedition to the Netherlands, where the queen had sent troops to aid the Protestant rebellion against Spain. Dudley, commander of the expedition, so admired his stepson's bravery at the battle of Zutphen (September 21, 1586) that he knighted the young man on the battlefield.

Upon his return to court in 1587 Devereux soon caught the queen's interest. Dudley had grown jealous of **Walter Raleigh** (1552–1618; see entry), who had become a favorite of the queen, and he encouraged his stepson to develop a close relationship with Elizabeth in order to reduce Raleigh's influence on her. This was not a difficult task. Though the queen was by this time in her fifties, she still enjoyed flattery and flirtation with young men. Almost from the start she doted on the dashing young Devereux. He was often alone with her, and observers remarked that he would often visit with the queen all night, staying with her until dawn. When Dudley died in 1588 Elizabeth made Devereux her Master of the Horse, a high position that included responsibility for scheduling all of the queen's social engagements.

Provokes queen's displeasure

Despite the fact that the queen favored him, Devereux was impatient for his career to advance quickly. He had inherited many debts from his father and was eager to improve his fortunes. Hoping for the opportunity for glory and riches, he joined **Francis Drake** (1540–1596; see entry) on a naval expedition in 1589 to the coast of Spain and Portugal. England was at war with Spain and had won a significant victory over the formidable Spanish Armada (navy) in 1588. With Spain thus considerably weakened, the queen ordered her fleet to sail into Spanish waters, burn Spain's Atlantic fleet, and capture the city of Lisbon, Portugal. This campaign, she hoped, would force the Spanish king, **Philip II** (1527–1598; see entry), to petition for peace.

Elizabeth had expressly forbidden Devereux to participate in this campaign, and she sent him a furious letter expressing her disapproval of his actions. Returning to England after the failure to take the city of Lisbon, he managed to regain the queen's favor. But he angered her once again when, in 1590, he married Frances Walsingham, widow of **Philip Sidney** (1554–1586; see entry) and daughter of Elizabeth's secretary of state, **Francis Walsingham** (1530–1590; see entry). The queen was notoriously jealous, and she resented her courtiers' attentions to other women. In fact, she had thrown Raleigh into prison when she discovered that he had married. With Devereux, however, she was more lenient, and she allowed him back at court after only two weeks. Devereux's marriage produced three children: Frances, Robert, and Dorothy. Robert became the third earl of Essex.

This pattern of provoking the queen and then obtaining her forgiveness became characteristic of Devereux's conduct. The young courtier, who had noble blood through his mother and therefore seemed to consider himself the queen's social equal, often lost his temper with the queen and staged tantrums like a spoiled child. And, like an indulgent mother, Elizabeth forgave him. According to one report Devereux once lost his temper during an argument with the queen. Disrespectfully, he turned his back on her. She slapped him angrily in response and told him to be hanged. Furious, he placed his hand on his sword—a gesture that could be considered treasonous—and cried that he would never have tolerated such rude treatment even from Elizabeth's father, **Henry VIII** (1491–1547; see entry). He then stormed out of the room. After barely apologizing, he was allowed to return to court three months later. Such behavior from anyone else could very well have resulted in the death penalty.

Serves on Privy Council

In 1591 Devereux was given command of a military expedition to aid Protestant rebels in France. The campaign was short-lived, however, and

Ulster Rebellion

Ireland had been conquered by the English in 1172, but over the centuries the English governors there had intermarried and adopted Irish ways. Rather than accepting English law, the Irish lived according to customary rivalries between competing clans. They raided enemy settlements, stole cattle, and practiced piracy along the coast. English economic interests there were increasingly threatened, particularly by pirate ships that demanded steep bribes from merchant vessels seeking to dock in Irish ports. Henry VIII attempted to subdue the chieftains by offering them land grants in exchange for their promise to accept English law. But he did not vigorously enforce this policy. Under Elizabeth, however, the policy was resumed in the 1570s. Many chieftains resented the fact that they would have to pay taxes to England on lands that they had owned for generations. They resisted, and England responded with military force. For several years England struggled to subdue the Irish, but resistance continued.

By the early 1590s Hugh O'Neill (c. 1540–1616), the third earl of Tyrone, had come to power in the northern province of Ulster. England sent troops against him, but Ulster, which was surrounded by bogs, mountains, and woodlands, was difficult territory to attack. O'Neill had rallied other chieftains to fight with him, and he had also received help from Philip II of Spain. In 1599 Devereux arrived in Ireland with the largest English force ever sent there. But instead of marching to Ulster, he decided to try to establish order in the south of the country. He established garrisons, or military posts, throughout the region, assigning numerous troops there. His force suffered heavy casualties in the south, and his garrisoned soldiers suffered from unsanitary conditions and inadequate food. Thousands died from typhoid, dysentery, and other diseases. When he finally turned north, Devereux had insufficient troops to win against O'Neill. He negotiated a truce, which was denounced in London as a humiliation.

Hugh O'Neill, Earl of Tyrone, led the Ulster Rebellion.
HULTON ARCHIVE/GETTY IMAGES.

To defend his actions in front of the queen, Devereux left Ireland without official permission in 1600. Elizabeth appointed another governor in Ireland. The general in charge of southern Ireland, George Carew (1555–1629), used a combination of diplomacy and force to stop the rebellion in that region by mid-1601. But the leader of the Ulster force, Arthur Chichester (1563–1625), burned crops and massacred the civilian population. When 3,500 Spanish troops arrived in Cork, on the southern coast of Ireland, later that year to aid the rebels, the Ulster chieftains rejoiced. They went south with a new strategy, and on December 24 launched an attack on the English at Kinsale, near Cork. The battle proved disastrous for the Irish, who fled back to Ulster to protect their own lands. O'Neill held out until March 30, 1603, when he surrendered. Elizabeth had died the week before. The new king, **James I** (1566–1625; see entry) gave O'Neill and the other chieftains full pardons and returned their estates. In return, they had to swear loyalty to the English crown and give up their private armies. The war in Ireland had cost England the lives of at least thirty thousand soldiers and £2 million, while as many as one hundred thousand Irish lives were lost.

Devereux was recalled to England in January 1592. He was appointed to the Privy Council in 1593, and he focused on advancing his career as a statesman. (The Privy Council is the board of advisors that carried out the administrative function of the government in matters of economy, defense, foreign policy, and law and order, and its members served as the queen's chief advisors.) By 1595 he had achieved significant power. He found himself increasingly at odds, however, with William Cecil's son, Sir Robert Cecil (1563–1612), who had become secretary of state in 1590.

When Devereux strongly urged the queen to authorize an attack on Spanish ports in 1596, she agreed to give him command of the land troops for the expedition. He became a hero after capturing the city of Cádiz, Spain. But Cecil, back in London, took every opportunity to criticize Devereux to the queen. Devereux responded by forging alliances with others who were opposed to the dominance of the Cecil family. After leading an unsuccessful naval expedition to the Azores islands, where he had hoped to capture Spanish treasure ships, Devereux found himself pitted more dramatically against Cecil and his supporters. While they argued for peace with Spain, Devereux pressed for continued aggression against Spanish targets.

England also faced a growing problem in Ireland, where the earl of Tyrone had launched a rebellion against English political control. Devereux, intent on earning honors and fame, begged the queen to let him lead the expedition against the rebels. She gave him command of seventeen thousand troops, the largest force ever sent to Ireland, in 1598. Devereux failed miserably. Defying orders, he conducted several small engagements in the south of the country instead of confronting Tyrone's forces in the north. Receiving a written complaint from the queen, Devereux insisted he was right to take this action and that his enemies at court had poisoned her against him.

When Devereux finally met with Tyrone in September 1599, his troops and supplies were so diminished that he had to negotiate a truce with the rebels, again without official permission. This was considered an extreme humiliation for England, and the queen was outraged. She sent Devereux another furious letter, which prompted his quick return to England. He rushed to the queen's private chamber without an appointment and fell to his knees before her. Though she smiled at him, she was extremely displeased. She had specifically ordered him to remain in Ireland, and once again he had disobeyed her.

Disgrace

Devereux was called before the Privy Council, which found that his truce with Tyrone had been unjustified. In addition the council charged him with desertion for leaving his post in Ireland without permission. It ordered him placed under house arrest at his home at York House. Refusing to accept responsibility for his own disgrace, Devereux blamed Cecil and Raleigh for poisoning the queen's mind against him. Fearing that Devereux would be restored to power, Raleigh urged Cecil to take steps to make sure this would not happen.

For a time Devereux lived quietly at York House. Under pressure from Cecil the Privy Council put him on trial on June 5, 1600. Kneeling before the council, Devereux was found guilty and deprived of public office. He was also refused the right to continue receiving import taxes on sweet wines, which had been his chief source of income. He begged Elizabeth to renew the license, but she refused. She also refused to send him back to Ireland.

Heavily in debt, Devereux plotted a way to salvage his finances and his reputation. He was able to gather together a group of frustrated nobles who helped him escape from York House in February 1601 and march to London. His plan was to force the queen to meet with him and to restore his place at court. Raleigh, however, discovered the plan immediately and was able to prepare the council. When Devereux and a few hundred followers entered the city, they tried to persuade the townspeople that they were trying to protect the queen from Raleigh. But the people of London saw through this lie, and they refused to support Devereux. Cecil then ordered his arrest.

On February 19, 1601, Devereux was put on trial for treason. Even those who had once supported him, including the philosopher **Francis Bacon** (1561–1626; see entry), whose early career Devereux had promoted, refused to come to his defense. Devereux was found guilty and sentenced to death. He was beheaded at the Tower of London on February 25, 1601. (The Tower of London was a fortress on the

Thames River in London that was used as a royal residence, treasury, and, most famously, as a prison for the upper class.) According to some reports Raleigh watched the execution from a window, disdainfully smoking a pipe where Devereux could see him.

Though Elizabeth signed Devereux's death warrant without complaint, she was saddened by his death. He had been given important responsibilities for which he had no real talent, and he had failed to execute them in a satisfactory way. He had involved himself in many arguments at court, and had challenged the queen's authority. Yet he was also a passionate man who was generous with his affections. Many, including the queen, were willing to forgive him much because of these positive qualities.

For More Information

BOOKS

Lacey, Robert. *Robert, Earl of Essex: An Elizabethan Icarus.* London: Phoenix Press, 2002.

Strachey, Lytton. *Elizabeth and Essex: A Tragic History.* San Diego, CA: Harvest Books, 2002.

Weir, Alison. *The Life of Elizabeth I.* New York: Ballantine Books, 1998.

WEB SITES

"Robert Devereux." *BBC: Historic Figures.* http://www.bbc.co.uk/history/historic_figures/devereux_robert.shtml (accessed on July 11, 2006).

"Robert Devereux." *Tudor Place.* http://www.tudorplace.com.ar/Bios/RobertDevereux(2EEssex).htm (accessed on July 11, 2006).

Francis Drake

BORN: 1541 • Tavistock, England

DIED: January 28, 1596 • Puerto Bello, Honduras

English explorer

"It isn't that life ashore is distasteful to me. But life at sea is better."

Francis Drake was the most famous seaman of the Elizabethan Era, the period associated with the reign of Queen Elizabeth I (1558–1603) that is often considered to be a golden age in English history. Drake was the first Englishman to circumnavigate, or sail around, the world. He achieved fame and glory for raiding Spanish treasure ships and ports in the Western Hemisphere, and for helping England defeat a major naval assault by the mighty Spanish Armada (navy). The Spanish regarded him as a ruthless pirate, but the English saw him as a daring hero. His exploits helped to strengthen English naval power at a time when Spain dominated the seas.

Learned seafaring skills

Francis Drake was the oldest child of Edmund Drake, a farmer from a prosperous peasant family in Tavistock, Devon, in southwestern England. Edmund became a Protestant preacher and left the family to

Francis Drake. COURTESY OF THE LIBRARY OF CONGRESS.

find parish work when Francis was still a child. Francis received little schooling. While still a young boy, he was sent to live with relatives, the Hawkins family, in the nearby town of Plymouth on England's southwest coast.

William Hawkins was a wealthy and powerful merchant whose ships traded in the Canary Islands and along the west coast of Africa. In his household Drake learned the skills of seafaring, which at that time often included piracy. Pirates attacked ships at sea and stole the valuable cargo. Though this practice was illegal, they often escaped punishment by arguing that the ships had belonged to rival countries.

In the late 1550s Drake accompanied his cousin, **John Hawkins** (1532–1595; see entry), on voyages to the French coast and other parts of Europe. Drake also sailed along when Hawkins began his ventures into the slave trade between Africa and the Americas. Though these excursions made Hawkins and his partners rich, they infuriated the Spanish, who had enjoyed exclusive rights to explore and trade in this part of the Western Hemisphere since 1494. Spain had no intention of letting England take a share of the huge wealth to be found in the Americas.

During Hawkins's third slaving voyage, in 1567, Drake participated as captain of the *Judith,* one of about nine ships in Hawkins's fleet. Expecting another extremely profitable excursion, he and Hawkins succeeded in selling most of their slaves in Rio de la Hacha and other Venezuelan ports. But soon after the fleet turned north for the home journey, the ships were hit by a devastating hurricane. Hawkins ordered them to shelter in the harbor of San Juan de Ulúa near Veracruz, Mexico. By now Spain had grown frustrated that the English continued to defy them about trade in the Caribbean. A large number of Spanish ships attacked the English, and after a fierce battle, Hawkins and Drake barely escaped with two ships. When Hawkins finally made it back to England, he claimed that Drake had slipped away with the *Judith* in the middle of the night, abandoning Hawkins and the remaining men on one overloaded ship with few supplies. Drake insisted he had followed orders. It was a scandal that troubled him for the rest of his life.

Privateering in the Americas

The experience caused Drake considerable bitterness toward Spain. He resented the riches he had lost in the attack, and he believed that this theft gave him the right to raid Spanish ships and territories in revenge. **Queen**

Elizabeth I (1533–1603; see entry) agreed, granting him a privateering commission in 1572. (Privateers are seafarers who own and operate their own ships independently but are authorized by their government to raid the ships of enemy nations, often capturing the entire ship with all its cargo.)

Drake took two small ships to the Caribbean, then known as the West Indies, in May 1572. He and his men attacked the settlement of Nombre de Dios, Panama, where they stole vast amounts of silver. Though he was wounded in the attack, Drake did not turn back because he wanted more treasure. He befriended the region's escaped African slaves, known as Cimaroons, who hated the Spanish and were eager to help Drake punish them. The Cimaroons showed Drake the route across the Isthmus of Panama by which the Spanish transported valuable goods. With this information Drake's party was able to raid Spanish ships carrying a fortune in silver. But Drake's brother, John, who had remained behind aboard one of the ships, was killed by Spanish gunfire. Soon afterward yellow fever attacked the ship, killing twenty-eight men, among them Drake's other brother, Joseph.

The voyage to the Caribbean made Drake a rich man. It also made him famous. But by the time he returned to Plymouth in 1573, England and Spain had agreed to try to maintain peaceful relations. Though the queen was enormously pleased that Drake had seized so much treasure from the Spanish colonies, she could not publicly welcome him or allow him to be treated as a hero.

Circumnavigates the world

Realizing that Elizabeth would not allow another privateering expedition at this time, Drake joined **Robert Devereux's** (Earl of Essex; 1566–1601; see entry) father, on a naval mission to defeat an uprising in Ireland in 1575. He was gone for about two years. Meanwhile the queen and her advisors were busy planning a secret expedition. They wished to send a fleet around South America to explore what lay beyond it. The fleet's commander would negotiate trading rights wherever possible, and he would also try to find an unknown continent called Terra Australis that was thought to lie south of the Strait of Magellan, a passage separating the southernmost part of the South American continent from the islands of Tierra del Fuego. The queen and those who invested in this expedition, including **Robert Dudley** (Earl of Leicester; 1532–1588; see entry) and secretary of state **Francis Walsingham** (1530–1590; see

A replica of The Golden Hind, *the ship in which Drake circumnavigated the globe.* © JOEL W. ROGERS/CORBIS.

entry), wanted this expedition to bring them wealth as well as weaken Spain's power.

Drake was appointed commander of the expedition. He was given official permission to take whatever wealth he could for himself and for the queen, and, at the same time, to attack Spanish ships and ports. He set out in December 1577 with five small ships and fewer than two hundred men. His flagship, the *Pelican,* was named in honor of the queen, who admired the pelican as a religious symbol. Drake later renamed this ship the *Golden Hind.*

Drake sailed from Plymouth, England, to the Cape Verde Islands off the coast of Africa. From there he turned west, crossing the Atlantic Ocean and heading toward South America. He reached the coast of Brazil in the spring of 1578. During the voyage tensions had arisen between himself and an officer, Thomas Doughty, in command of the *Swan.* In June, after stripping the *Swan* of all its supplies and equipment and ordering it to be burned, Drake put Doughty on trial for attempted

Ferdinand Magellan

Portuguese explorer Ferdinand Magellan (1480–1521) led the first European expedition to circle the world. In the service of Spain, Magellan led a fleet of five small ships to explore the seas that lay beyond South America. These regions were little known to Europeans, but Magellan believed that a passage existed by which he could sail from the Atlantic into the Pacific, reaching the Spice Islands in the Indian Ocean. Previously European traders had sailed around Africa to reach these Asian ports.

Magellan set out on September 8, 1519, and reached the coast of Brazil in December. He spent several months exploring the coast of Argentina and defeating an attempted mutiny. On October 31, Magellan finally entered the passage that, as it turned out, did lead to the Pacific. It took more than a month for his ships to navigate the passage, which wound among numerous islands and contained many channels. When he finally reached the western ocean, Magellan broke down and cried with joy. This passage became known as the Strait of Magellan.

Magellan's voyage across the Pacific was difficult. Hunger, thirst, and scurvy, a vitamin deficiency, took the lives of many of his crew. Sailors were forced to eat rat-gnawed biscuits and even leather from parts of the boat. On March 5, 1521, the ships arrived at Guam where they gathered supplies. Magellan then set sail for the Philippines. He had sailed thirteen thousand miles by the time he anchored in Cebu. There he befriended the ruler, but several weeks later, Magellan was killed in a fight on nearby Mactan Island.

Only one ship from Magellan's fleet, the *Victoria*, returned to Spain. The voyage, which ended on September 6, 1522, had taken almost three years. Of the original 270 men who sailed with Magellan, only eighteen survived. The sea route that Magellan discovered allowed European ships to navigate around South America. It remained an important sea route for hundreds of years, until the Panama Canal, which opened in 1914, provided a much shorter passage.

mutiny. He also stripped and abandoned a second ship, the *Christopher*. Though a lawyer on board argued that these actions were not legal, Drake insisted that he did not care about the law. Doughty was found guilty and beheaded. Drake later bragged about the incident when he wished to frighten Spanish prisoners aboard his ship.

On August 21, 1578, Drake entered the Strait of Magellan. (The Strait of Magellan is a body of water on the southern end of South America that connects the Atlantic and Pacific Oceans. It is named after explorer Ferdinand Magellan, who discovered the passage.) The trip through this difficult passage, which winds around numerous islands, took sixteen days. Once Drake reached the Pacific Ocean, however, huge winds battered his fleet. One ship sank, and the *Golden Hind* became separated from the remaining ship, the *Elizabeth*. Thinking the *Golden Hind* had sunk, the *Elizabeth* sailed back to England.

The *Golden Hind* was blown southward toward Cape Horn, at the southern tip of Tierra del Fuego. Exploring these treacherous waters, Drake was able to confirm his theory that the region south of Chile contained only open seas—and not an unknown continent. This discovery was an important advancement to geographic knowledge of the time. Though Drake did not actually sail through the waterway south of Tierra del Fuego, where storms and ice create great dangers, it became known as the Drake Passage. The passage was successfully sailed for the first time in 1616.

Turning back north, Drake sailed up the coast of Chile looking for riches. Never having experienced an attack in these waters, the Spanish were completely unprepared. In the port of Valparaiso Drake captured a large merchant ship and then looted the town. Finding less treasure than he had hoped, he continued up the coast, raiding settlements at will. His biggest prize, however, was the Spanish ship the *Cacafuego,* filled with gold, silver, and jewels. By the time Drake was ready to plot a return course to England, the *Golden Hind* was so crammed with riches that it sat dangerously low in the water.

Drake claimed to have sailed along the Pacific coast of the Americas as far north as Vancouver, Canada, before turning west. Historians, however, believe he exaggerated this story. Some evidence suggests he went as far as San Francisco, California, but other records show he may only have reached San Diego, California. In July 1579 he turned west across the Pacific. After sixty-eight days he sighted a group of islands that may have been the Palau Islands, near Indonesia. He then landed in the Philippines, where he gathered supplies. Drake went on to the Moluccas Islands, part of present-day Indonesia. Here, the ruling sultan entertained him and authorized him to trade for spices.

After repairing damage that the *Golden Hind* had sustained after hitting a reef, Drake sailed across the Indian Ocean and around the Cape of Good Hope in Africa. On September 26, 1580, two years after entering the Strait of Magellan, the *Golden Hind* returned to Plymouth harbor. Though the ship was loaded with treasure, only fifty-six of Drake's original crew of one hundred had survived. Drake had, however, become the second person to successfully circumnavigate, or sail around, the world—the first had been Magellan.

Wealth and fame

According to documents quoted by Harry Kelsey in *Sir Francis Drake: The Queen's Pirate,* Drake brought back to England "twenty of [Spain's] tons of silver, each one 2,000 pounds; five boxes of gold, a foot and half in length; and a huge quantity of pearls, some of great value." In addition, there were 650 ingots of silver weighing almost 23,000 pounds, as well as 36 parcels of gold weighing about 100 pounds. Those who had invested in the voyage got double their money back. The crew reportedly shared £40,000 among themselves, while the queen authorized Drake to take an extra £10,000 worth of gold for himself.

Queen Elizabeth was delighted with Drake's success, and she knighted him on April 1, 1581. (A knight is a man granted a rank of honor by the monarch for his personal merit or service to the country.) He was now immensely rich and famous. He enjoyed talking about his adventures, and he often told tales that were not quite true about his own bravery. He was elected to Parliament, England's legislative body, in

Queen Elizabeth I knights Francis Drake. © BALDWIN H. WARD AND KATHRYN C. WARD/CORBIS.

1581. He also became mayor of Plymouth that year. One of his accomplishments as mayor was the creation of a new water system for the town.

Drake had married in 1569, but his wife died in 1583, leaving him with no children. In 1585 he married Elizabeth Sydenham, whose family wealth further enhanced his fortune. He bought a large estate, Buckland Abbey, and settled down to enjoy his wealth and power.

War with Spain and the Armada crisis

Soon, however, Drake was at sea once again. By 1585 it was clear that war with Spain was likely, and, in order to weaken Spanish forces as much as possible, the queen sent Drake to raid Spanish territories. He set out with twenty-five ships on September 14. He captured Santiago, a Spanish port in the Cape Verde Islands, and then he raided the cities of Cartagena, Colombia; St. Augustine, Florida; and San Domingo, Hispaniola (now the Dominican Republic). Turning north for the return to England, he stopped at Roanoke Island, the settlement organized by **Walter Raleigh** (1552–1618; see entry). The settlers there were running out of supplies, and Drake decided to take them back with him to England.

In 1587 Drake was ordered to plan attacks on merchant ships sailing into or out of ports in Spain and Portugal. He sailed into the city of Cadiz and destroyed or captured thirty-seven ships in its harbor. Later he occupied Sagres, Portugal. He also seized a large Portuguese merchant ship in the Azores, a group of nine islands off the coast of Portugal. Despite this damage, the powerful Spanish Armada (navy) remained ready for an attack on England. If this naval assault succeeded, **King Philip II** (1527–1598; see entry) of Spain would be able to invade the country, overthrow Queen Elizabeth, and install a Roman Catholic government.

The queen placed Drake second in command of the English fleet. In 1588 the Armada sailed into the English Channel. According to English legend, Drake was playing a game of bowls, a game much like bowling that is played on a lawn, when he heard the news that the Armada was nearby. The fearless Drake calmly finished the game while English fleet commanders prepared their ships for battle. After several inconclusive skirmishes in the Channel, the English were able to break the Armada's formation and then chase the Spanish ships toward the north. On its route back to Spain, the Armada was almost completely destroyed by a powerful storm. Though Drake tried to take credit for playing a major role in the Armada's defeat, he did not act with complete regard for

England's defense. Early in the fighting he ignored orders and captured the *Rosario,* one of the Spanish pay ships, which was carrying a large amount of gold coins. Later he quarreled with another naval officer, Martin Frobisher (1535–1594), about dividing up the treasure. Frobisher claimed that Drake had withdrawn from the battle during an English attack on the *San Mateo,* and, according to Kelsey, called Drake "a cowardly knave or a traitor."

Nevertheless, the queen continued to trust Drake. In 1589 she sent him and Sir John Norris (1547–1597) to Spain with about 180 ships. But this fleet failed to inflict any significant military damage on Spanish or Portuguese targets. Most humiliating was its failure to capture the city of Lisbon. After losing several thousand men, the fleet sailed back to England. It was Drake's first naval failure.

Final voyage

Drake returned to Devon, where he was again elected to Parliament in 1593. Yet he was never entirely happy on land. When the queen offered him a commission in 1595 he immediately accepted. With John Hawkins, he would lead twenty-seven ships and about 2,500 men to the West Indies. Their mission was to attack the Spanish settlement there. The fleet sailed in August.

This expedition was a disaster from the start. When the fleet reached the Caribbean, Drake insisted on going ashore on Grand Canary Island. But local residents killed several crew members and captured others, who revealed the fleet's plans. Spain was warned, and a fleet was sent from Lisbon to stop Drake and Hawkins before they could capture the Spanish treasure ships in Puerto Rico.

While preparing the assault on San Juan, Puerto Rico, Hawkins died aboard ship. Several other officers were killed in the fighting. Drake left Puerto Rico, eventually reaching Curacao, an island off the coast of Venezuela. Finding little treasure there, he ordered the towns looted and burned. Realizing that the Spanish would be guarding the rich city of Cartagena, he decided to sail to Panama instead. Here the fleet encountered bad weather and Spanish resistance. In January 1596 Drake ordered the fleet to sail toward Honduras and Nicaragua. Soon afterward he fell seriously ill with dysentery, an inflammation of the lower intestines that causes severe diarrhea. Drake realized he would not survive this journey. After dictating final changes to his will, he died aboard his ship on January 28, 1596. Though he had stated his desire to be buried on land, Drake's body was sealed in a lead casket and buried at sea. The surviving ships, empty of treasure, returned to England in April and May.

Drake was a legend in his own time. The writer **Richard Hakluyt** (1552–1616; see entry) published accounts of Drake's voyages that focused on Drake's bravery and heroism. The queen and others who grew rich from Drake's plunder admired and encouraged his daring exploits. But, though Drake was fearless, he was also greedy and violent. Both a pirate and a patriot, Drake remains one of the most famous figures in English history.

For More Information

BOOKS

Cummins, John. *Francis Drake: Lives of a Hero.* New York: Macmillan, 1997.

Jugden, John. *Sir Francis Drake.* New York: Henry Holt and Company, 1990.

Kelsey, Harry. *Sir Francis Drake: The Queen's Pirate.* New Haven, CT and London: Yale University Press, 1998.

PERIODICALS

Cummins, John. "'That Golden Knight' Drake and His Reputation." *History Today,* January, 1996, p. 14.

Schwarz, Frederic C. "1573: Drake Sees the Pacific." *American Heritage,* February-March, 1998, p. 94.

WEB SITES

Pretty, Francis. "Sir Francis Drake's Famous Voyage Round the World, 1580." *Modern History Sourcebook.* http://www.fordham.edu/halsall/mod/1580Pretty-drake.html (accessed on July 11, 2006).

"Sir Francis Drake." *National Maritime Museum, Royal Observatory, Greenwich.* http://www.nmm.ac.uk/server/show/conWebDoc. 140 (accessed on July 11, 2006).

"Sir Francis Drake." http://www.sirfrancisdrakehistory.net/ (accessed on July 11, 2006).

Robert Dudley

BORN: 1532 • England

DIED: September 4, 1588 • Oxfordshire, England

English statesman; courtier

"I knew [Elizabeth I] better than anyone else from when she was eight years old, and from that age she always said that she would never marry."

Robert Dudley, a close friend of **Elizabeth I** (1533–1603; see entry) since childhood, became the queen's favorite courtier and a trusted advisor. (A courtier is a person who serves or participates in the royal court or household as the king's or queen's advisor, officer, or attendant.) He and Elizabeth felt such affection for one another that some observers believed they might have been lovers. Indeed, Dudley hoped to marry the queen, and even after her persistent rejections he maintained his close bond with her. As the Protestant queen's faithful supporter, Dudley was dedicated to her safety, pursuing ruthless policies against English Catholics whose loyalty he distrusted.

Though Dudley loved the queen, he did not always serve her well as a statesman. His advice often conflicted with that of Elizabeth's more experienced councilors; her willingness to listen to him caused considerable resentment among many of the queen's advisors. Dudley

Robert Dudley. HULTON ARCHIVE/GETTY IMAGES.

made many enemies, and he influenced the queen to take some actions that proved costly and unsuccessful, including the support of Protestant rebellions in France and the Netherlands. An advocate of extreme policies that did not always advance England's best interests, Dudley was nevertheless devoted to Elizabeth and remained one of her closest friends.

Early life

Robert Dudley was the fifth son and one of thirteen children born to John Dudley (Duke of Northumberland; 1501–1553), the most powerful noble in the government of Edward VI (1537–1553). Edward had taken the throne at age nine after the death of his father, **Henry VIII** (1491–1547; see entry). Since Edward was too young to make governmental decisions, John Dudley, one of Henry VIII's chief councilors, acted as his regent. This meant, in essence, that John Dudley would rule for the king until the boy reached adulthood. Robert and his siblings, three of whom survived into the 1560s, grew up surrounded by royalty and power. One sister, Mary, became the mother of the famous poet, **Philip Sidney** (1554–1586; see entry).

Robert first met Edward's half sister, the future Elizabeth I, at age eight, when the two children became good friends. They may have taken lessons together; both were exceptionally bright and interested in academic subjects. Unlike Elizabeth, however, who favored the study of Greek and Latin, Robert preferred mathematics and science. He was also an especially talented horseman.

Though a romantic link between Robert and Elizabeth was widely rumored, he married a Norfolk heiress, Amy Robsart, in 1550. Elizabeth herself attended the lavish wedding. Amy died ten years later after a fall, arousing suspicion that Robert may have caused the accident in order to become available as a marriage candidate for Elizabeth.

When Edward VI died in 1553 England was thrown into turmoil. Henry had named his daughters, **Mary I** (1516–1558; see entry) and Elizabeth, next in line to succeed Edward, but many nobles were unwilling to see Mary become queen. Not only was she a woman, but she was also a Catholic. Protestantism had become firmly established during Edward VI's rule, largely through the efforts of the Protestant lords who served as his councilors. They had no wish to see Mary try to restore Catholic rule in a country that was still struggling to subdue Catholic resistance to the new religion. John Dudley led an attempt to place Lady

Jane Grey (1537–1554), his daughter-in-law and a Protestant great-granddaughter of Henry VII (1457–1547) on the throne. Though Grey did become queen of England for nine days, Mary's supporters defeated Dudley's plot and restored Mary to power. John Dudley and his sons were imprisoned in the Tower of London. (The Tower of London was a fortress on the Thames River in London that was used as a royal residence, treasury, and, most famously, as a prison for the upper class.) John Dudley was beheaded for treason, but Robert and his brothers were released after a year.

A period of struggle followed. Robert and his brother, Henry, went to France to fight on the side of Mary's husband, **Philip II** (1527–1598; see entry), king of Spain. Henry was killed in battle, and Robert returned to England, where he faced financial difficulties. Not until Elizabeth took the throne in 1558 did his fortunes significantly improve.

The queen's favorite

Elizabeth named Dudley, whom she called her "Sweet Robin," Master of the Queen's Horse, an honor that brought him into frequent personal contact with the queen. He was given charge of organizing her public schedule and her personal entertainments. Handsome, athletic, witty, and flirtatious, he quickly became her favorite courtier. Elizabeth bestowed many lavish gifts on him, including property, money, and titles. In 1562 she made Dudley a member of her Privy Council, despite objections from the other councilors. (The Privy Council was the board of advisors that carried out the administrative function of the government in matters of economy, defense, foreign policy, and law and order, and its members served as the queen's chief advisors.) When she became ill with smallpox that year she requested that, if she were to die, Dudley be made Lord Protector of the Realm. In 1564 she made him earl of Leicester and Baron Denbigh. Many at the royal court began to gossip about a romance between the queen and Dudley. Rumors suggested that they were lovers, and even that the queen was pregnant with Dudley's child.

Those who resented Dudley's influence on Elizabeth grew to hate him. They saw him as an arrogant and ambitious man who held more power over the queen than he deserved. He spent money irresponsibly and was known for his many romantic affairs. He soon became, according to many accounts, one of the most widely detested men in England. Nevertheless, he remained Elizabeth's close friend throughout his life.

Dudley in Literature

Though Dudley was not widely popular during his life, he received some respectful tributes after his death. Some historians believe that the play *Endymion, the Man in the Moon,* written by John Lyly (1554–1606) and performed for the queen on New Year's Day of 1591, was an allegory, or symbolic representation, of the love between Dudley and Elizabeth. In the play, which is based on a Greek myth, a humble shepherd, Endymion, falls in love with Cynthia, the goddess of the moon. Cynthia has never fallen in love or even kissed a man, but she is so moved by Endymion's youth and beauty that she grants him immortality with a kiss: "When she, whose figure of all is the perfectest and never to be measured, always one yet never the same, still inconstant yet never wavering, shall come and kiss Endymion in his sleep, he shall then rise; else never." (Act III, Scene 4). This scene symbolizes the power of the queen to bestow honors on her beloved that will endure after his life has ended.

The poet **Edmund Spenser** (1552–1599; see entry), who entered Dudley's service in 1579, honored Elizabeth with a monumental allegorical epic, *The Faerie Queene,* published between 1590 and 1609. Throughout this work the figure of Arthur, the perfect knight and suitor of Queen Gloriana, appears. Many scholars believe that Spenser intended Arthur to symbolize Dudley, while Gloriana symbolized Elizabeth.

When Dudley's wife, Amy Robsart, was found dead of a broken neck at the bottom of a staircase in 1560, Dudley's enemies immediately suspected Dudley of foul play. Dudley was called before a jury and examined, but insufficient evidence existed to convict him of a crime. Nevertheless, the scandal damaged his reputation and stood in the way of any hopes that he might marry the queen. Nevertheless, he actively courted Elizabeth. She rejected him, however, and even suggested that he consider a marriage with her Catholic cousin, **Mary Stuart** (Queen of Scots; 1542–1587; see entry). Since Mary had powerful Catholic allies who felt that she had a more legitimate claim to the English throne than Elizabeth did, the queen had reason to doubt Mary's loyalty. Marriage to Dudley, whom Elizabeth trusted completely, would help to neutralize any threat that Mary might pose. But Mary was insulted at the idea that she should accept a suitor whom Elizabeth had rejected; she refused to consider the proposal.

Although it became increasingly clear that Elizabeth would never agree to wed Dudley, he was a jealous man and objected to all other marriage proposals that she received, pressuring her to reject each one. At the same time, though, he conducted numerous scandalous love affairs, including one with Lady Douglas Sheffield (c. 1545–1608) that produced a son, Robert. In 1578, convinced that Elizabeth would never accept him as a husband, he married the queen's cousin, Lettice Devereux (1540–1634), widow of the earl of Essex. This made Dudley the step-father of her nine-year-old son, **Robert Devereux** (later Earl of Essex; 1566–1601; see entry), who would in time surpass him as Elizabeth's favorite at court. Lettice gave birth to a son, also named Robert, who died in infancy. Dudley had no other children. His marriage to Lettice caused the queen intense displeasure; from then on, Elizabeth's affection for Dudley was tempered with disappointment.

Anti-Catholic policies

As a statesman Dudley emphasized the need to strengthen Protestant control in England. He understood that Elizabeth had many powerful enemies both at home and abroad, and he made it his mission to protect her from danger wherever it might be found. He was wary of develop-ments in France and in Spain, both strongly Catholic countries and traditional rivals of England. Some English Catholics had fled to these countries to escape persecution, and they had succeeded in gaining some political support. In France, especially, there was growing interest in the cause of Mary Stuart, who was related to the French nobility and had grown up at the French royal court. Mary's supporters believed that she, as a great-granddaughter of the English King Henry VII (1457–1509), had a better legal claim to the English throne than did Elizabeth, whose mother was Henry VIII's second wife. Because the Catholic Church did not grant Elizabeth's father a divorce from his first wife—he obtained a divorce through the Protestant Church instead—her birth was not con-sidered legitimate under Catholic law. When war broke out between the Catholic majority in France and the small but influential Protestant minority, called Huguenots, in 1562, Dudley urged the queen to assist the Huguenots.

Elizabeth agreed to send troops and money. However, she was motivated not only by religious loyalty but also by the desire to recapture territories in northern France that had once been English possessions. In return for her support she demanded that the Huguenots give her the cities of Dieppe and Le Havre as pledges for the eventual return of Calais, which the French had seized during the reign of Elizabeth's predecessor, Mary I. But the English expedition failed. Once **Catherine de Medici** (1519–1589; see entry), who ruled France for her adolescent son, Charles IX (1550–1574), discovered that England was gaining a foothold into

French territory, she convinced both of the French factions to unite and drive England out of the country. Elizabeth was forced to give up hopes of ever reclaiming Calais for England. The failure of this campaign in France did nothing to improve Dudley's reputation among the Privy Council, where he soon had many enemies, chief among them the queen's most trusted advisor, **William Cecil** (Lord Burghley; 1520–1598; see entry).

In 1584 Dudley helped to form the Protestant Association, whose members vowed to protect Elizabeth with their lives. He relentlessly pursued the punishment of English Catholics who might pose a threat to Protestant power. He grew increasingly fearful of Spain, a strongly Catholic country that had become associated with various plots to overthrow Elizabeth and install Mary Stuart, who had been forced to flee Scotland and was now living under guard in England, as queen. Dudley became one of the strongest voices on the queen's Privy Council to urge direct intervention against Spain. This extreme position pitted him against the more moderate Cecil, who hoped to avoid open war with Spain.

Dudley's enemies detested him, and in 1584 they published a pamphlet, *Leicester's Commonwealth,* that attacked his character. Biographer Elizabeth Jenkins, quoted in *Shakespeare Oxford Newsletter,* described the publication as a "racy piece of journalism" that made Leicester look like a "master criminal, with his tribe of poisoners, bawds [prostitutes] and abortionists. . . ." The pamphlet went on to accuse Dudley of having murdered Amy Robsart and of poisoning the earl of Essex so that Dudley could then marry Essex's widow. Historians believe that this anonymous pamphlet, which presented a distorted picture of Dudley, was probably written in retaliation for Dudley's relentless aggression toward English Catholics.

In 1585 Elizabeth finally agreed to send military support to Protestants in the Netherlands who had launched a rebellion against Spain. She gave Dudley command of six thousand troops. He proved to be a poor military leader. Furthermore, without obtaining the queen's permission, he accepted a Dutch offer making him governor-general of the provinces that had declared themselves independent of Spain. Dudley's assumption of this position infuriated the queen, who worried that it would cause Philip II to believe that she wished to rule the Netherlands. She sent Dudley an angry letter, quoted in Derek Wilson's *The Uncrowned Kings of England,* expressing surprise and displeasure that "a man raised up by ourself and extraordinarily favoured by us above any other subject of this land, would have in so contemptible a sort broken our commandement." She demanded that he obey her orders to the letter or else face the "uttermost peril." Shocked by the queen's anger, Dudley wrote apologetic letters in return, but his arrogant tactics and lack of military skill caused Elizabeth to call him back to England in 1587.

Despite his failures in the Netherlands, Dudley received another military commission from the queen in 1588, when England was preparing to defend itself from an expected attack by Spain. Elizabeth appointed him lieutenant general of the army at Tilbury. As it turned out, the invasion failed when the mighty Spanish navy, the Armada, was chased into northern waters and then destroyed by devastating storms. Dudley, in charge of a defensive force on land, never saw action in this campaign.

Heavily in debt, Dudley died of a fever on September 4, 1588, at his home in Oxfordshire, and he was buried at St. Mary's Church, Warwick. His enemies said that their great joy at the defeat of the Spanish Armada was nothing compared to their joy in Dudley's death.

Although by the end of his life Dudley had begun to lose some of the queen's favor, he nevertheless remained her close friend to the end of his life. She mourned for him and reportedly refused to see or speak with anyone for several days after he died. Regardless of the wisdom of his political counsel, Dudley provided Elizabeth with unwavering friendship and an intimate affection that she found in no one else.

For More Information

BOOKS

Dersin, Denise, ed. *What Life Was Like in the Realm of Elizabeth: England A.D. 1533–1603.* Alexandria, VA: Time-Warner Books, 1998.

Wilson, Derek. *Sweet Robin: A Biography of Robert Dudley, Earl of Leicester, 1533–1588.* London: H. Hamilton, 1981.

———. *The Uncrowned Kings of England: the Black History of the Dudleys and the Tudor Throne.* New York: Carroll & Graf Publishers, 2005.

WEB SITES

Moore, Peter R. "Demonography 101: Alan Nelson's *Monstrous Adversary.* " *Shakespeare Oxford Newsletter,* Winter 2004. http://72.14.203.104/search?q=cache:OxnF52ZYqzsJ:www.shakespeare-oxford.com/demngraf.htm+leicester%27s+commonwealth&hl=en&gl=us&t=clnk&cd=8 (accessed on July 11, 2006).

"Robert Dudley." *Elizabeth I.* http://www.elizabethi.org/us/queensmen/robertdudley.htm (accessed on July 11, 2006).

"Robert Dudley." *Tudor Place.* http://www.tudorplace.com.ar/Bios/RobertDudley(1ELeicester).htm (accessed on July 11, 2006).

"Works of John Lyly: Endimion—The Man in the Moone. 1591." *Elizabethan Authors.* http://www.elizabethanauthors.com/endmodGloss.htm (accessed on July 11, 2006).

Elizabeth I

BORN: September 7, 1533 • Greenwich, England

DIED: March 24, 1603 • Richmond, Surrey, England

English queen

"I know I have the body but of a weak and feeble woman; but I have the heart and stomach of a king, and of a king of England too."

Queen Elizabeth I. COURTESY OF THE LIBRARY OF CONGRESS.

When Elizabeth I became queen of England in 1558, she inherited a weak and backward island that had been severely divided by three religious upheavals in two decades. Most of her subjects doubted the ability of a woman to lead the troubled country and anxiously waited for her to marry. But Elizabeth chose to play her role as the monarch of the realm alone. Applying her instinct, intelligence, energy, and stubborn willfulness to the task, she would become the strongest and most beloved monarch the island had seen in centuries. During Elizabeth's reign England became one of Europe's most powerful and sophisticated countries and a growing empire. In military strength, exploration, commerce, and above all the arts, the nation experienced a golden age that changed the culture of England, as well that of Europe and North America, forever.

Birth and early childhood

Despite her royal birth, Elizabeth suffered some terrible hardships as a child. At the time of her conception (when her mother became pregnant with her) her father, **Henry VIII** (1491–1547; see entry), had been married to the Spanish princess Catherine of Aragon (1485–1536) for over twenty years. The royal couple had only one surviving child, **Mary I** (1516–1558; see entry). Henry, who desperately wanted a male heir to the throne, sought to get out of his marriage. He had developed a passion for Anne Boleyn (c. 1504–1536), his wife's well-educated and attractive lady-in-waiting, and he wished to marry her. (A lady-in-waiting is a woman in the queen's household who attends the queen.) Henry hoped the Catholic pope, the head of the Catholic Church, would quietly terminate his marriage. When the pope refused, Henry secretly married the already pregnant Boleyn, claiming his first marriage had been illegitimate. As the pope prepared to excommunicate the king, depriving him of membership in the church, Henry broke off England's centuries-old relationship with the Roman Catholic Church and named himself head of the church in England. English citizens who continued to practice Catholicism under the pope's leadership had their property taken away or were imprisoned.

Elizabeth was born on September 7, 1533. Her father had changed the course of English history in order to provide a male heir to the throne, so he was not happy to find out his child was a girl. Within a few months the infant Elizabeth, tended by a small group of noblewomen, or women born to families of high rank, was sent to live in her own household about twenty miles north of London. Boleyn visited her child and sent her gifts of clothing, but she had other challenges to face. It was not long before Henry lost interest in his new queen. Less than three years after their marriage Boleyn was arrested on charges of committing adultery. Few people, even those who disliked her, believed the charges, but Henry overpowered all objections. Boleyn was beheaded on May 19, 1536. Within two weeks of her death Henry married Jane Seymour (c. 1509–1537). From this third marriage he finally got a son, Edward VI (1537–1553), although his new wife died twelve days after giving birth.

Elizabeth was not yet three years old when her mother was executed. She never spoke publicly or wrote about her feelings about her mother's death or her father's part in it.

A royal education

Elizabeth was raised in a series of royal households under the loving care of her governess, Kat Ashley. Her older half-sister, Mary, often lived in her household, and the sisters got along well with each other. After years of separation from their father, Elizabeth and Mary were invited to Henry's sixth and final marriage to Katherine Parr (c. 1512–1548) in 1543. Parr was a loving stepmother, creating a warm family life Elizabeth had not experienced before. Under Parr's influence, the aging Henry made certain that both his daughters were in line to inherit the throne, making it official that upon his death the English throne was to pass to Edward. If Edward died without an heir, Mary was next in line, and then Elizabeth.

The top educators in England were hired to teach Edward, and Elizabeth, who was already an outstanding student, was allowed to study under them as well. The tutors had all participated in the new humanist movement that had spread from Italy to England's Cambridge University in the beginning of the century. Humanism stressed educating students in the ancient Latin and Greek languages, preparing them to study about human virtue and morality from the classic texts. Elizabeth surpassed all expectations as a student. Well before reaching her teens, she was fluent in Latin, French, Italian, and Welsh, and knew a considerable amount of Greek. She was fond of translating ancient Latin and Greek works into English or French, and she studied the Bible and the works of the classical philosophers as well as history on a daily basis. Revealing the prevailing notion of his day that women were inferior, her teacher, the humanist Roger Ascham (1515–1558), quoted in Simon Schama's *A History of Britain: At the Edge of the World? 3500 BCE–1603 CE* wrote: "Her mind has no womanly weakness, her perseverance is equal to that of a man, and her memory long keeps what it quickly picks up." Ascham took the unusual step of teaching Elizabeth oratory, or the art of public speaking, which was not considered a useful skill for women. She excelled in it.

Katherine Parr had become intrigued with the era's religious reformers, people of the new Reformation movement who believed there was corruption in the Catholic Church and disliked some of its practices. This movement resulted in the establishment of several Protestant churches. The Protestants preferred a simple, pious study of the Bible and more personal experiences in seeking truth and faith. Parr held daily religious meetings, and both Elizabeth and Edward eagerly attended. Ascham was a Protestant as well.

The child king

When Henry VIII died in 1547, nine-year-old Edward took the throne as Edward VI. By the orders of Edward's regents, the people appointed to rule England in his name while he was under age, Catholic traditions and rituals (established ceremonies performed in precise ways according to the rules of the church) were forbidden and a new Protestant prayer book was introduced that outlined the services for all English churches. Catholics were expelled from the council of royal advisors, Catholic bishops were fired and replaced by Protestants, and those English people who would not accept the Protestant faith were persecuted. Faithful Catholics watched in silent horror as mobs destroyed their churches, smashing the altars and the images of the Virgin Mary and other Catholic symbols.

After her father's death, Elizabeth lived with Katherine Parr, who had hastily married a former love, Thomas Seymour (c. 1508–1549). Seymour was the ambitious and good-looking uncle of the young king. He was also the younger brother of Edward's first regent, the Duke of Somerset. Seymour began to make inappropriate romantic advances toward the fourteen-year-old Elizabeth, who evidently found him intriguing. Parr died due to complications in childbirth and Seymour began to consider the possibility of marrying Elizabeth. Though she never agreed to marriage, Elizabeth did not object to his attentions. In the end Seymour's ambitions got the better of him. He made plans to kidnap Edward and take over his brother's role as regent. The plot was uncovered, and Seymour was sent to the Tower of London. (The Tower was a fortress on the Thames River in London that was used as a royal residence, treasury, and, most famously, as a prison for the upper class.) Details of the relations between Elizabeth and Seymour quickly became a matter of public knowledge, and Edward's councilors questioned Elizabeth to find out if she had participated in Seymour's conspiracy. The young princess maintained a quiet dignity even when, two weeks later, Seymour was beheaded for treason. No one has ever known how Elizabeth felt about Seymour and his execution; she had learned at a very early age to keep her thoughts and feelings to herself.

Imprisoned during Mary's rule

In 1553 Edward died at the age of fifteen. Mary, a devout Catholic, took the throne, determined to restore England to Catholicism. She soon became engaged to marry the heir to the Spanish throne, **Philip II** (1526–1598; see entry). It was a very unpopular marriage in England. Spain was the richest and most powerful nation in Europe. The English people, Catholic and Protestant alike, feared that Philip would make England a province of Spain. A group of English noblemen hastily planned to overthrow Mary before she could wed Philip and place Elizabeth on the throne. The effort failed, but it left Mary suspicious that Elizabeth had participated in the plot. The queen imprisoned her younger sister in the Tower of London. There Elizabeth spent two miserable months, sick and afraid for her life. When she was released, she was placed under house arrest at the home of one of her sister's loyal followers. Mary married Philip in 1554.

Elizabeth imprisoned in the Tower of London. HULTON ARCHIVE/GETTY IMAGES.

Elizabethan World: Biographies

After a failed pregnancy Mary turned her attention to forcing Protestants to conform to the Catholic Church, beginning by enacting harsh laws against heresy, religious opinions that conflict with the church's doctrines. The most prominent religious leaders and statesmen of Edward's reign as well as more humble Protestants who refused to deny their religious beliefs were sentenced to burn at the stake. About three hundred people died in this manner during Mary's short rule, earning her the nickname "Bloody Mary." Many Protestants fled to Europe.

Elizabeth, living under constant watch, attended Catholic masses and kept her ideas about religion to herself. For good reason, she spent much of Mary's reign wondering if she would live to see the next day. Despite fears for her life, Elizabeth was observing the reigns of her brother and sister. If she succeeded to throne, Elizabeth did not wish to repeat their mistakes.

Elizabeth takes the throne

Mary died of cancer in 1558. English legend has it that when the lords arrived to bring Elizabeth the news, they found her reading a Bible under an oak tree in her garden. (The oak tree is an English symbol of the nation's stability and duration.) Upon hearing of Mary's death, Elizabeth fell to her knees, and the messengers heard her recite a verse from Psalm 118 in Latin: "This is the Lord's doing: and it is marvelous in our eyes" (as quoted in Peter Brimacombe's *All the Queen's Men*).

Mary had left the nation in poor shape. Its military powers were diminished, the royal government was deeply in debt, poverty was widespread, and the population had become bitterly divided by the rapid religious changes imposed by three monarchs in a row. Elizabeth got to work before her sister was buried. She began by reorganizing the Privy Council, the board of advisors that carried out the administrative function of the government in matters of economy, defense, foreign policy, and law and order, and its members served as the king's or queen's chief advisors. Elizabeth dismissed thirty of Mary's councilors. Her first appointment to the council was **William Cecil** (Lord Burghley; 1520–1598; see entry) as secretary of state and her chief advisor. No one but Elizabeth herself was to have greater power during her reign. Though Cecil began his office holding the firm belief that a woman alone could not rule England, he would serve Elizabeth faithfully for forty years. He was a voice for caution and moderation and a valuable counterbalance to some of the dashing, but rash, statesmen that flocked to Elizabeth's court.

One of these courtiers, or royal attendants, was her long-time favorite, **Robert Dudley** (Earl of Leicester; 1532–1588; see entry), a childhood companion who was, in these first days, named Master of Horse. Cecil and Dudley would be at odds with each other for many years to come. Elizabeth seemed to enjoy the conflict and valued both of their points of view.

At her coronation, or crowning as queen, Elizabeth immediately demonstrated her royal dignity and her understanding of her subjects. She knew that many viewed her as the illegitimate child of Anne Boleyn and that few believed a woman was fit to lead them, but she gave no sign of self-doubt as she appeared before thousands of Londoners. Observers noted that Elizabeth gave her attention to each person, listening to the speeches of children, attentively watching the plays in her honor, accepting gifts, smiling upon all, and constantly stopping to offer her thanks for the outpouring of love she received. Somehow she appeared as both goddess and warm personal friend. At twenty-five the red-haired Elizabeth was very attractive. She was tall and slender, with high cheekbones and piercing dark eyes, and she was very proud of her beautiful long-fingered hands. She created a worthy royal display, wearing Mary's coronation garments of silk, gold, and ermine (a type of fur) under her own purple velvet robes. Thousands of attendants waited upon her, and all of them had been exquisitely outfitted in silk, gold, silver, and velvet.

The religious settlement of 1559

No one was certain what Elizabeth's personal religious beliefs were, but her goal was clear: she wished to create a united church in which all English people could worship. In her 1559 religious settlement she devised a compromise between the Catholics and the Protestants. Elizabeth's church retained some of the religious objects of Catholicism—the candles, crucifixes, priests' robes, and altars. But in Elizabethan England there would be no Catholic Mass, the service at which an ordained priest performs transubstantiation, blessing the Eucharist (bread and wine) and miraculously changing it into the blood and body of Christ, while maintaining the appearance of bread and wine. Protestants objected to this ceremony because they believed that only God, not human priests, could perform such miracles. Elizabeth restored the *Book of Common Prayer,* which set out all the services, ceremonies, and rituals of the new church. The book was from Edward VI's Protestant reign, but the wording was made so vague that Protestants and Catholics alike could follow their own beliefs while using it. Services of the new church were conducted in English, as opposed to the Latin Catholic services, and the translated Bible was readily available to all. Elizabeth intended to be the head of the new Anglican Church, but Parliament, England's legislative body, objected strongly to a woman serving in this role. Elizabeth compromised, calling herself the supreme governor of the church and leaving final decisions on religious matters to the church authorities.

Elizabeth made it known that she meant to enforce an outward appearance of conformity, and that everyone could believe as they wished as long as they were private about it. "There is only one Jesus Christ. The rest is a dispute over trifles," Elizabeth told a French diplomat, as quoted by Alison Weir in *The Life of Elizabeth I.* Nevertheless, the act made Protestantism the religion of England. Everyone in England was required to attend the local Anglican Church. For Catholics, these changes were unwelcome and for many Protestant reformers, the changes were not nearly enough. But most people accepted the religious compromise.

The question of succession

As soon as Elizabeth took the throne, Parliament and her Privy Council urged her to marry. They wanted an heir to the throne when she died, but that was not the only reason. Most believed that no woman could be a capable ruler. There were many suitors for the young and attractive queen of England. Her sister's husband, Philip, now the king of Spain, asked for her hand, as did the king of Sweden and the archduke of Austria. Elizabeth seems to have enjoyed the attention and did her best to keep her suitors guessing what her intentions were. But she repeatedly said she did not want a husband. She accepted her role as England's ruler and had no intention of sharing it. Furthermore there were problems with almost any choice of husband for Elizabeth. The English people did not want a foreign king, as she had seen when her sister married Philip; and Elizabeth considered most English matches beneath her.

There was one other problem. Elizabeth was apparently in love with her Master of Horse, Robert Dudley, whom she called her "Bonny Robin." Though Dudley was married when he took his post, he and Elizabeth spent hours together every day. Their intimacy raised eyebrows around the court. One of the first scandals of Elizabeth's reign occurred when Dudley's wife, who was ill with cancer, died under suspicious circumstances. Although an investigation found the death to be an accident, Elizabeth knew that suspicion remained, making marriage between Dudley and herself impossible. She made Dudley the earl of Leicester and gave him many powers in her court, remaining close to him through the years. In the meantime Elizabeth began to promote her image as the Virgin Queen, married only to her kingdom.

The queen and her court

Elizabeth's court traveled with her to her many palaces, usually consisting of from one thousand to fifteen hundred attendants and servants. The royal court was England's main place of government, business, entertainment, and art—in fact some have called it the center of English culture. Attending court was vital for all who wanted to advance their careers or be noticed. Along with statesmen and foreign representatives, the best musicians, artists, philosophers, and explorers were found at court. Young women of England's highest-ranking families sought positions at court as maids of honor. Their reward for a job well done was a marriage arranged by the queen. All who attended court dressed in the latest fashions and knew the proper manners to use in the presence of royalty. Elizabeth maintained regal magnificence in her court night and day. She believed the strength of her rule depended on a lavish display of grandeur. She dressed extravagantly and followed the elaborate royal traditions.

Elizabeth spent most of her day in the well-guarded Privy Chamber, where she conducted her business or entertained herself. Only a few privileged attendants could enter the Privy Chamber. Others met with the queen in the more public Great Hall, usually gaining entrance by paying one of her staff for the privilege.

Elizabeth was remarkably energetic. She loved sports, especially riding horses and hunting. She also loved to dance. Well into her sixties, she was frequently seen on the dance floor executing intricate hops and twirls with one of her favorites. Elizabeth's favorites were the many bold and handsome young men that she kept in her presence. Most were able flatterers, as well as good dancers, dressers, or horsemen. The queen enjoyed interesting young men who could challenge her intellect, and she preferred them to be handsome. She was very vain about her own looks. Males who wished her favor acted as though they were in love with her, even as she got older. Elizabeth expected a great deal of time and loyalty from her favorites. She had a fiery temper, once throwing a shoe in a tantrum. With her intimates she swore like a sailor, and spared no one from her sharp tongue when annoyed. But the queen also showed warm and loyal affection to her closest associates. Most of her attendants were genuinely drawn to her magnetic presence. Writer Sir John Harington (1561–1612), as quoted by Brimacombe, summarized: "When she smiled, it was a pure sunshine, that everyone did chose [choose] to bask in if they could."

Elizabeth applied her vast energy wholeheartedly to her work, involving herself in every detail of her rule, often working late into the night. Elizabeth's work included propaganda, or creating a persuasive heroic image of herself. She carefully staged her public appearances and made an effort to travel regularly to be seen by her people. During the summer she often took her whole court on progresses, lengthy and expensive visits to the estates of favored attendants.

Plots for the throne

Elizabeth's councilors constantly feared conspiracies to overthrow her. No one caused them more alarm than **Mary Stuart** (Queen of Scots; 1542–1587; see entry). Mary had become the queen of Scotland as an infant, but she was raised in France and at the age of fifteen had married the heir to the French throne. She was the great-granddaughter of Henry VII (1457–1509), Elizabeth's grandfather, and had a strong claim to the English throne. Mary, a devout Catholic, returned to rule Scotland in 1560 after the death of her husband.

In 1565 Mary married Henry Stewart, Lord Darnley (1545–1567), the next heir after herself to the English throne. Darnley was an arrogant man who drank too much and offended everyone, including his wife. The couple had a son, James (1566–1625). A year after their child was born, Darnley was murdered. Many in Scotland suspected Mary had been involved. When she married the man suspected of committing the murder, the Scottish people rose up against her and forced her to give up the throne in favor of her infant son, who then became James VI of Scotland. Mary fled to England in 1568, where she asked Elizabeth for protection.

Elizabeth had much to fear from her Scottish cousin. Spain, France, the Catholic Church in Rome, Catholics in England, and exiled English Catholics abroad would all have liked to see Mary take the English throne and restore Catholicism as the nation's official religion. Elizabeth's Privy Council urged her to send Mary back to Scotland where she would be imprisoned, but Elizabeth believed strongly in the God-given authority of kings and queens. She also viewed Mary as family and did not want to be the instrument of her downfall. Elizabeth placed Mary in the watchful care of some loyal followers. As feared, Mary became a symbol of the Catholic cause and the focus of several conspiracies against Elizabeth.

The first conspiracy arose in 1569 in the distant and largely Catholic northern provinces. The rebels successfully restored some northern cathedrals to Catholicism before Elizabeth gathered a large army to suppress the rebellion, which became known as the Northern Rising. More than four hundred northern rebels were executed. The Catholic Church in Rome had supported the uprising, and in 1570 Pope Pius V (1504–1572) belatedly excommunicated Elizabeth, calling on her Catholic subjects to rise against her. At the same time Philip II became involved in a plan, known as the Ridolfi plot, for Spain to invade England and install Mary Stuart on the throne. This conspiracy failed quickly. An uneasy peace, with Mary living in captivity, continued for fifteen more years. In 1586 Elizabeth's spymaster **Francis Walsingham** (1532–1590; see entry) intercepted a letter in which Mary consented to a plan to kill Elizabeth. She was found guilty of treason and Elizabeth reluctantly signed the death warrant. In 1587 Mary was beheaded. After so many plots, Elizabeth's government became far less tolerant of Catholics. Hundreds of English Catholics, many of them priests, who worked to promote Catholicism were executed.

War with Spain

Spain and England had traditionally been friendly with each other, but by the 1580s, tensions between them were high. The major reason was that Philip had dedicated himself to defending the Catholic faith, and he began to feel it a point of honor that he would one day restore England to Catholicism. But there was more to it than that. England was beginning to resent Spain's monopoly (exclusive right) on trade with the Americas. Spain's monopoly had made it immensely rich and powerful. Elizabeth began allowing English privateers to attack Spanish ships. (Privateers are seafarers who own and operate their own ships independently but are authorized by their government to raid the ships of enemy nations, often capturing the entire ship with all its cargo.) This practice infuriated Philip.

Protestants in the Spanish-dominated Netherlands rose up against Philip in 1585. They asked for Elizabeth's help, and she sent them troops in a direct confrontation with Spain. Philip began planning an invasion of England immediately. By early July 1588 the Spaniards had assembled the Great Armada, a fleet of one hundred and thirty vessels, and sailed for the English Channel. The English navy of about sixty-six ships set out to meet the Armada. The sea battle began on July 19, 1588. Although the English were outnumbered, their ships were smaller, faster, and easier to maneuver. They carried cannons on their decks that could damage enemy boats from a distance. The two navies fought for more than a week without a decisive battle. Then the English waged a second attack, setting fire to several ships and sending them directly into the Spanish fleet. The Armada scattered to avoid fires. Just as they were about to get back into position, a fierce windstorm arose, further scattering the remaining Armada. The Spanish fleet retreated only to face a severe storm. About thirty-five of the Spanish ships were lost. The English had won the fight.

Meanwhile, not knowing who was winning the battle at sea, England prepared for a Spanish invasion on its soil. Elizabeth, attended by Dudley, fearlessly rode to Tilbury, a camp at the mouth of the Thames River, to appear before her troops. Dressed in silver and white velvet and holding a silver helmet and the sword of state, she spoke to the soldiers from her white horse. The speech at Tilbury enthralled her troops and became one of the defining moments of the queen's reign.

Having defeated Europe's most powerful navy, England could claim to be the greatest sea power in the world. But as her nation celebrated, Elizabeth was cast into mourning. Dudley died two weeks after escorting her to Tilbury, and this loss was only the beginning of difficult times for the queen. As the years passed and more of her closest advisors died, the aging Elizabeth sank into loneliness and depression. She mourned the loss of her old governess, Kat Ashley, and her trusted advisor, William Cecil.

The last years

In her last decades Elizabeth continued to have young favorites such as the renowned explorer, poet, and statesman **Walter Raleigh** (1552–1618; see entry). Her strongest affection was given to a handsome but temperamental and highly ambitious young man, **Robert Devereux** (Earl of Essex; 1566–1601; see entry). Elizabeth granted Devereux many favors, but she did not place him in the powerful positions he wanted, probably distrusting his abilities. In 1599 Devereux convinced Elizabeth, against her better judgment, to give him command of a force intended to stop a rebellion in Ireland. The mission failed, with Devereux unaccountably making a truce with the enemy and returning to England without orders to do so. He soon found himself out of the queen's favor and denied access to her presence. Devereux found this disgrace too humiliating to endure. He organized a poorly planned rebellion against his queen and was arrested in the act of treason. Elizabeth, in her late sixties, was forced to sign the death warrant of her last favorite. Devereux was beheaded in 1601.

Though she wore a red wig to cover her thinning hair and thick white powder to cover her wrinkles, Elizabeth's magnificence faded in her old age. In the winter of 1603 she became ill. Refusing medical treatment and food, she prepared herself for the end. She died in her bed in March. James VI of Scotland was proclaimed **King James I** (see entry) of England a few hours after Elizabeth's death.

At the time of her death Elizabeth was sixty-nine and had ruled England for forty-five years. Her reign was over, but the culture that had found its center in her court continued to inspire humankind with its spirit of adventure and conquest and its thirst for the arts and theater. The image that Elizabeth had cultivated over the years as "Gloriana," the symbol of a newly discovered national pride in England, survived long after the queen was gone.

For More Information

BOOKS

Brimacombe, Peter. *All the Queen's Men: The World of Elizabeth I.* London: Sutton Publishing, 2000.

Schama, Simon. *A History of Britain: At the Edge of the World? 3500 BCE –1603 CE.* New York: Hyperion, 2000.

Starkey, David. *Elizabeth: The Struggle for the Throne.* New York: HarperCollins, 2001.

Weir, Alison. *The Life of Elizabeth I.* New York: Ballantine Books, 1998.

WEB SITES

"Elizabeth I." *Historic Figures: BBC.* http://www.bbc.co.uk/history/historic_figures/elizabeth_i_queen.shtml (accessed on July 11, 2006).

"Elizabeth I: Biography." http://www.elizabethi.org/uk/biography.html (accessed on July 11, 2006).

Rodriguez-Salgado, Mia and Joan Pau Rubies. "England Under Elizabeth." *Kingship in the Modern World.* London School of Economics and Political Science. http://www.fathom.com/course/21701738/session1.html (accessed on July 11, 2006).

Richard Hakluyt

BORN: 1552 • London, England

DIED: November 23, 1616 • London, England

English geographer; writer; priest

"Richard Hakluyt contributed more to English letters, and has had more effect on English writing, than any other man who ever lived, with the possible exception of Shakespeare."

— Delbert A. Young. *According to Hakluyt: Tales of Adventure and Exploration.*

Though he never traveled very far from his native England, Richard Hakluyt (pronounced Hack-loot) inspired a great interest in exploration and adventure. A scholar and priest, Hakluyt was fascinated with geography and maps. He was one of the first people in England to practice geography, or the study of the Earth's surface, and he collected and published the stories of ship captains, merchants, adventurers, and common sailors who voyaged to distant parts of the world. Readers loved these accounts, and Hakluyt's work helped to promote interest in England's colonization, or settlement, of North America.

Early fascination with geography

Richard Hakluyt was born in 1552. Some accounts give his birthplace as London, while others say he was born in Herefordshire, where his ancestors had lived for many generations. His father, also named Richard, was a merchant who sold skins and furs. Historians believe that the family, which was most likely of Welsh origin, was relatively wealthy since it could afford to send Richard and his three brothers to school. (Richard also had two sisters.) Richard's parents both died when he was five. A cousin, also named Richard Hakluyt (1535–1591), became guardian of the Hakluyt children.

95

The young Hakluyt attended Westminster School and then entered Christ Church College at Oxford University. He received some financial support during his university years from the Skinners' Company in London, an association of fur traders. He completed his bachelor's degree in 1574 and his master's degree in 1577. The next year he was ordained as a priest.

When he was sixteen and still a student at Westminster, Hakluyt paid a visit to his cousin. The older Richard Hakluyt was a lawyer who collected maps, charts, and travel writings. At that time European countries including England, Spain, and Portugal were sending ships to explore regions of the world that few Europeans had ever seen. Maps of these regions—North and South America, India, and Southeast Asia—were often incomplete or inaccurate, if they existed at all. The materials that Hakluyt's cousin collected were very important to people who wanted to organize new expeditions. This is because better knowledge of geography could help explorers make safer voyages. Explorers could also venture farther into territories that were new to them. Young Hakluyt became fascinated with his cousin's collection, and the cousin told him all he could about geography and the sights that European explorers described in their travels. The cousin finished by quoting a passage in the Bible: "Some went down to the sea in ships, doing business on the great waters; they saw the deeds of the Lord, His wondrous works in the deep."

Tales of adventure

This experience deeply impressed Hakluyt, and he returned to school determined to complete his education and devote his life to promoting geographical knowledge. Although he became a priest and supported himself through his church work, geography and travel writing remained his primary interest. Just three years after earning his master's degree, Hakluyt published the story of French explorer Jacques Cartier's (1491–1557) first two voyages to North America. Cartier was hoping to find something known as the Northwest Passage, which would give European sailing vessels a shortcut to Asia. European traders bought and sold many valuable products in Asia, but the region was very far away from Europe. Ships had to sail all the way around Africa to get there. If a shorter route could be found, trade could become even more profitable. By the 1500s explorers hoped that such a route could be found through the waters north of Canada. Cartier sailed to eastern Canada in 1534. He explored

Hakluyt's first publication was the story of French explorer Jacques Cartier (pictured).
© BETTMANN/CORBIS.

the coast of Newfoundland and eastern Quebec. In 1535 he made a second voyage, sailing farther up the St. Lawrence River to the site of present-day Quebec City. An account of these voyages had been written by an Italian historian, and Hakluyt asked John Florio (1553–1625), a specialist in Italian literature at Oxford, to translate this material into English. Hakluyt published this book in 1580. For the first time English people could read about Cartier's adventures.

Hakluyt published his own book, *Divers [Various] Voyages,* in 1582. He dedicated this volume to **Philip Sidney** (1554–1598; see entry), a poet and courtier. (A courtier is a person who serves or participates in the royal court or household as the king's or queen's advisor, officer, or attendant.) The book contained the stories, in their own words, of several men who had sailed on voyages of exploration. Historians believe that Hakluyt had begun collecting material for this book while he was still a student at Oxford. It is likely that he interviewed several men who sailed with explorer Martin Frobisher (1535–1595), who explored northeastern Canada in the 1560s and 1570s looking for the Northwest Passage. Hakluyt talked with as many people as he could, and he wrote down their stories in their own direct language. As Delbert A. Young noted in his introduction to *According to Hakluyt: Tales of Adventure and Exploration,* "Any sailor, merchant prince or between-decks seaman, fascinated him."

Government leaders considered Hakluyt's work so important that **William Cecil** (Lord Burghley; 1520–1598; see entry), secretary of state to **Queen Elizabeth I** (1533–1603; see entry) arranged financial support for him. In 1582 Hakluyt traveled to Paris where he worked as a priest for the English ambassador to France. He held this job until 1587. England and Spain had become political enemies, but France had remained neutral. As the possibility of war increased, England and Spain sent spies to France, hoping to get information there about enemy plans. Though it is not known whether Hakluyt was actually a spy, he did sometimes carry secret papers back to England. In France Hakluyt was able to study materials relating to French, Portuguese, and Spanish voyages of exploration.

After Hakluyt returned to England he was given a prebend, or financial allowance, from the church in Bristol. In 1590 he was appointed to a parish job in Wetheringsett, Suffolk, and he held this job for the rest of his life. In addition he received a prebend from Westminster in 1602. From 1603 to 1605 he served as Archdeacon of Westminster, and in 1604 he was appointed chaplain, or attending priest, at the Hospital of the Savoy.

Hakluyt, a priest in the Anglican church, married for the first time in 1587, but his wife died the following year after giving birth to a son. In 1598 he married the widow of a London merchant.

Hakluyt's translation of the account of French explorer Rene Goulaine de Laudonniere's (1529–1582) expedition to Florida was published in 1587. This book described the explorer's attempt to establish a colony at Fort Caroline, near present-day Jacksonville. This colony encountered many difficulties, including hunger and rebellion, and it was finally destroyed by Spanish troops. Hakluyt dedicated the book to **Walter Raleigh** (1552–1618; see entry), an English explorer who was interested in building colonies in North America. Among other tales of exploration that Hakluyt translated and published were those of Hernando de Soto (1496–1542), a Spanish adventurer who explored South America and the southern regions of North America.

Published epic work

In 1589 Hakluyt published the first version of his most famous book, *The Principal Navigations, Voyages, and Discoveries of the English Nation.* This book described the whole history of English explorations, and it created great excitement among English readers. He went on to expand this book and published a new version of it, in three volumes, between 1598 and 1600. This enormous book, which included accounts of more recent explorations, contained 1.5 million words. "No reader who has ever delved seriously into this work," wrote Young, "would call it anything other than the prose epic of the English people." For many generations, Young explained, "Hakluyt's tales were ... the only adventure reading young people had. His characters are as vital, as colourful, and as dynamic as those created by Shakespeare—and Hakluyt's characters were real."

Hakluyt's book described people, plants, and animals that most Europeans had never seen before. His account of John Winter's voyage around South America, for example, included this description of the people who inhabited the region near the southernmost part of the continent: "From our observation they are a people much given to jollity. They laugh easily and were entranced by the sound of our trumpets and the music of our viols [stringed instruments]. Too, they were amused beyond belief when Master Winter danced for them." The narrator continues, "They are a people of middle stature [height], well made, and brown-skinned. Some of them paint their faces in divers [various] colours; their clothing is made entirely from the skins of beasts while upon their heads they wear a certain kind of cap, or hat, with ends which hang down over their shoulders." The book also provides a fascinating description of penguins: "The third isle ... had a numberless store of great fowls which cannot fly because their wings are so small they are of use only for swimming. In colour these birds are black on the back, while their underparts are speckled black and white. They do not even walk as do other fowls. Instead, they stand upright on their short legs so that, seen from afar, they might well be mistaken for little children."

But *The Principal Navigations* contained stories of hardship and danger as well. Pirates, sickness, starvation and thirst, storms, shipwrecks, and mutinies—revolts by the sailors against their captain—were common. Hakluyt's book described these things in exciting detail. The account of Martin Frobisher's (1535–1594) explorations, for example, showed the harsh weather he often encountered: "Ice came thick about the ships, some of it in such monstrous pieces that even the least of them could have shivered [broken] a ship into portions [pieces]." The story of Thomas Cavendish's voyage to South America told how he cruelly ordered sick crewmembers to be put ashore near the Strait of Magellan, where they died of hunger and exposure. (The Strait of Magellan is a body of water on the southern end of South America that connects the Atlantic and Pacific Oceans. It is named after explorer Ferdinand Magellan, who discovered the passage.) Other accounts described battles between sailors and the regions' native peoples. Details about fights and raids on Spanish ships also added excitement to the narratives. In some cases sailors told of ships that returned to England after difficult voyages with only a handful of men still alive.

Hakluyt's ability to describe the personalities of the various men he interviewed played a major role in the book's popularity. As Richard David explained in the introduction to his edition of Hakluyt's *Voyages,* "The man with a story to tell may be officer or seaman, merchant, gentleman-adventurer, servant, or curious tripper. Each tells his story in his own style, which may be polished or semi-literate, jocular [joking] or pious, critical or naïve." Furthermore, these distinct voices often gave different points of view about a particular event or person. For example, captains or men of high rank often spoke of their journeys in ways that made their own behavior look intelligent and brave. The members of their crews, however, would sometimes complain about unfair treatment, poor food, and the stupidity of orders that placed them in danger of shipwreck or attack.

Supported exploration

In addition to recording and publishing these important stories, Hakluyt actively promoted England's continued exploration of the Americas. In 1584 he petitioned the queen to support Walter Raleigh's plan to build a colony in Virginia. In 1589 Hakluyt served as a director of the Virginia Company, a business organization that raised money to create English settlements on the eastern coast of North America. He was also a member of a second Virginia Company in 1606, and he was a charter member of the Northwest Passage Company. In addition he served as a consultant to the East India Company, which focused on exploration in Asia.

Mercator's Projection

The earth is a sphere, but maps are flat. For this reason, no map can be completely accurate, and in the early 1500s maps were often badly distorted. Gerhard Mercator (1512–1594), a Belgian cartographer (mapmaker), created a more accurate map that was especially useful for ocean navigators. He imagined a globe of the earth inside a cylinder made of paper. Then he imagined the cylinder folding around the globe. On this paper he could then draw circles of latitude that would be parallel. (Latitude is a series of imaginary lines that run from east to west on the globe measuring the angular distance north or south from the Earth's equator, measured in degrees.) Mercator's projection distorted the size of land masses that were far away from the equator, but preserved their outlines fairly accurately. More important for navigators, it preserved the angles that they used to determine their location and plot their courses at sea. Nautical charts today are still based on the Mercator projection.

Hakluyt contributed to important advances in cartography, the science of making maps. In the second volume of the second edition of his *Principal Navigations,* published in 1599, he included a new map of the world, the Molineux-Wright world map. Based on the globe created by Emery Molineux (also spelled Molyneux) in 1592, it used Mercator's projection to create the most scientifically advanced map of that time. Historians believe that Hakluyt asked Molineux himself to draw the map, and that navigator John Davis (1550–1606) also worked on it. Unlike many earlier maps, the Molineux-Wright map did not contain fancy illustrations or drawings of places that Europeans had not yet explored. For example, sailors had heard about a place called Terra Australis but did not know its exact location. Traditional cartographers drew it on their maps anyway, guessing where to put it and what its shape might be. Hakluyt, though, wanted the new map to be scientifically accurate. It included only information that explorers had confirmed. Historians consider the Molineux-Wright map to be one of the best world maps of the sixteenth century.

Hakluyt died in 1616 and was buried at Westminster Abbey in London. He has been honored for the contributions that he made to English literature and to the study of geography and cartography. The Hakluyt Society, which was inspired by his work, was founded 1846 and remains active today. This organization continues Hakluyt's work by publishing books about voyages of discovery and the history of maritime (sea) exploration.

For More Information

BOOKS

David, Richard, ed. *Hakluyt's Voyages.* Boston, MA: Houghton Mifflin Company, 1981.

Parks, George Bruner. *Richard Hakluyt and the English Voyages.* Edited and with an introduction by James A. Williamson, 2nd ed. New York: Ungar, 1961.

Quinn, David B., ed. *The Hakluyt Handbook.* London: The Hakluyt Society, 1974.

Watson, Foster. *Richard Hakluyt.* London: The Sheldon Press; New York: Macmillan, 1924.

Young, Delbert A. *According to Hakluyt: Tales of Adventure and Exploration.* Toronto and Vancouver, Canada: Clark, Irwin & Company Limited, 1973.

WEB SITES

"The New World In Maps: The First Hundred Years." *The Newberry Library.* http://www.newberry.org/smith/slidesets/ss09.html (accessed on July 11, 2006).

"Richard Hakluyt." *The Galileo Project.* http://galileo.rice.edu/Catalog/NewFiles/hakluyt.html (accessed on July 11, 2006).

"Richard Hakluyt." *The Literacy Encyclopedia.* http://www.litencyc.com/php/speople.php?rec=true&UID=1930 (accessed on July 11, 2006).

Bess of Hardwick

BORN: 1527 • Derbyshire, England

DIED: February 13, 1608 • Derbyshire, England

English landowner

"There is no lady in this land that I better love and like [than Bess of Hardwick]."

— Elizabeth I. Quoted by A. L. Rowse in *Eminent Elizabethans.*

Bess of Hardwick. © MARY EVANS PICTURE LIBRARY/THE IMAGE WORKS.

Elizabeth Hardwick, known as Bess of Hardwick, rose from modest origins to become the wealthiest woman in Elizabethan England after the queen herself. Bess owned enormous estates on which she built magnificent great houses that made her famous throughout the country. She used her fortune to increase her status and to promote the ambitions of her children. As a lady-in-waiting, or a woman in the queen's household who attends the queen, to **Elizabeth I** (1533–1603; see entry), Bess associated with some of the most powerful members of the royal court and used these contacts to enhance her own position in society. Admired as an extraordinary businesswoman, she created splendid buildings that stand as examples of the best architecture of the era. She has also been acknowledged as a woman who managed her husbands' properties with great success.

Early life

Bess was born into a family of modest means. She was the third surviving daughter of John Hardwick of Hardwicke, Derbyshire, and his wife, Elizabeth Leake. It was customary in Elizabethan times for families to give their daughters marriage settlements, which consisted of income or property that the girl would bring with her when she married. A generous marriage settlement could improve a girl's chances of finding a wealthy husband. But John Hardwick died when Bess was still a child, leaving her and her sisters with little to inherit. Since this poverty made it unlikely that Bess would be able to find a wealthy and powerful husband, it was necessary for her to make her own way. At age fourteen she began work as a servant on the Barlow estate nearby. There she fell in love with Robert Barlow, the twelve-year-old heir to the estate. Robert was ill, and Bess nursed him. He fell in love with her and they were married, but he died soon afterward. As a widow Bess inherited one-third of the income from the Barlow estate.

At age twenty Bess married again. Her husband, Sir William Cavendish (1505–1557), whose two previous wives had died and who had two daughters, was more than twice her age. The marriage, a happy one, produced eight children, of whom six survived. Cavendish became quite wealthy as one of the officials in charge of seizing property belonging to Roman Catholic monasteries and transferring it to the government. **Henry VIII** (1491–1547; see entry) had authorized this action after rejecting the authority of the pope and making himself the supreme head of the church in England in the 1530s. The monasteries possessed a fortune in gold and silver, and they also owned an enormous amount of land—as much as ten percent of the land in England. By taking over these goods and properties for the state, Henry greatly enriched his treasury. He rewarded the "visitors of the monasteries," as these officials were called, by allowing them to take a share of the confiscated properties.

As a trusted servant of Henry VIII and of his successor, Edward VI (1537–1553), Cavendish had social contacts among the most important Protestant nobility in England. In fact, he and Bess were able to name several high-ranking people as godparents to their six children. Edward's half-sister, Princess Elizabeth—later to become Queen Elizabeth I—became godmother to Bess's first son, Henry Cavendish. Elizabeth's half-sister, **Mary I** (1516–1558; see entry), stood as godmother to Bess's third son, Charles Cavendish.

Bess advised Cavendish to sell his properties in southern England and buy the Chatsworth estate in Derbyshire. Bess and her husband began enclosing large portions of their property, which meant fencing off areas that local people had traditionally been able to use. Bess planned and oversaw extensive improvements to the great house at Chatsworth, a task that took many years to complete.

Close acquaintance with the queen

After Cavendish's death, Bess married a third time in 1559. Once again she chose a rich and powerful spouse. Her husband, Sir William St. Loe, was captain of the guard to Elizabeth I and chief butler of England. He owned magnificent estates at Tormarton in Gloucestershire and Chew Magna in Somerset. Bess had no children with St. Loe, who died in 1564 or 1565 and left all of his property to Bess. St. Loe's two adult daughters and his brother, who was suspected of having poisoned St. Loe, were left out of his will.

Through St. Loe, Bess had become a lady-in-waiting to Queen Elizabeth. This position gave Bess the opportunity to become a close friend of the queen, and she used this role to great advantage. But her relationship with Elizabeth, who could often be demanding and easily offended, was not always smooth. In 1561 Elizabeth imprisoned Bess in the Tower of London, a fortress on the Thames River in London that was used as a royal residence, treasury, and, most famously, as a prison for the upper class. Bess had angered the queen because she had kept a secret from her. Lady Catherine Grey (1540–1568), daughter of Bess's friend, Frances Brandon (1517–1559), had secretly married Edward Seymour (Lord Hertford; 1537–1621) and Bess had refused to tell the queen. Because Catherine had been named in Henry VIII's will as next in succession (the legal sequence in which individuals inherited the throne) after Elizabeth, Catherine's marriage was a matter of state concern. Elizabeth strongly preferred that Catherine should remain unmarried, thereby not producing an heir. When she found out about the secret marriage, she threw both Seymour and his wife into prison, and kept Bess in the Tower for seven months. Eventually Bess, known for showering the queen with lavish gifts, was able to regain Elizabeth's favor.

By the time her third husband died, Bess was the wealthiest woman in England except for the queen. Her income was estimated at £60,000 per year, which today would equal millions of dollars. She remained attractive and healthy, catching the interest of several eligible men. In

1568, with the queen's approval, Bess married George Talbot (Earl of Shrewsbury; 1528–1590), a widower with seven children. Talbot was one of the richest and most powerful aristocrats in England. He owned seven mansions and was one of Queen Elizabeth's leading noblemen. Though Talbot admired Bess at first, he quickly grew to dislike her. Once speaking affectionately of her as his "sweetheart" or his "jewel," as quoted in John Guy's *The True Life of Mary Stuart, Queen of Scots,* within a few years Talbot called Bess "my wicked and malicious wife" or "my professed enemy." They separated around 1580 and the earl refused thereafter to spend a single night under the same roof with her.

Mary Stuart's keeper

In 1568 Elizabeth gave Talbot the job of guarding **Mary Stuart** (Queen of Scots; 1542–1587; see entry). Mary had fled to England after the Protestant lords in Scotland had removed her from power and forced her to give the Scottish throne to her infant son, the future **James I** (1566–1625; see entry). She begged Elizabeth, her cousin, to allow her to remain in England. Elizabeth allowed this, but ordered Mary to be watched carefully. There was good reason to fear that Mary might inspire English Catholics to rebel against their Protestant queen and put Mary, a great-granddaughter of Henry VII (1457–1509), on the throne instead. It was necessary to keep a close watch over Mary to prevent any rescue attempts or uprisings. For fifteen years Talbot and Bess acted, in essence, as Mary's jailers.

Keeping Mary Stuart housed and safe was a huge responsibility that placed a considerable strain on Talbot's finances. The queen provided a modest sum for Mary's upkeep, but this was not sufficient to cover all of Mary's expenses. The queen of Scots kept several ladies-in-waiting and other servants, and these all had to be supported. Talbot himself was forced to pay these considerable extra costs. Occasionally Elizabeth's spies uncovered various conspiracies to rescue Mary; when this happened, Mary had to be moved to a new location with better security. This responsibility, too, fell to Talbot to organize and finance.

Life under guard was stressful and boring for Mary. Often forbidden even to go outdoors, she passed much of her time doing embroidery with Bess. After fifteen years Mary was finally passed into the custody of another noble. By this time, however, Bess had accused Talbot of having entered into a romantic affair with Mary. Historians do not consider this charge very likely, but it added further stress to the marriage between Bess and Talbot, who separated permanently soon thereafter.

Arbella Stuart

As the childless Queen Elizabeth grew older, the question of the succession to the throne became increasingly important. England had no clearly established laws regarding the succession, and families with royal blood held competing claims to the throne. Bess's granddaughter, Arbella Stuart, was a cousin of the young king of Scotland, James VI (later James I), who had Tudor royal blood through his mother, Mary Stuart. Since Arbella was a Catholic and had been born in England, many who objected to a Protestant monarch supported Arbella's claim to the throne over James's. Bess raised her granddaughter to believe she was destined to become queen of England. She was given a good education and was treated like royalty.

Though Bess hoped for an advantageous marriage for Arbella, Elizabeth demanded that Arbella should remain single. The queen had named James VI of Scotland to be her successor; if Arbella were to marry and bear a child, this heir would have a claim on the succession that would compete with that of James's children. Despite Elizabeth's wish, Arbella devised a plan to escape from her grandmother and elope with Edward Seymour (1586–1618), the oldest grandson of Lady Catherine Grey. Since the Greys had royal blood, a union between Arbella and Seymour was seen as particularly threatening to Elizabeth and James. The queen ordered Arbella to be sent to live in the custody of the earl of Kent, where the girl could be kept under close watch.

James, too, remained wary of Arbella, who was associated with several plots against him soon after he took the English throne in 1603. But in 1608 he allowed her to come back to the royal court. Two years later she secretly married William Seymour (1588–1660), the younger brother of her first intended husband. This marriage caused alarm at court, and James ordered Seymour and Arbella imprisoned. Seymour was sent to the Tower of London, while Arbella was placed under house arrest at the home of Sir Thomas Perry. Arbella plotted an escape; dressed in men's clothes, she fled her captors and boarded a ship for France, where she hoped to meet her husband. James's agents, however, captured Arbella in Calais, France, and returned her to England. James ordered her placed in the Tower of London. Though she attempted another escape, this failed and she never saw her husband again. She died in the Tower on September 27, 1615—according to some stories, after having starved herself—and was buried at Westminster Abbey, London. Arbella became known in England as the "Queen That Never Was."

Promotes interests of her children

In 1574 Bess invited Margaret Douglas (Countess of Lennox; 1515–1578) to visit her. Margaret was the niece of Henry VIII and granddaughter of Henry VII (1457-1509), which gave her children a strong claim to the succession. During the visit Bess's daughter, Elizabeth Cavendish, fell in love with Charles Stuart (1555–1576), the Countess's son and brother of Mary Stuart's second husband, Henry Stewart (Lord Darnley; 1545–1567). Because the Lennox family had a claim to the throne of England, Elizabeth could not marry Charles without the queen's permission. Otherwise, the marriage could be considered an act of treason. But Bess, intent on securing a prominent social position for her daughter, arranged for the marriage to take place without the queen's prior knowledge. When Elizabeth received this news, she ordered Margaret Douglas imprisoned for several months. She also demanded that Bess come to London and explain herself. But Bess ignored this order and remained at her home in Sheffield until the queen's anger weakened.

Elizabeth Cavendish and Charles Stuart had one daughter, Arbella Stuart (1575–1615). Bess doted on this granddaughter, whom she raised after the girl was orphaned in infancy. Bess even hoped that Arbella might one day become queen of England, but the girl grew up to be so spoiled and disobedient that Bess eventually cut Arbella out of her will. Denied official permission to marry, Arbella eloped and was imprisoned in the Tower of London, where she died.

Major building projects

Among Bess's most notable building projects was Chatsworth House, in Matlock, Derbyshire. Chatsworth is the seat of the dukes of Devonshire, whose family name is Cavendish; this family is descended from William Cavendish, Bess's second husband. The house, on the River Derwent, contains an extensive art collection and its garden is one of the most famous in England. Bess and her husband began building it in 1553. Bess finished the house in the 1560s after Cavendish's death, and lived there with her fourth husband, Talbot. Mary Stuart was lodged at Chatsworth several times from 1570 onward.

Hardwick Hall in Doe Lea, Chesterfield, Derbyshire, became a secondary residence for the dukes of Devonshire. The great house was designed for Bess by Robert Smythson (1535–1614). The house is considered a symbol of Bess's wealth and power. It became particularly famous for its numerous large windows. Since glass was an expensive material in Elizabethan times, this architectural detail demonstrated that Bess could afford great luxuries.

Bess died in the middle of a particularly cold winter, on February 13, 1608. People said that she was so disappointed that the snow outside had halted her building projects that this caused her death. She was buried in a vault in Derby Cathedral, where a memorial to

Hardwick Hall was a symbol of Bess of Hardwick's wealth and power. © ERIC CRICHTON/ CORBIS.

her was built. She has been remembered as perhaps the best example of the powerful Elizabethan woman who managed both her husbands and her children with great authority.

For More Information

BOOKS

Dunn, Jane. *Elizabeth and Mary: Cousins, Rivals, Queens.* New York: Alfred A. Knopf, 2004.

Guy, John. *The True Life of Mary Stuart, Queen of Scots.* Boston and New York: Houghton Mifflin Company, 2004.

Rowse, A. L. *Eminent Elizabethans.* Athens: University of Georgia Press, 1983.

WEB SITES

"Arbella Stuart." http://www.elizabethan-era.org.uk/arbella-stuart.htm (accessed on July 11, 2006).

"Bess of Hardwick." *Tudor Place.* http://www.tudorplace.com.ar/Bios/ BessofHardwick.htm (accessed on July 11, 2006).

"Hardwick Hall—Derbyshire." *UK Heritage.* http://www.ukheritage.net/ houses/hardwick.htm (accessed on July 11, 2006).

"History of Chatsworth and the Cavendish Family." *Chatsworth.* http:// www.chatsworth.org/ (accessed on July 11, 2006).

John Hawkins

BORN: 1532 • Plymouth, England

DIED: November 12, 1595 • West Indies

English admiral; merchant; slave trader

"One fearing God / And loyal to his Queen, / True to the State / by trial ever seen."

— Inscription on the Memorial to Hawkins at St. Dunstan in the East Church.

The first English merchant to participate in the African slave trade, John Hawkins is considered one of the leading seafarers of the 1500s. He led several sea expeditions that challenged Spanish and Portuguese control of the Atlantic Ocean and lands in the Western Hemisphere. His actions helped to bring vast profits to England, but his raids on Spanish ships and territories also contributed to tensions between England and Spain.

Many of Hawkins's actions—bribery, attacks on towns, and raiding enemy ships—caused political trouble for England. But Hawkins was also an effective administrator who improved the English navy. Hawkins built an efficient modern fleet that helped make England a major sea power.

Pirate or privateer?

John Hawkins was born into a wealthy family in the busy seaport of Plymouth, in southwest England. His mother was Joan Trelawney; his

John Hawkins. TIME LIFE PICTURES/MANSELL/TIME LIFE PICTURES/GETTY IMAGES.

111

father, William Hawkins, was a successful businessman involved with the sea trade. William was a powerful man who was often in trouble with the law. In 1527, for example, he was charged with beating a Plymouth man almost to death, but he did not receive a harsh punishment. In 1545 he was accused of piracy and sent to prison for a short time. (Piracy is the illegal practice of robbing ships at sea.) William was not afraid to take risks to make money, and in 1530 became the first Englishman to sail from Plymouth to Africa and then across the Atlantic Ocean to Brazil to trade various goods. This general route became known as the triangular transatlantic route.

Like his father, John Hawkins could be daring and even violent. When he was only twenty years old, he killed a man in Plymouth. The authorities who investigated the crime decided that he had acted in self-defense.

Hawkins and his older brother, William, worked with their father and learned much from him about seamanship and trade. They also perfected their skills at piracy and privateering. (Privateers are seafarers who own and operate their own ships independently but are authorized by their government to raid the ships of enemy nations, often capturing the entire ship with all its cargo.) Privateers were expected to give the treasure they stole to the government—though privateers often tried to keep as much as they could for themselves. Hawkins considered himself a privateer, but many of his actions came close to being piracy.

When Hawkins's father died, in 1553 or 1554, he and his brothers inherited the business, which continued to thrive. In 1559 Hawkins moved to London. He still spent much time in Plymouth, but he also began to establish a powerful career in London. Around this time Hawkins became a father, but he did not marry until 1567. Though his only son, Richard, was born out of wedlock, Hawkins accepted him as his legitimate child.

In London Hawkins hoped to find financial support for a daring new plan: an expedition to Africa to buy slaves, who would then be sold at a large profit in the Americas. Portuguese and Spanish explorers were already conducting a busy slave trade between Africa and the Americas, and they were stealing gold, silver, and other precious resources from lands in the Western Hemisphere. If England could participate in this trade, it, too, would become an extremely wealthy nation.

European slave traders considered African people nothing more than a cargo that could be bought and sold, like sugar or cloth. In fact, slaves were worth much more than most other types of cargo because they could be put to work on the new plantations that Europeans were building in Brazil and other parts of the Americas. With slave labor these plantations produced products such as sugar and coffee, which were then sold for enormous prices in Europe. Plantation owners needed slave labor in order to build huge fortunes. If they employed paid workers instead of slaves, they could not make such large profits.

First slaving voyage

Hawkins met several influential businessmen in London, and he began to establish connections with those in political power. Among these individuals was Benjamin Gonson, treasurer of the Royal Navy. Gonson helped to persuade a group of London merchants and investors to finance Hawkins's project. In 1562 Hawkins set out on his first slaving voyage.

Most Elizabethan ships were small and crowded, but Hawkins always traveled with chests full of fancy clothes, fine dishes, and other luxuries. He even hired musicians on his voyages to play for his own enjoyment. Though his sailors often endured hardships, Hawkins treated himself to the very best.

Hawkins sailed to West Africa. On the way he captured several Portuguese ships and stole their cargoes of slaves, spices, ivory, and other goods. With three hundred to four hundred slaves, Hawkins then set sail for the island of Hispaniola in the Caribbean. Forced to live in brutally overcrowded conditions, half of the slaves died on this voyage. Despite this loss Hawkins made huge profits from the sale of the surviving slaves. With these profits he bought goods to sell back in England. He acquired so much gold, silver, pearls, sugar, hides, and other merchandise that he did not have enough room for it all on his ships.

Finding two empty Spanish vessels, Hawkins arranged for them to carry the extra goods to Spain. He then took his own ships back to England. But Spanish authorities seized the two ships that had arrived in Spain, claiming that the English had no legal right to trade in the Western Hemisphere. In 1494 the pope had divided the Americas between Spain and Portugal. No other country could trade in the Western Hemisphere without first obtaining permission. But Hawkins had ignored this law. Spain took possession of the ships' cargoes and refused to return them to Hawkins. Even with the loss of these goods, however, Hawkins made an enormous profit from the voyage and immediately began planning a second venture.

Second slaving voyage

Eager to share in the profits that the slave trade could bring, many high-ranking individuals in England agreed to help pay for Hawkins's second voyage. Among them were some of the most influential advisors to **Queen Elizabeth I** (1533–1603; see entry), including **William Cecil** (Lord Burghley; 1520–1598; see entry); Lord Admiral Clinton, the Earl of Pembroke; and **Robert Dudley** (Earl of Leicester; 1532–1588; see entry). Even the queen herself became involved. Although she had said earlier that the buying and selling of African people was a "detestable" action, as quoted in Nick Hazlewood's *The Queen's Slave Trader: John Hawkyns, Elizabeth I, and the Trafficking in Human Souls,* she now agreed to lend Hawkins one of her own ships, the *Jesus of Lubeck.* She also granted Hawkins permission to have a coat of arms, a type of honorary badge. At the top of the design was the picture of an African slave, bound with a rope.

Hawkins sailed from Plymouth in 1564, with the young **Francis Drake** (1540–1596; see entry), a relative, sailing with him. When the ships reached Africa, Hawkins sent raiding parties ashore to capture slaves. Leading a raid himself in December, he was attacked by local fighters and barely made it back to his ship with his men. In all, Hawkins obtained about four hundred slaves to carry across the Atlantic. But the voyage encountered trouble, including several storms and a period without any wind, which prevented the ships from making any progress. The ships almost ran out of food and water.

Reaching the coast of Venezuela in the spring of 1565, Hawkins discovered that the Spanish authorities there had forbidden residents to trade with him. To persuade the residents to cooperate, he sent groups of armed men ashore to pretend to capture certain towns where he wanted to trade. This way the local merchants could buy his goods and then tell Spanish authorities that they had been forced into it. No real fighting occurred, however. This strategy worked well, and Hawkins made even more money on this voyage than he had on his first one.

Third slaving voyage

Back in England after this second voyage, Hawkins began planning a third slaving expedition. But the queen's advisors wanted him to wait. Impatient, he kept his fleet in Plymouth harbor for more than a year. When Spanish ships sailed into this area, Hawkins fired shots at them. In 1567 he set sail for Africa. As before, he raided the coast for slaves and then, after enduring severe storms in the Atlantic, he brought this cargo to the Americas. By bullying and bribing the local authorities, he was able to trade in several ports. But then a severe storm came, forcing him to anchor in the port of San Juan de Ulúa, Mexico. There he hoped to sell his remaining cargo and repair damage to his ships. Only one day later, though, a large fleet of Spanish ships entered the harbor. The Spanish did not believe Hawkins when he told them he had come in peace. Fierce fighting broke out, and the English were almost completely destroyed. Hawkins lost many men and almost all his goods. Only two of his ships survived.

Hawkins had command of one of the remaining ships, the *Minion*, and Drake commanded the other, the *Judith*. When the two ships were separated Drake sailed back to England alone. Hawkins later accused Drake of abandoning him, though Drake insisted that he was just following orders. The battered ships, full of wounded men, had been forced to flee the fighting before they had taken on any new supplies. There was almost no food or water. As Hazlewood described it, "Men chewed on cowhides and chased rats and mice. Cats and dogs became delicacies." The men aboard the *Minion* grew so desperate that they begged Hawkins to set them ashore on a remote part of the Mexican coast. But when he agreed, and asked for volunteers to leave the ship, they changed their minds. So Hawkins ordered them ashore. He abandoned 114 men in Mexico, promising to return for them a year later if he ever made it back to England.

The return journey was filled with horrors. According to an account of the voyage published in Hakluyt's *Principal Navigations* and quoted by Hazelwood, "Our men being oppressed with famine died continually, and they that were left grew into such weakness that we were scantly able to manage our ships." By the time the *Minion* reached European waters off the coast of Spain, its men had been without adequate nutrition or fresh water for more than three months. Many suffered from scurvy, a vitamin deficiency. Hawkins and his ship finally returned to England in January 1569. This third voyage was Hawkins's last venture as a slave trader.

Hawkins began working for the release of the men he had left behind, whom the Spanish had captured and sent back to Spain. Because the queen's government did not wish to anger Spain any further by fighting for the release of these hostages, it suggested that Hawkins try to trick the Spanish government into releasing the prisoners. Hawkins befriended

Scurvy

Elizabethan sailors had no method of storing fresh fruits and vegetables during long sea voyages. Without these important foods in their diets, sailors frequently developed scurvy, a condition caused by Vitamin C deficiency. Symptoms included blackened skin, difficulty in breathing, and diseased gums that caused teeth to fall out. Sailors with scurvy became so tired they could scarcely move, and their flesh and breath smelled so rotten that others could barely stand to be near them. Scurvy was often deadly; indeed, when the Portuguese explorer Ferdinand Magellan (1480–1521) made his famous trip around the world in 1520, more than 80 percent of his crew died of scurvy. Seafarers in the 1500s had no idea what caused scurvy and were helpless to prevent it. It was not until the 1700s that the Scottish doctor James Lind (1716–1794) discovered that scurvy could be prevented by stocking ships with large amounts of lemons and limes. This is because citrus fruits are high in Vitamin C.

King Philip II of Spain (1527–1598; see entry) and offered to become his agent. Philip was fooled. He not only released the prisoners but made Hawkins a grandee, the highest rank for a noble in Spain. He also gave Hawkins a fortune in cash.

Having next gained the trust of the Spanish ambassador, Hawkins was able to obtain secret information about a Spanish plot against Elizabeth in 1571. English Roman Catholics, who were forbidden to practice their religion, hoped to overthrow the queen with Spain's help, and then make the Catholic **Mary Stuart** (Queen of Scots; 1542–1587; see entry) queen of England. This plan became known as the Ridolfi plot. Hawkins revealed the plan to the English government, and the English conspirators were arrested.

Becomes naval treasurer

During the 1570s and 1580s Hawkins busied himself with dealings in London and in Plymouth. In 1571 he was elected to Parliament, England's legislative body, as a representative from Plymouth. He had married Katherine Gonson, whose father was treasurer of the Royal Navy, in 1567. In 1577 Hawkins became royal treasurer after his father-in-law, and in 1589 he became the naval controller, in charge of finances. He made many improvements to the English navy. For example, he invented a method of smearing the part of a ship that was underwater with a thick mixture of tar and horsehair to protect the wood from rotting. He also introduced the chain pump, which helped keep water out of the bottom parts of ships. He ordered older ships to be rebuilt, and he promoted the design of faster and more heavily armed ships. These, it turned out, helped make it possible for the English to defeat the powerful Spanish navy, the Armada, in 1588.

By 1585 Philip II had started planning a naval assault on England. The Spanish fleet, which had about 130 ships and 19,000 infantry soldiers as well as 8,000 seamen, sailed for England in 1588. Spain hoped to overwhelm the English navy, invade the country, and overthrow the queen. The English, with Hawkins third in command, were well prepared. After several battles in the English Channel with no clear winner, the English initiated a major battle on August 7 and 8. They forced the Armada ships to break formation, which gave the smaller and faster English ships room to maneuver effectively and inflict great damage. The Armada tried to escape, sailing north toward Scotland. It encountered a devastating storm that wrecked several ships and drove others off course. Only about 60 of the original 130 ships made it back to Spain. The powerful Armada had been defeated.

In recognition of Hawkins's bravery and leadership during the Armada crisis, Queen Elizabeth made him a knight. (A knight is a man granted a rank of honor by the monarch for his personal merit or service to the country.) Those who had criticized his decisions during his disastrous third slaving voyage now began to respect him again. He worked hard to oversee repairs that the English fleet needed after the fighting. But as the years passed, the queen began to disapprove of the high costs involved in making naval improvements. She criticized Hawkins for spending too much, and he feared that she would send him to prison. He petitioned to be released from his job as naval treasurer, but the queen refused.

In 1590 Hawkins's wife died. The marriage had been a happy one, and he grieved for her. After a few years Hawkins married Margaret Vaughan, who had been one of the queen's ladies-in-waiting, a woman in the queen's household who attends the queen. Around this same time Hawkins organized the construction of a hospital for seamen at Chatham. In 1594 this institution received a royal charter and was named the Hospital of Sir John Hawkins.

Death at sea

Hawkins sailed on his final sea voyage in 1595. Francis Drake had persuaded the queen to approve of an expedition to the Caribbean, where English ships would attack Spanish ports and raid treasure-filled

Spanish ships. The queen made Hawkins second in command after Drake. The fleet anchored at Guadeloupe, West Indies, on October 29, and the commanders began considering various plans to attack the Spanish. But Hawkins became seriously ill. He died on November 11, 1595, off the coast of Puerto Rico, and was buried at sea.

A privateer and slave trader, Hawkins nonetheless made significant contributions to English history. He was respected as a daring seaman and fighter who helped England become a leading naval power.

For More Information

BOOKS

Hazlewood, Nick. *The Queen's Slave Trader: John Hawkyns, Elizabeth I, and the Trafficking in Human Souls.* New York: William Morrow, 2004.

Kelsey, Harry. *Sir John Hawkins: Queen Elizabeth's Slave Trader.* New Haven, CT and London: Yale University Press, 2003.

WEB SITES

"Admiral Sir John Hawkins." *Tudor Place.* http://www.tudorplace.com.ar/Bios/ JohnHawkins.htm (accessed on July 11, 2006).

"The Pirates: Sir John Hawkins." *Elizabeth's Pirates.* http://www.channel4.com/ history/microsites/H/history/pirates/piratesjhawkins.html (accessed on July 11, 2006).

"Sir John Hawkins." *The Encyclopedia of Plymouth History.* http:// www.plymouthdata.info/PP-Hawkins.htm (accessed on July 11, 2006).

"Spain vs. England: The Early History of the Slave Trade." *The Middle Passage: Slaves at Sea.* http://beatl.barnard.columbia.edu/students/his3487/lembrich/ seminar51.html (accessed on July 11, 2006).

Henry VIII

BORN: June 28, 1491 • Greenwich, England

DIED: January 28, 1547 • London, England

English king

"I do not choose anyone to have in his power to command me, nor will I ever suffer it."

By breaking away from the authority of the Roman Catholic Church, Henry VIII initiated a revolution that resulted, after his death, in a golden age for England. But his reign was marked by controversies and problems. Intent on ensuring that his family line would inherit the throne, he persecuted his political rivals and created religious conflicts that threatened to tear the country apart. His ill-advised military actions, intended to enhance his own glory, almost bankrupted the country and led to further discontent among his subjects. By emphasizing his supreme power as king, Henry strengthened the position of the monarchy in England, but he also caused resentment among the nobles who wanted a larger share of power. He left his successors to rule a country that was divided by religious strife and remained vulnerable to rival European powers.

A royal upbringing

King Henry VIII. © GIANNI DAGLI ORTI/CORBIS.

The second son of Henry VII (1457–1509) and Elizabeth of York, daughter of Edward IV (1442–1483), Henry VIII grew up without

119

much training in the art of ruling a country because his older brother, Arthur, was expected to assume the throne when their father died. Highly intelligent, Henry was interested in scholarly subjects and received a relatively good education. He became fluent in six languages and was interested in mathematics, astronomy (the study of the stars, planets, and other celestial bodies), geometry, and theology (the study of religion). He was also a talented musician. He could play several instruments, and he composed music as well.

Tall, strong, and strikingly handsome, Henry was a superb athlete. He loved to ride horses, hunt, and play sports, including tennis. He could dance all night without getting tired. He enjoyed tournaments and jousting—a type of athletic contest in which participants on horses tried to unseat their opponents by riding toward them and striking them with lances. Henry also admired the arts, and he gave them generous financial support.

Arthur died in 1502, making Henry heir to the throne. When Henry became king after his father's death in 1509, it was England's first peaceful succession (the sequence in which persons legally become king or queen) since 1422. Henry's father, who came from a family of mostly Welsh ancestry, had taken the throne after defeating his rival, Richard III (1452–1485) in battle in 1485. This ended the long and bitter War of the Roses (1455–1485), in which the Lancaster family and the York family fought for their right to rule England. Henry VII became the first English king in the Tudor family.

Early rule

Lacking a clear sense of what he wished to accomplish as king, Henry VIII often focused more on his image than on policy. Wanting his subjects to hold him in awe, he cared very much about ceremonies and luxuries that emphasized his majesty and authority. He relied heavily on the advice of his councilors when he had to make decisions about governing. Even so, Henry never let it look as if he were not in total control of his realm.

Just a few weeks after becoming king, Henry married Catherine of Aragon (1485–1536), daughter of the Spanish monarchs Ferdinand (1452–1516) and Isabella (1451–1504). Catherine was the widow of Henry's brother, Arthur, and Henry received special permission from the pope, head of the Roman Catholic Church, to marry her. In 1511 Catherine gave birth to a son, but the baby lived only a few weeks. Several later pregnancies resulted in miscarriages.

Did Henry VIII Suffer from Syphilis?

Some of the symptoms that made King Henry VIII's later life so miserable suggest that he could have been suffering from syphilis, a sexually transmitted disease that had no cure in his day. Left untreated, the syphilis bacterium stays in the body and damages internal organs, including the brain, nerves, heart, blood vessels, liver, joints, bones, and eyes. Henry's leg sores, for example, have sometimes been explained as the result of a serious jousting accident he suffered as a young man, but could also have been the result of syphilis. His increasingly irrational behavior as he aged has also been attributed to syphilis. In addition, his difficulty in fathering a child could have been related to this disease. His first wife, Catherine of Aragon, suffered several miscarriages—a pattern that can be typical when one parent has syphilis. Or Catherine herself may have been infected by her husband; some 40 percent of pregnancies among women who have syphilis result in a miscarriage. Henry's daughter, Mary, had various health problems that may have been caused by a congenital (from birth) syphilitic condition.

Many doctors in Henry's own time believed the king had syphilis, which was commonly known as "the pox." But the question has never been satisfactorily answered. Some modern doctors believe the evidence strongly supports a diagnosis of syphilis, but others say that there is not enough information to confirm or reject this disease as a cause of Henry's medical problems.

Frustrated that he had not yet fathered an heir, the young king decided to join Spain in a war against France. He hoped that military success would bring him glory. But this decision prompted James IV of Scotland (1473–1513), an ally of France, to invade England. Under the military leadership of Thomas Howard (Earl of Surrey; 1443–1524), the English defeated the Scots at Flodden Field in 1513. James died in battle. Though England could claim military victory, the war was expensive and contributed to England's worsening financial problems.

In 1515 Henry made Thomas Wolsey (1474–1530), who was Archbishop of York and a cardinal of the Catholic Church, his primary advisor. Wolsey, an ambitious and greedy man, was known for his corruption and hypocrisy. Hoping to become pope one day, Wolsey advised Henry to meddle in affairs between Spain and France in the 1520s. The cardinal wanted to make a political alliance that would strengthen support for his own position of power in the church. But Spain resented England's interference, and the Spanish government retaliated by blocking English access to the cloth trade with the

Netherlands. Because this trade was an important part of the English economy, its loss caused great anger in England.

Increasing financial problems also created discontent. In 1523 Wolsey agreed to call Parliament, England's legislative body, into session to consider raising taxes. But Parliament approved amounts that were far too low, and the next year Wolsey attempted to impose an additional tax. This move proved so unpopular that Henry cancelled it. By 1527 England had almost no money left in its treasury.

"The King's great matter"

Unpopular as a result of his bad financial policies, Henry also faced more personal frustrations. After several years of marriage he still had no male heir. Only one of his children by Catherine, **Mary I** (1516–1558; see entry) had survived; since then, the queen had not become pregnant again. Fearing that a female succession would be challenged, Henry wanted to dissolve his marriage, which would leave him free to marry again and father a legitimate son.

With Wolsey as his spokesperson, the king petitioned the pope to dissolve his marriage to Catherine. But the pope feared angering Catherine's nephew, Charles V (1500–1558), Holy Roman Emperor and king of Spain. For six years he refused to give an answer. Meanwhile, Henry convinced himself that he had committed a sin by marrying Catherine. He became obsessed with obtaining the divorce, which he began calling "the King's great matter."

In 1529 Henry removed Wolsey as his advisor and had him arrested. He was angry that the cardinal had failed to persuade the pope to grant the divorce. If Wolsey had not died of natural causes on his way to prison, Henry would likely have ordered him executed for treason. In 1531 Thomas Cromwell (1485–1540) became Henry's chief advisor. Cromwell devised a plan: pass a law stating that the English church would make its own decisions without appealing to the pope. This law enabled Archbishop of Canterbury Thomas Cranmer (1489–1556) to declare Henry's marriage to Catherine void in 1533. By this time Henry had made his mistress, Anne Boleyn (1507–1536) pregnant and had secretly married her. At the same time that he announced Henry's divorce, Cranmer legitimated this new marriage. After the princess **Elizabeth I** (1533–1603; see entry) was born, the pope excommunicated Henry, depriving him of the right to worship as a Catholic.

The Reformation in England

In 1534 Parliament passed the Act of Supremacy, which declared the king the supreme head of the church in England. This step, the result of Henry's concern about the succession, created a complete break with the Catholic Church in Rome and led to revolution. Concerned about maintaining the loyalty of his subjects, Henry prosecuted prominent leaders who refused to accept his new religious authority. Among these was the king's former friend and counselor, Thomas More (1478–1535), who was beheaded for treason in 1535.

Henry then took over England's monasteries, which owned huge treasures, including gold and silver religious objects as well as valuable land. The English people had been required to pay income to these monasteries, and this substantial income now went to the government. The sale of monastic lands and objects also provided the royal treasury with huge profits, and shifted new wealth to the nobles. This allowed the nobles, in time, to assume more influential roles in England's affairs.

Henry's goal had never been to create religious dissent. He disapproved of Martin Luther (1483–1546), for example, a German monk who in 1517 had protested Catholic policies that he and other reformers considered corrupt. These reformers wanted to restore the church to the purity and simplicity that they believed had been its original state. They objected to the influence of the pope and the clergy, who were often wealthy and did not live by the principles they preached to others. But Henry did not disapprove of Catholicism. In fact, he had written a best-selling book in 1521 attacking Luther, which had inspired the pope to give Henry the title of Defender of the Faith. But the Act of Succession, in effect, supported the same cause that Luther championed in Europe—the Protestant Reformation, a sixteenth-century religious movement that aimed to reform the Roman Catholic Church and resulted in the establishment of Protestant churches. Henry's break with the pope created deep conflicts in England between those who wished to remain loyal to the Catholic Church and those who wanted to embrace a reformed, Protestant religion. Religious conflict continued throughout Henry's reign and the reigns of his heirs, resulting in years of controversy and bloodshed. In the end England became an officially Protestant country, but enduring anti-Catholic feeling shaped attitudes in England for centuries.

King Henry VIII (center) and his six wives, shown clockwise from the top: Anne of Cleves (4th), Catherine Howard (5th), Anne Boleyn (2nd), Catherine of Aragon (1st), Katherine Parr (6th), and Jane Seymour (3rd). © BETTMANN/ CORBIS.

A sequence of marriages

Soon after Elizabeth was born, Henry grew tired of Anne Boleyn, who had failed to give birth to a son. In 1536 he ordered Anne executed for adultery—a charge that many considered false. Henry then married Jane Seymour (1509–1537), who in 1537 gave the king what he had long wanted: a son, Edward (1537–1553). But Jane died in childbirth, leaving Henry free to marry again. This time, on Cromwell's advice, he took

Anne of Cleves (1515–1557) as his wife. But the king disliked her so much that he divorced her six months later. He also ordered Cromwell's execution.

In 1540 the aging king married Catherine Howard (1520–1542), a twenty-year-old beauty. Though this marriage brought Henry some brief happiness, Catherine's flirtations with other men caused the king to order her execution in 1542. His final marriage, to Katherine Parr (1512–1548), took place in 1543. Henry got along well with Katherine, who helped him renew his relationship with his daughters.

By this time Henry was no longer a handsome and athletic man. He had grown extremely fat. His waistline was at least 57 inches around, and he was said to weigh almost 400 pounds. He suffered from many illnesses, including headaches and sores on his legs that often became infected and gave off a bad odor. Unable to walk, he had to be carried around in a chair and hauled up stairs by ropes and pulleys. His moods grew unpredictable, and he could often act in cruel ways. When Catherine of Aragon died in 1536, for example, he held a ball to celebrate the occasion. Fearful of anyone with royal blood who might become a rival to the Tudor dynasty, he found ways to charge them with treason and ordered their executions. He even supervised the passage of the "Acte for Poysoning" in 1531, which declared that willful murder by poison was high treason and punishable by a new form of execution: boiling to death. Once admired by his subjects as a magnificent king, Henry became an object of fear and ridicule.

Final years

Henry's last years were marked by increasing ill health and bad temper. As tensions worsened between Catholics and Protestants, Henry struggled to keep his kingdom united. He often lost his temper with his councilors, and he complained that his subjects did not appreciate what a splendid ruler he was.

Though his health was poor, Henry remained active in government. But he did not have a clear vision of what he wanted to achieve for his country; many of his decisions, historians believe, resulted from his wish for personal glory. His actions toward Scotland, for example, proved disastrous. When hostilities between Spain and France resumed in 1542, Henry decided to join Spain, prompting Scotland to ally itself with France. England then invaded Scotland. In response the Scots marched into northern England but were defeated at Solway Moss in November.

Shortly after this battle, the Scottish king died, leaving his infant daughter, **Mary Stuart** (1542–1587; see entry), queen of Scotland. Scotland and England negotiated peace terms in the Treaties of Greenwich in 1543, which stated that Mary would marry Henry's son, Edward. But when the English Parliament refused to ratify the treaties, the Scottish Parliament changed its decision and rejected them.

Furious, and determined to bend Scotland to his will, Henry ordered a series of further attacks. Known as the "Rough Wooing," these raids only hardened the Scots' resolve to resist English control. Scotland strengthened its alliance with France, and arranged for Mary Stuart to marry the heir to the French throne. War with Scotland continued until 1546 and drained England's economy. To pay for the war Henry was forced to sell off monastic property, which deprived the country of a source of future income. He also devalued the currency, which allowed him to pay some debts but soon led to extreme inflation.

By the end of 1546 Henry was near death. Catherine Parr helped to persuade him to change his will, naming his daughters Mary and Elizabeth as next in line to the succession after their brother, Edward. Henry died at Whitehall Palace in Westminster, London, on January 28, 1547.

Legacy

Henry VIII achieved some notable successes, but his foremost act, the split with the Roman Catholic Church, had significant historical consequences. This act propelled England into a revolution that led, during Elizabeth's reign, to a golden age of exploration, expansion, and learning. Yet Henry's own reign was marked by curious shortcomings. He became so obsessed with the idea of keeping the Tudor dynasty in power that he ignored one of the most important developments of the time: the exploration of the Western Hemisphere, in which Spain and Portugal were already busily engaged. Exploitation of the Americas was making Spain and Portugal extremely rich, but because Henry did not support voyages of exploration, England did not become a major participant in this trade until Elizabeth's reign.

Henry VIII strengthened the position of the monarchy and improved government administration. He supported the creation of a navy, incorporated Wales into the kingdom and granted equal rights to the Welsh, declared himself king of Ireland, and strengthened the role of Parliament. He was able to impose some order in a country that was divided by religious conflict as well as rivalries for the throne, but he did so through fear and the brutal suppression of dissent. He persecuted his enemies, Protestant and Catholic alike, and he destroyed whole families that he feared might oppose him. Henry succeeded most of all in making himself into the image of a magnificent and all-powerful king who was more feared than admired.

For More Information

BOOKS

Bernard, G. W. *The King's Reformation: Henry VIII and the Remaking of the English Church.* New Haven, CT and London: Yale University Press, 2005.

Oliver, Marilyn Tower. *The Importance of Henry VIII.* San Diego, CA: Lucent Books, 2004.

Weir, Alison. *Henry VIII: The King and His Court.* New York: Ballantine Books, 2001.

Wilson, Derek. *In the Lion's Court: Power, Ambition, and Sudden Death in the Reign of Henry VIII.* New York: St. Martin's Press, 2001.

PERIODICALS

Kesserling, K. J. "A Draft of the 1531 'Acte for Poysoning.'" *English Historical Review,* September 1, 2001.

Walker, Greg. "Henry VIII and the Invention of the Royal Court." *History Today,* February 1, 1997.

WEB SITES

"Henry VIII." *BBC: Historic Figures.* http://www.bbc.co.uk/history/historic_figures/henry_viii_king.shtml (accessed on July 11, 2006).

"Henry VIII." *Kings and Queens of England.* http://www.royal.gov.uk/output/Page19.asp (accessed on July 11, 2006).

Hutton, Ronald. "Henry VIII: Majesty with Menace." *Church and State: Monarchs and Leaders.* http://www.bbc.co.uk/history/state/monarchs_leaders/majesty_menace_01.shtml (accessed on July 11, 2006).

"Letter of Thomas Cranmer on Henry VIII's Divorce, 1533." *Medieval Sourcebook.* http://www.fordham.edu/halsall/source/cramner-hen8.html (accessed on July 11, 2006).

James I

BORN: June 19, 1566 • Edinburgh, Scotland

DIED: March 27, 1625 • Hatfield, England

Scottish king

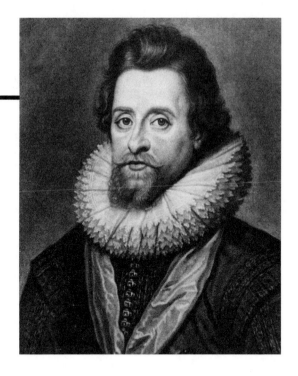

"Look not to find the softness of a down pillow in a crown, but remember that it is a thorny piece of stuff and full of continual cares."

The first king of a united England and Scotland, James I brought relative peace and stability to a realm that had known tremendous turmoil during the reigns of his predecessors, the Tudor monarchs. Intense religious conflicts and hostilities with rival European kingdoms had troubled England since the reign of **Henry VIII** (1491–1547; see entry), who was crowned in 1509. After James took the English throne in 1603, he ended England's prolonged war with Spain and strengthened the official position of the Church of England. While this policy supported moderate Protestantism, it frustrated Catholics and led to a plan to blow up the houses of Parliament (England's legislative body), and overthrow the English government. Exposed at the last moment, the plot nearly succeeded.

King James I. RISCHGITZ/ GETTY IMAGES.

James also spent more than his treasury could afford, and he alienated the English Parliament because he insisted that his lawful powers as king

129

were more extensive than Parliament would accept. This conflict heightened the demand among many English statesmen for constitutional reform, which intensified after James's death and contributed to civil war in the 1640s. Many historians have judged James an ineffective king. But others have pointed out that James had shown good ability as a ruler in Scotland, and that the complexity of the problems he faced in England had much to do with his failures there.

An unhappy childhood

James Stuart, the only son of the Scottish queen **Mary Stuart** (1542–1587; see entry) and her second husband, Henry Stewart (Lord Darnley; 1545–1567), was the undisputed heir to the Scottish throne. He also inherited a strong claim to the throne of England. His mother was a great-granddaughter of King Henry VII (1457–1509) of England. Mary Stuart's grandmother, Margaret Tudor (1489–1541) was Henry VIII's sister. Margaret had married King James IV (1473–1513) of Scotland; their son, James V (1512–1542), became Mary Stuart's father. After James IV died, Margaret married a second time. Her daughter by this marriage became Henry Stewart's mother. Thus, both of James's parents were related to the ruling Tudor family in England.

James's childhood was marked by traumatic events that profoundly influenced him and shaped his attitudes toward kingship. He encountered grave danger before he was even born. His mother, a Catholic, had returned to rule Scotland after having grown up in France. Facing resistance from Protestant lords who objected to a Catholic monarch, Mary kept a precarious hold on power by compromising with the lords, but many continued to disapprove of her. After she married Lord Darnley, her actions caused some further criticism. Mary was not happy with her second husband, and rumors circulated that she had fallen in love with her secretary, David Rizzio (1533–1566). Some even said that Rizzio was the real father of the child she was expecting. One evening during Mary's pregnancy, a band of Scottish Protestant rebels broke into the queen's private rooms and murdered Rizzio. The rebels threatened the queen herself when she attempted to save her secretary. Addressing the English Parliament many years later in 1605, James said that his fearful nature could be traced to this incident when he was still in his mother's womb.

Mary Stuart's reign in Scotland came to an end before the infant James reached his first birthday. James's father was murdered on

February 10, 1567, and suspicion fell on James Hepburn (Earl of Bothwell; c. 1536–1578), whom the queen married three months later. Convinced that the queen had been involved in the murder, the outraged lords rose against her and forced her to give her crown to her infant son. Soon afterward she fled to England, where she lived in exile for the rest of her life. James, crowned King James VI of Scotland on July 29, 1567, at age thirteen months, never saw his mother again.

Because the infant king could not rule on his own, a regent was appointed to rule until the boy came of age. The first regent was assassinated in 1570. The second regent held power for only one year before he was killed in a civil rebellion. Young James witnessed his death. The third regent, who died of natural causes, also held power for only about one year. The fourth regent lasted for ten years, but he was then executed for his part in the death of James's father. James grew up without any consistent emotional support, and historians believe that this harsh environment contributed to his deep need for love and friendship throughout his adult life.

James coped with his unhappiness by devoting himself to learning. Fluent in French, he studied Latin and Greek and demonstrated good intellectual ability. Indeed, he became known as one of the most learned monarchs ever to take the English throne. But lessons were not always pleasant for the young king. His tutor, George Buchanan (1506–1582), would beat James when the boy challenged him.

Though he was not athletic, James loved to hunt on horseback. He spent almost half of his time at this activity, which helped him to feel strong. In fact, he believed that he could strengthen his weak legs by dipping them into the bellies of freshly killed deer. According to Adam Nicolson in *God's Secretaries: The Making of the King James Bible,* the young king once killed every deer in the royal hunting ground at Falkland in Fife.

Religion and politics

Beginning in 1581 James ruled Scotland without the help of a regent. Though the Scottish Parliament had established an official Protestant Church of Scotland in 1560, religious conflict continued throughout James's rule, as some Catholics resisted the new religion. James had been baptized a Catholic, but he had been crowned in a Protestant ceremony that included an oath to maintain the official religion of Scotland. Though James did not want to alienate Catholics, he realized that he needed the cooperation of the Protestant lords if he was to survive.

James relied to a great extent on the support and advice of close friends. Among these was his older male cousin, Esmé Stuart (1542–1583), who had arrived in Scotland from France in 1579 when James was thirteen. James was strongly attracted to this Catholic cousin, and some believed them to have been lovers. According to a contemporary account quoted by Alan Stewart in *The Cradle King: The Life of James VI & I, the First Monarch of a United Great Britain,* the king "is in such love with [Esmé], as in the open sight of the people, oftentimes he will clasp him about the neck with his arms and kiss him." The Protestant lords disapproved of Esmé Stuart and resented the influence he had on the king. In 1582 a group led by William Ruthven (Earl of Gowrie; c. 1541–1584) took James captive and banished Esmé, who returned to France. They held the king for almost one year at Ruthven Castle before he was able to escape with another of his close courtiers, or royal attendants, James Stuart. To help eliminate future Protestant threats, James convinced Parliament to pass the Black Acts in 1584, which declared him head of the Scottish church. This move alienated him from the church leaders, who feared he might push the church toward the type of Protestantism practiced in England.

In 1586 James and **Elizabeth I** (1533–1603; see entry) agreed, through the Treaty of Berwick, that Scotland and England would become allies. Since England was a Protestant country, this event pleased the Scottish Protestant lords. This alliance also strengthened James's claim to the English succession, since Elizabeth had no children. One year later, his mother, who had been implicated in a conspiracy to assassinate Elizabeth and make herself queen of England, was executed for treason. This event placed James, Elizabeth's closest relative, next in line for the English throne.

Following a Catholic uprising in 1588, James was forced to improve his relationship with the leaders of the Scottish church. He agreed in 1592 to the repeal of the Black Acts. But his insistence on granting a pardon to some of the Catholic rebels resulted in another Protestant conspiracy against him in 1600, led by John Ruthven, son of the conspirator who had captured James in 1582. The plot failed and the rebels were executed.

In 1589 James married a Protestant princess, Anne of Denmark (1574–1619). Though close friends early in their marriage, they eventually drifted apart and agreed to live separately. They had seven children. Their second son, Charles (1600–1649), succeeded James as king of England in 1625.

As king of Scotland James strengthened law and order in the country and minimized the influence of rebellious Catholic lords. He also concerned himself with abolishing witchcraft. When a severe storm

James I arrives in London for his coronation. HULTON ARCHIVE/GETTY IMAGES.

threatened the ship on which James and his new bride were returning to Scotland after their marriage in Norway, authorities accused several people of using witchcraft to create the storm and thereby kill the king. Many of the accused were executed. James, who attended the witch trials at Berwick, was inspired to write *Daemonologie,* an article on witchcraft that he hoped would convince skeptics that witches were really at work in Scotland.

Becomes king of England

During the final years of Elizabeth's life, her secretary of state, Robert Cecil (1563–1612), had secretly written to James to instruct him on how to rule England. But when James succeeded to the English throne after Elizabeth's death in 1603, he made it clear that he had his own ideas about being king. He believed in the divine right of kings, a doctrine which stated that a monarch ruled due to the will of God, not the will of the people or any government body. The English Parliament, however, expected the king to share power with its members—a circumstance for which James was unprepared.

The King James Bible

Many scholars consider the King James Version of the Bible to be the greatest work of prose (non-poetry) ever written in the English language. Church leaders, recognizing the numerous errors in the many versions of the Bible, wanted to create an official text that would conform to church teachings. In particular, they wanted to replace the Geneva Bible, a text that had been created in Switzerland by English Protestants there who had fled England after **Mary I** (1516–1558; see entry) took power and attempted to restore Catholicism in England. The Geneva Bible had been influenced by Puritan doctrines that mainstream English Protestants considered too extreme.

No single person compiled the King James Bible. The completed translation was the work of fifty-four scholars on six separate committees. They were not paid for their work, which took several years. The finished book was an oversized volume intended to be used in churches, not in private homes.

The rich, lyrical, yet direct style of the King James Bible profoundly affected the development of the English language. The poet John Milton (1608–1674) read from the King James Bible every day; in his works, including *Paradise Lost,* he used many phrases and images from its pages. American writers, too, were influenced by the style of the King James Version. For example, Herman Melville's (1819–1891) masterpiece, *Moby Dick,* is filled with religious symbolism and word patterns that reflected biblical prose. Poet Walt Whitman (1819–1892) wrote innovative poetry, such as *Leaves of Grass* and *Song of Myself,* that showed the influence of the psalms. In the twentieth century civil rights leader Martin Luther King Jr. (1929–1968) delivered impassioned and influential speeches that reflected the dramatic and poetic language of the King James Bible. As Adam Nicolson wrote in *God's Secretaries,* "Nothing in our culture can match its breadth, depth, and universality . . . [except] the great tragedies of Shakespeare."

James was crowned king of England at Westminster Abbey in London on July 25, 1603. This event created a "personal union" between England and Scotland, which meant that the two countries shared a ruler but remained technically separate states. The new king faced several immediate challenges, including a budget crisis. Prices had risen by almost 50 percent during Elizabeth's reign; she left a government in significant debt and plagued by growing corruption. James was not able to correct these financial woes. He spent large sums, giving generous amounts to his friends and increasing the budget deficit each year. Five years after taking the throne, James had increased the royal debt by 600 percent.

As in Scotland, James also faced religious conflicts in England. At the insistence of the Puritans (a group of Protestants who follow strict religious standards) who wanted more extensive reforms in the English

Protestant church, he met with reformers at the Hampton Court Conference in 1604. James rejected most of their demands, but he did agree to authorize an official translation of the Bible into English. This work, first published in 1611, became known as the King James Bible. Admired for its elegant poetic language, it had a deep and lasting influence not only in the church but also on English literature as a whole.

In 1604 James signed the Treaty of London, ending England's twenty-year war with Catholic Spain. James also took care to support religious tolerance, but Catholic extremists felt he was not doing enough to ensure their rights and they engaged in several conspiracies to remove him from power. **Walter Raleigh** (1552–1618; see entry) was implicated in one of these plots, though many believed his political enemies had falsely accused him. Raleigh was imprisoned for several years, and he was eventually executed for treason.

The Gunpowder Plot

The most serious attempt on James's life occurred in 1605, when a group of Catholic conspirators led by Robert Catesby (1573–1605) plotted to blow up the Houses of Parliament during the annual opening ceremony, when James would be present. They hoped to kill the king and his entire government, and place his oldest daughter, whom they would persuade to become a Catholic, on the throne. After the explosion they hoped to inspire a huge rebellion. This conspiracy became known as the Gunpowder Plot.

The conspirators planned to tunnel under the Parliament buildings and put gunpowder in place there. But their task was made easier when they were able to obtain the lease for a cellar directly under the House of Lords. They filled this room with thirty-six barrels containing approximately 2.5 tons of gunpowder—enough to blow up Parliament as well as many of the nearby buildings, including the Palace of Westminster and Westminster Abbey. It would have killed everyone within 100 meters of the blast.

The king's chief minister, Robert Cecil, discovered the plot after a Catholic member of Parliament had received a warning not to attend the session and had shown this message to Cecil. Guy Fawkes (1570–1606), an English soldier with training in explosives, was arrested at the scene. The king signed a warrant authorizing Fawkes to be interrogated under torture. Two days later Fawkes confessed, naming his fellow conspirators.

Guy Fawkes, a member of the Gunpowder Plot, attempted to plant gunpowder in the cellar of the Houses of Parliament.
HULTON ARCHIVE/GETTY IMAGES.

Though many had fled to the surrounding countryside, they were found and all were either killed during capture or executed. The incident traumatized England, and it was a further setback for the cause of equal rights for Catholics.

Conflicts with Parliament

Meanwhile James continued to act in ways that angered Parliament. Frustrated that Parliament had not voted him sufficient funds, he imposed customs duties (taxes on goods entering England from foreign countries) without Parliament's consent. In 1610 Cecil presented a plan to the king and Parliament that would increase the royal income. This Great Contract, as it was known, would grant the crown an annual sum if the crown agreed to give up some royal rights, including the right to seize goods and services for its own use. Nothing came of this plan, though, because of disagreement among members of Parliament. Angry at this outcome, James dissolved Parliament in 1611.

To cope with the increasing debt, James began selling titles for cash. A person could become an earl, for example, if he paid £20,000 to the government. But these measures did little to improve finances, and in 1614 a new Parliament was called to session in order to impose new taxes. It achieved nothing, however, and James dissolved it shortly afterward. He ruled without a Parliament for the next seven years.

In 1618 war between Catholics and Protestants broke out in Europe. James had no wish to involve his kingdom in this conflict. But his daughter, Elizabeth, was married to Frederick V (1596–1632), a German prince, and most of the fighting was taking place in Germany. His son, Charles, joined the man who was now James's favorite courtier, George Villiers (1592–1628), in urging James to aid the Protestant cause. Parliament criticized Villiers, whom many suspected was the king's lover, for having too powerful an influence on James. Parliament also complained about the king's policy of selling titles and impeached his lord chancellor, **Francis Bacon** (1561–1626; see entry) for corruption. James dissolved Parliament again in 1624.

In March 1625, while on a hunting trip, James became ill. Modern historians believe that he probably suffered a stroke. He was unable to speak and grew extremely weak. He died on March 27 and was buried at Westminster Abbey.

Though James was not a popular king, he did achieve some significant goals. He ended England's long and costly war with Spain and stabilized relations with foreign powers. This peace contributed to the growth of English trade. James also worked to ease religious tensions. He left his successor, his son Charles I, with a government that, despite financial problems and calls for constitutional reform, was relatively stable.

For More Information

BOOKS

Fraser, Antonia. *King James.* New York: Knopf, 1975.

Hogge, Alice. *God's Secret Agents: Queen Elizabeth's Forbidden Priests and the Hatching of the Gunpowder Plot.* New York: HarperCollins, 2005.

Nicolson, Adam. *God's Secretaries: The Making of the King James Bible.* New York: HarperCollins, 2003.

Stewart, Alan. *The Cradle King; The Life of James VI & I, the First Monarch of a United Great Britain.* New York: St. Martin's Press, 2003.

WEB SITES

Butler, John. "James I of England." *Luminarium.* http://www.luminarium.org/sevenlit/james/jamesbio.htm (accessed on July 11, 2006).

The Gunpowder Plot. House of Commons Information Office, 2004. http://www.parliament.uk/factsheets (accessed on July 11, 2006).

"What if the Gunpowder Plot Had Succeeded?" *BBC: Church and State: Monarchs and Leaders.* http://www.bbc.co.uk/history/state/monarchs_leaders/gunpowder_hutton_01.shtml (accessed on July 11, 2006).

John Knox

BORN: 1513 • Haddington, Scotland

DIED: November 24, 1572 • Edinburgh, Scotland

Scottish religious reformer

"England and Scotland shall both know that I am ready to suffer more than either poverty or exile, for the profession of that … heavenly religion, whereof it has pleased His merciful providence to make me … a simple soldier and witness-bearer unto men."

John Knox. STOCK MONTAGE/GETTY IMAGES.

Religious reformer John Knox was the leader of the Protestant Reformation in Scotland. His passionate anti-Catholicism led him to denounce Catholic rulers such as **Mary I** (1516–1558; see entry) of England and the Scottish queen **Mary Stuart** (1542–1587; see entry). He played a major role in fueling the rebellion that led to Mary Stuart's removal from power, which increased religious and political tensions in both Scotland and England. His intense disapproval of women rulers alienated **Elizabeth I** (1533–1603; see entry), who supported the Protestant cause but found Knox's views distasteful and extreme.

139

Early life

John Knox was born into a middle-class Catholic family in Haddington, Scotland, around 1513. He attended the local school and left home at age fifteen to study at St. Salvatore's College, University of St. Andrews. He received a bachelor of divinity degree, and he was ordained a priest on April 15, 1536.

The exact reason that Knox rejected Catholicism remains unclear. In 1543 he was serving as a Catholic priest under the archbishop of St. Andrews, but he was becoming exposed to reformist ideas. During this time, the Reformation, a sixteenth-century religious movement that aimed to reform the Roman Catholic Church and resulted in the establishment of Protestant churches, was well underway. A Protestant lord, Hugh Douglas of Longniddry, who had hired Knox to tutor his two sons, embraced Protestantism in late 1545.

Though Catholicism was still the official religion of Scotland at this time, Protestant ideas were gaining ground. Students and merchants returning to Scotland from Europe smuggled in the writings of religious reformers such as Martin Luther (1483–1546), a German monk who in 1517 denounced the Catholic Church for its sale of indulgences, which according to church doctrine cancelled the punishment for sins. Luther and his followers saw much corruption in the church. It controlled vast wealth; its highest-ranking clergy held personal riches and ignored the needs of the poor. Furthermore, in the view of reformers, few priests followed true Christian ideals in their own lives. Reformers wished to free the church from these practices and return it to the principles on which it was originally founded. Such ideas, however, were considered dangerous. In 1525 Scotland's Parliament, or legislative body, passed a law banning the importation of literature that preached heresy, or religious belief that contradicted the church's doctrines. The law had little effect, however, and stricter measures were enacted, including the death penalty—by burning at the stake—for those who preached heresy.

Circumstances were complicated even more by the situation in England, where **Henry VIII** (1491–1547; see entry) had officially broken with the Roman Catholic Church in the 1530s. In order to obtain a divorce—which the pope, the head of the Catholic Church, had refused to allow—Henry declared himself the supreme head of the church in England. Though he had no interest in creating a reformed church, his action gave political support to those in England who did. As a result England under Henry became a Protestant country. The Scots, always suspicious that Henry wished to dominate them politically, rejected his proposal that their infant queen, the Catholic Mary Stuart, marry his only son and heir, Edward VI (1537–1553). Henry responded by launching military raids into Scotland, prompting the Scots to seek a military alliance with France, a strongly Catholic country. England's aggression gave Scotland renewed cause to fear the rise of Protestantism.

Martyrdom and rebellion

In 1545 George Wishart (1513–1546), a Scottish Protestant preacher who had acted as one of Henry's representatives during these unsuccessful marriage negotiations, was placed under government surveillance in Scotland. Knox joined a group of Protestant lords bent on protecting him. Armed with a two-handed sword, Knox remained with Wishart for five weeks until Wishart finally persuaded him to return to his teaching duties. One day later Wishart was arrested. He was strangled and burned at the stake for heresy.

This event only strengthened the resolve of the reformers. Recognizing that the Scottish cardinal, David Beaton (1494–1546), had called for Wishart's arrest and execution, some Protestant lords broke into the cardinal's castle at St. Andrews and stabbed him to death. Besieged in the castle, the rebels held out for a little more than a year against Scottish government forces. In April 1547 Knox decided to join the rebels to provide them with spiritual support. By mid-July, however, French ships had arrived with military aid for the Scottish troops, and the castle fell on July 31. Knox was captured and sentenced to work as a galley slave on a French ship.

Never a particularly robust man, Knox suffered terribly in the galleys, where he was forced to work to exhaustion and was underfed. His health was weakened by the experience, but he kept his spirit strong through his belief that God would soon free him. After nineteen months, in March 1549, he was released.

Life in exile

Faced with persecution in Scotland, Knox went to England, where the king's Privy Council gave him a preaching position in Berwick. (The Privy Council was a board of advisors that carried out the administrative function of the government in matters of economy, defense, foreign policy, and law and order, and its members served as the king's chief advisors.) Here he was able to recover his health and continue his

Knox's Time as a Galley Slave

John Knox spent nineteen months as a galley slave for the French navy. Galleys were a class of ship powered by both sails and oars. They were about 100 to 150 feet long, with twenty-five oars that passed through oar-holes on the ship's side. Each oar was about 40 to 50 feet long. Normally six men rowed on each oar, but during battle only four men did the job, in order to leave room for the crew's movements.

Galley slaves were chained to their benches by their legs day and night; they ate and slept at their seats. They were forced to row for hours at a time, with only biscuits and water each day and vegetable soup three times a week. They were whipped for any misbehavior. Not surprisingly, no sailor would volunteer to row in the galleys, and the French used convicted criminals and prisoners of war as slaves. The prospect of being captured and forced to row in the galleys of the French terrified the English, and boosted their resolve to defend their country from attack.

Galley slaves on French ships were expected to attend Catholic Mass, which Knox and his fellow Scottish rowers refused to do. In his *History of the Reformation in Scotland* Knox described an incident in which the French brought an image of the Virgin Mary to him and demanded that he kiss it. He called it an idol and refused to touch it, but they thrust it into his hands. When no one was looking, he threw it into the water.

In addition to being overworked, underfed, and kept in unsanitary conditions, galley slaves risked being killed in battle. Chained at their seats, they could not escape enemy fire. Nor could they save themselves in the event of shipwreck. If no one on board thought to unchain them, galley slaves died when their ships were destroyed. Knox became very ill in the galleys, and he almost died. He was given extra rations, and he gradually recovered his health. He later wrote that his faith helped him to maintain the will to live during this time of brutal suffering.

religious studies. He also met his future wife, Marjory Bowes, to whom he became engaged in 1553. Knox began to refine his beliefs and his teachings, particularly his rejection of the Catholic Mass, during which a priest performs transubstatiation, the miraculous change that occurs when a priest blesses the Eucharist (bread and wine) and it changes into the body and blood of Christ, while maintaining the appearance of bread and wine. He preached this so adamantly that in 1550 the Privy Council ordered him to appear before them to explain his beliefs in more detail. He argued that the authority of Scripture, the church's sacred texts, was supreme, and its teachings were above even those of the pope or the king. Because the Mass was not mentioned in Scripture, he said, it should not be performed. The council accepted his argument, and Knox soon became well known and respected. In 1551 he preached before John Dudley (Duke of Northumberland; 1501–1553), who in effect ruled

England for the adolescent king, Edward VI. Dudley was so impressed with Knox that he invited him to London to preach before Edward. Dudley also offered Knox a position as bishop, but Knox declined.

When Edward VI died in 1553, his Catholic half-sister, Mary I, became queen of England and immediately took steps to restore Catholicism there. Realizing that his life would be in danger if he remained in England, Knox fled to Europe, where he remained for the next five years, settling in Geneva, Switzerland. There he met the most influential leaders of the Protestant Reformation, including John Calvin (1506–1564).

In 1555 Knox made a trip to Scotland. Though Mary Stuart, a Catholic, was technically queen, she was still a child and was living in France while her mother, Mary of Guise (1515–1560), ruled on her behalf. Mary of Guise supported tolerant policies toward Protestants, making it safe for Knox to preach freely in Scotland. Nevertheless, Catholic feeling was still strong, and within about six months he was pressured to leave the country. After he left, he was burned in effigy, meaning that a representation of him was burned. During this period in Scotland Knox married Marjory Bowes, returning with her to Geneva in 1556.

Knox planned another trip to Scotland in early 1557. He had been invited by the Scottish Protestant lords to help them start a religious reformation there. But the lords later advised him to wait until conditions in Scotland would be more favorable for such a plan. Knox remained in Europe until 1559.

In Geneva Knox busied himself with writing. One of his most widely known pamphlets, *The First Blast of the Trumpet Against the Monstrous Regiment of Women* (1558), was an attack on the rule of female sovereigns. In this pamphlet, which was published anonymously, Knox wrote that women's rule was "repugnant to nature" and "a disgrace to God." He concluded that it was proper for the Protestant faithful to overthrow their Catholic leader by an armed uprising. Knox frequently denounced the Catholic Church, which he called a "synagogue of Satan" and a "harlot … polluted with all kinds of spiritual fornication." He called Catholic priests "pestilent papists" and "bloody wolves." In 1559, after the death of Mary, Knox published *A Brief Exhortation to England, for the Speedy Embracing of the Gospel Heretofore of Mary Suppressed and Banished.* This pamphlet urged the English to repent for the "shameful defection" of those who had gone back to Catholicism during Mary's reign. Knox's negative views of female rulers so angered England's newly crowned Protestant queen, Elizabeth I, that she refused to grant him safe conduct through England when he decided to return to Scotland in 1559.

Return to Scotland

By the time Knox returned to Scotland in May 1559, the Protestant lords were in open rebellion against Mary of Guise. A few days later Knox preached a sermon at Perth that inspired his listeners to loot neighboring religious houses. In October the lords removed Mary of Guise from power, and sent to England for support from Elizabeth, a Protestant. In February 1560 the Protestant rebels signed a treaty with England in which England promised military aid to the rebellion in Scotland. In effect, this ended any support for Mary of Guise, who died a few months later. Soon afterward France and England signed the Treaty of Edinburgh, in which both countries agreed to remove their troops from Scotland. At a parliament session in Edinburgh that August, Scotland enacted laws that abolished the authority of the pope, forbade the celebration of the Mass, and instituted a reformed Protestant church in Scotland.

Knox was appointed as the first Protestant minister of St. Giles Cathedral in Edinburgh. He was also asked to join a committee charged with preparing a program of religious reformation and reorganization, including a national system of education. This work became known as the *Book of Discipline.* One of its central provisions was that the clergy should be elected by democratic process, not through political patronage. Knox believed that those who did not embrace the reformed church were sons of Satan and did not deserve respect or fair treatment. In fact, he thought it permissible to cheat and torment them, and even rejoice in knowing that they would be condemned to hell. In Knox's view, the reformed church required that all members of society should act according to the teachings of the Bible. Even rulers should acknowledge the higher power of the Scriptures and act according to Christian ideals.

Rule of Mary Stuart

The return of Mary Stuart to the Scottish throne in 1561 did nothing to change Knox's hatred and distrust of Catholicism and women's rule. He publicly criticized the queen's love of dancing, causing her to call him before her court for questioning. He told her that he disapproved of her Catholic religion, her flirtation with Henry Stewart (Lord Darnley;

John Knox in an interview with Mary Stuart, Queen of Scots. HULTON ARCHIVE/GETTY IMAGES.

1545–1567), and her general conduct. Though many Protestant lords agreed with Knox, not all of them shared his hostility to Mary; their objections to his extreme views caused him to be officially reprimanded by the General Assembly of the Church of Scotland in 1564.

Through much of the 1560s Knox worked on his book, *History of the Reformation in Scotland.* He also preached regularly, but he did not participate actively in political matters. His first wife died in 1560, leaving him with two sons. In 1563 he married Margaret Stewart, daughter of a Protestant lord. Knox was fifty years old at this time; his bride was only seventeen. This marriage produced three daughters. Though his writings expressed extreme views and employed passionate and sometimes coarse language, in daily life Knox was known as a considerate man who got along well with his neighbors of all social classes.

In 1567 Mary Stuart's husband, Henry Stewart, was murdered. Immediately afterward the queen married James Hepburn (Earl of Bothwell; 1535–1578). The Scots firmly believed that Mary had been involved in Stewart's death, and even those Protestant lords who had previously taken her side now turned against her. Though Knox did not actively participate in the lords' uprising, he did approve of it; in fact, he urged that Mary be executed. Instead the queen rallied some troops to her side and attempted a defense. In 1567 she was defeated in battle and forced her to give up the throne in favor of her infant son, **James I** (1566–1625; see entry).

Knox allied himself with the Protestant lords who ruled in the infant king's name. But he grew increasingly bitter by what he saw as a betrayal by those Protestant lords who had defended Mary Stuart. He continued to denounce Mary so strongly that her supporters forced him out of Edinburgh. He lived in St. Andrews for one year until tensions died down, returning to Edinburgh in September 1572. By this time he had grown frail, and he soon lost the ability to walk or read. He died that November at the age of fifty-nine.

Though his extremism alienated some Protestants, Knox played a key role in establishing the reformed church in Scotland. The hatred that he preached against Catholics also contributed to religious and political tensions that pitted supporters of Mary Stuart against those who favored Protestant rule. These tensions spilled over into England, where Mary's cause inspired several attempts to overthrow Elizabeth and place Mary on the throne. Mary did have some claim to the English throne as Elizabeth's cousin and great-granddaughter of Henry VII (1457–1509). Largely as a result of Knox's teachings, the Church of Scotland developed along more extreme and intolerant lines than did Protestantism in England.

For More Information

BOOKS

Reid, W. Stanford. *Trumpeter of God: A Biography of John Knox.* New York: Scribner, 1974.

Ridley, Jasper. *John Knox.* London: Oxford University Press, 1968.

WEB SITES

"John Knox." *English Bible History.* http://www.greatsite.com/timeline-english-bible-history/john-knox.html (accessed on July 11, 2006).

"John Knox." *Mary, Queen of Scots.* http://www.marie-stuart.co.uk/knox.htm (accessed on July 11, 2006).

"John Knox." http://www.newgenevacenter.org/biography/knox2.htm (accessed on July 11, 2006).

Maclean, Diane. "John Knox." *The Scotsman: Heritage & Culture.* http://heritage.scotsman.com/timelines.cfm?cid=1&id=40872005 (accessed on July 11, 2006).

Selected Writings of John Knox: Public Epistles, Treatises, and Expositions to the Year 1559. http://history.hanover.edu/early/knox.html (accessed on July 11, 2006).

Christopher Marlowe

BORN: February 1564 • Canterbury, England

DIED: May 30, 1593 • Deptford, England

English playwright

"I hold the Fates bound fast in iron chains."

Christopher Marlowe was the most influential dramatist of the Elizabethan Era, the period associated with the reign of Queen Elizabeth I (1558–1603) that is often considered to be a golden age in English history. He was the first English playwright to show the dramatic possibilities of blank verse, the form that **William Shakespeare** (1564–1616; see entry) perfected in his own plays. Marlowe's work also introduced exciting new themes in Elizabethan drama by focusing on tragic protagonists who dared to challenge traditional ideas about morality. In his private life, too, Marlowe defied convention. Evidence suggests that he worked as a secret agent for the English government. At the same time, he was often accused of holding anti-religious beliefs, a serious crime in Elizabethan England. Some accused him of being a homosexual. Marlowe was killed at age twenty-nine. The official report of the incident determined that he had been killed in a fight that he had started. Some historians, however, believe he was assassinated by the government. Marlowe died before he had reached the height of his

Christopher Marlowe.
KEYSTONE/GETTY IMAGES.

149

artistic powers. Many believe that, had Marlowe lived longer, his works could have equaled or even surpassed those of Shakespeare.

Early life and education

One of nine children born to shoemaker John Marlowe and his wife, Katherine Arthur, Christopher Marlowe grew up in Canterbury, the site of one of England's oldest cathedrals. Though not actually poor, the family never quite achieved a comfortable standard of living; nevertheless, it was stable and happy. As a boy Christopher received a scholarship to attend the King's School, a prestigious choir school under the cathedral's administration. Here he studied Greek, Latin, religion, music, and history. He also obtained a thorough knowledge of poetic structure, and he was expected to be able to compose his own poems in Latin. Students at the King's School often performed plays in Greek and Latin, and they were required to speak in Latin at all times, even during their free time.

At age sixteen Marlowe enrolled as a scholarship student at Corpus Christi College, Cambridge University. Here he deepened his knowledge of Latin and began writing his own poetry and plays. He completed his bachelor's of arts degree in 1584 and received his master's degree in 1587. The university officials had been reluctant at first to grant Marlowe's master's degree because he had been absent from the university for an extended period of time. They suspected he may have gone to Europe to meet with Catholic exiles there who had fled Protestant rule in England. If Marlowe had Catholic sympathies, they judged, his loyalty to the English government might be in question; if this were the case, they would withhold his degree.

Marlowe may very well have been in Europe, but if so his purpose was probably quite different from what the university authorities suspected. Many historians believe that, during his university days, Marlowe was recruited by **Francis Walsingham** (1530–1590; see entry) as a secret agent for the English government. There was intense religious conflict in England at this time, and **Elizabeth I** (1533–1603; see entry), a Protestant whose right to the English throne was disputed by Catholics, was vulnerable to Catholic plots to assassinate her. Walsingham sought intelligent and educated men like Marlowe to work as spies in England and Europe to help expose anti-government conspiracies. Marlowe's frequent absences from the university in the mid-1580s may have occurred while he was on undercover missions for Walsingham. The details of any such assignments, though, are not known.

The queen's Privy Council sent a letter to the university in Marlowe's defense. (The Privy Council was the board of advisors that carried out the administrative function of the government in matters of economy, defense, foreign policy, and law and order, and its members served as the queen's chief advisors.) It informed the authorities that any rumor about Marlowe working for the English Catholic cause in Europe was false. As quoted in *The World of Christopher Marlowe* by David Riggs, the letter also told the university to grant Marlowe his degree because "it was not her Majesty's pleasure that anyone employed as he had been in matters touching the benefit of his Country should be defamed by those that are ignorant in the affairs he went about." The authorities granted the degree.

Moves to London

Soon afterward Marlowe moved to London, where he settled in the neighborhood of Norton Folgate just outside the city walls to the north. This was a suitable location for an aspiring playwright because it was free from city government control. Playhouses, of which the stricter Protestant faction called Puritans disapproved, could operate freely there. So could taverns, gambling dens, and houses of prostitution. Performances at playhouses often drew rowdy audiences, and robberies and fights were common.

Marlowe quickly developed a reputation for drinking and quarreling. He was arrested in 1589 after a street fight in Norton Folgate that resulted in the death of an innkeeper named William Bradley. Marlowe and Bradley were fighting in an alley when Thomas Watson, a poet, drew his sword to intervene. Bradley then attacked Watson, and Watson stabbed him to death. A jury ruled that Marlowe had not been involved in the killing, and that Watson had acted in self-defense. In 1592 authorities in Shoreditch, near Norton Folgate, demanded that Marlowe provide them with a guarantee that he would not disturb the peace. Later that year he was charged with damaging property in Canterbury.

A new age of drama

From his earliest days in London Marlowe became associated with a company of actors, the Admiral's Men, whose star performer was Edward Alleyn (1566–1626). Soon the Admiral's Men were staging the young dramatist's works. In late 1587 Marlowe's *Tamburlaine, Parts 1 and 2* was performed in London. According to James E. Ruoff in *Major Elizabethan Poetry & Prose,* this play "heralded in spellbinding cadences [rhythms] a new age of drama." It was the first play in English to exploit the full potential of blank verse, a type of poetry with regular meter (the pattern of stressed and unstressed syllables) but no rhyme. Theatergoers as well as Marlowe's fellow writers were entranced by this innovative use of blank verse; poet Ben Jonson (c. 1572–1637) called it "Marlowe's mighty line."

Tamburlaine also excited audiences with its subject matter. The play told the story of Tamburlaine, a poor shepherd from Scythia (a region near the Black Sea) who conquers the world. He is a cruel and pitiless tyrant, and the play is filled with scenes of graphic violence. For example, a captured emperor kills himself by smashing his head against the bars of the cage in which Tamburlaine exhibits him. Tamburlaine, played by Alleyn in a performance that brought him great fame, shocked Elizabethans because he openly enjoys his cruelty. Furthermore, he refuses to accept any social order that might limit his power. Though he was born poor, he decides to make his own destiny. "I hold the Fates bound fast in iron chains," he declares. This insistence on his own power to do as he chose made Tamburlaine a new type of hero, one who completely rejected the traditional virtues of Elizabethan England. As Ruoff explained, this play and Marlowe's other works glorified the new ideas of the Renaissance, which emphasized individual freedom. (The Renaissance was the era beginning around 1350 in Europe, in which scholars turned their attention to classical Greek and Latin learning and shifted to a more rational [based on reason rather than spiritual belief or church authority] approach to philosophy, religion, and science.)

Between 1588 and 1592 Marlowe wrote at least four other plays; another, *Dido, Queen of Carthage,* may date from his years at Cambridge University. *Tamburlaine* was published in 1590, but the dates of Marlowe's other plays, which were performed but not published until after his death, are not certain.

The Tragical History of Doctor Faustus, published in 1604 but first produced around 1589, was based on the German story of a magician who sells his soul to the devil in order to gain forbidden knowledge. Marlowe's play, scholars believe, was the first dramatization of this story. The play features Faustus's famous speech about his fear of death, and his descent into hell. *The Jew of Malta,* first produced around 1590 but published in 1633, was considered a major influence of Shakespeare's *The*

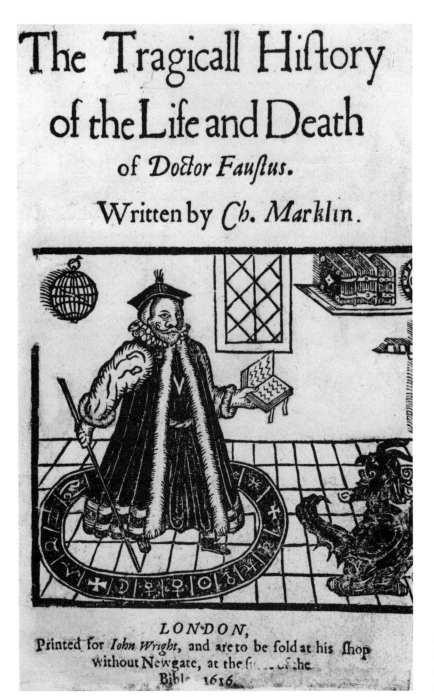

The Tragicall History of the Life and Death of *Doctor Faustus*.

Written by *Ch. Marklin*.

LONDON,
Printed for *Iohn Wright*, and are to be fold at his fhop
without Newgate, at the fi.... of the
Bibl. 1616.

The 1616 cover to Dr. Faustus
by Christopher Marlowe.
HULTON ARCHIVE/GETTY
IMAGES.

Merchant of Venice. In Marlowe's play, a Jewish merchant, Barabas, embarks on a violent campaign of revenge after authorities in Malta deprive him and other Jews of their wealth in order to pay a tax demanded by the Turks. *The Massacre at Paris* dramatized the events of the St. Bartholomew's Day Massacre in 1572, when Catholic mobs in Paris murdered thousands of Protestants. The Catholic Duke of Guise, one of the leaders behind the massacre, is the play's hero. *Edward II,* considered Marlowe's best-constructed play, is based on the reign of King Edward II of England (1284–1327), a homosexual ruler who struggled against powerful barons who eventually assassinated him. It focuses more closely on character development than previous examples of history plays, or plays about historical figures and events. It is also one of only a very few plays from this period that dealt with the subject of homosexuality.

Accused of atheism

Marlowe's actions and writings stirred up controversy, and almost from the start of his career he found himself accused of atheism, or not believing in God—a serious crime in Elizabethan England punishable by burning at the stake. In 1588 a rival writer and critic, Robert Greene (c. 1560–1592), published a pamphlet that hinted at atheism in *Tamburlaine.* Greene also wrote a play, *Friar Bacon and Friar Bungay,* that appeared to criticize the lack of repentance and redemption in *Doctor Faustus.* In 1592 Greene published another pamphlet that more specifically associated Marlowe with atheism.

The playwright found himself in other kinds of trouble as well. When the plague, a disease that killed nearly one-fourth of the city's population, came to London in 1592, playhouses were temporarily closed. Around this time Marlowe went to the Netherlands, where Protestants had been engaged in a years-long rebellion against Spanish Catholic rule, at times with English military support. Marlowe was arrested in Flushing, a town under English control, and accused of counterfeiting and of intent to aid the enemy. Marlowe was sent back to London but was never punished. This incident has caused historians to theorize that Marlowe had received another espionage assignment.

In early 1593, with the plague still raging in London, Marlowe worked on the long narrative poem *Hero and Leander.* (A narrative poem is a poem that tells a story.) He died before completing it. The poem was based on a Greek legend about lovers who lived on opposite sides of a narrow strait, the Hellespont. Every night Leander swam across, guided by his lover's lamp. In the ancient legend Leander is drowned one night when a storm extinguishes the light. Marlowe's poem, however, breaks off after the lovers' first night together. The unfinished portion was published in 1598, and a version completed by poet George Chapman (c. 1559–1634) was published later that year. The other major poem for which Marlowe is known is "The Passionate Shepherd to His Love."

A violent death

In May 1593 more allegations surfaced about Marlowe's alleged atheism. Several bills, or pamphlets, had been posted around the city that threatened Protestant refugees from Europe. One of these, put up on the wall of the Dutch churchyard, was written in blank verse, contained references to Marlowe's plays, and was signed "Tamburlaine." Alarmed, the queen ordered city authorities to crack down on the authors of these bills. Thomas Kyd (1558–1594), a playwright with whom Marlowe shared a workroom, was one of those arrested. A search of Kyd's room unearthed papers expressing views that contradicted official religious teachings. The authorities described these views, in a report quoted by Riggs, as "vile heretical Conceits denying the deity of Jesus Christ."

After being tortured in prison, Kyd told the authorities that the papers were not his but Marlowe's. On May 18 the Privy Council issued a warrant for Marlowe's arrest. He was taken into custody at the estate of his powerful patron, Thomas Walsingham, nephew of the secretary of state who was also involved in the English espionage network. The council did not imprison the playwright, but it did insist that he provide daily reports on his activities. On May 26 Richard Baines, an informer, provided the council with a document that became known as the Baines Note. As quoted by Constance Brown Kuriyama in *Christopher Marlowe: A Renaissance Life,* the note accused Marlowe of "damnable judgment of religion and scorn of God's word." Four days later Marlowe was dead.

On May 30 Marlowe was killed at the house of Widow Bull in Deptford, an area south of the river from London near several theaters. Witnesses reported that Marlowe had picked a fight with his companions about the bill for their food and drink, and he had attacked and wounded Ingram Frizer in the head. Frizer then killed Marlowe with an accidental stab wound just above the eye. Marlowe died instantly. A coronor's jury on June 1 found that Frizer had acted in self-defense. Marlowe was buried that day at St. Nicholas Church, Deptford.

The Passionate Shepherd and the Nymph's Satirical Reply

Although Marlowe is best known for dramas with powerful, violent heroes, his "The Passionate Shepherd to His Love" is a very different work. Its first stanza contains one of the best-known opening lines in English poetry.

The Passionate Shepherd to His Love
Come live with me and be my Love,
And we will all the pleasures prove
That valleys, groves, hills, and fields,
Woods, or steepy mountain yields.

And we will sit upon the rocks,
Seeing the shepherds feed their flocks,
By shallow rivers to whose falls
Melodious birds sing madrigals [songs].

And I will make thee beds of roses
And a thousand fragrant posies,
A cap of flowers, and a kirtle [skirt]
Embroidered all with leaves of myrtle;

A gown made of the finest wool
Which from our pretty lambs we pull;
Fair lined slippers for the cold,
With buckles of the purest gold;

A belt of straw and ivy buds,
With coral clasps and amber studs:
And if these pleasures may thee move,
Come live with me, and be my Love.

The shepherd's swains shall dance and
      sing
For thy delight each May-morning:
If these delights thy mind may move
Then live with me and be my Love.

Several contemporary poets wrote parodies of this poem. The best known is "The Nymph's Reply to the Shepherd" by **Walter Raleigh** (1552–1618; see entry):

The Nymph's Reply to the Shepherd
If all the world and love were young,
And truth in every shepherd's tongue,
These pretty pleasures might me
      move
To live with thee and be thy love.

Time drives the flocks from field to fold
When rivers rage and rocks grow cold,
And Philomel [the nightingale] beco-
      meth dumb;
The rest complains of cares to come.

The flowers do fade, and wanton
      fields
To wayward winter reckoning yields;
A honey tongue, a heart of gall
Is fancy's spring, but sorrow's fall.

Thy gowns, thy shoes, thy bed of
      roses,
Thy cap, thy kirtle, and thy posies
Soon break, soon wither, soon
      forgotten—
In folly ripe, in season rotten.

They belt of straw and ivy buds,
Thy coral clasps and amber studs,
All these in me no means can move
To come to thee and be thy love.

But could youth last and love still
      breed,
Had joys no date nor age no need,
Then these delights my mind might
      move
To live with thee and be thy love.

SOURCES: "THE PASSIONATE SHEPHERD TO
   HIS LOVE," *BARLEBY.COM* AND "THE
   NYMPH'S REPLY TO THE SHEPHERD,"
   LUMINARIUM.ORG.

Despite this official version of events, suspicions of foul play later arose. The men who were with Marlowe that day, who included Nicholas Skeres and Robert Poley in addition to Frizer, had all worked for Walsingham, and some historians believe that they may have been part of a secret plot to assassinate the playwright. There may have been powerful individuals who feared what Marlowe might reveal about their own activities if he were brought to trial on the atheism charge. The queen herself may have wished to silence him. But other historians point out that Marlowe had a well-deserved reputation for violence, and he could very well have simply started a fight that turned deadly.

At the time Marlowe's enemies considered his death the logical result of his atheism. His friends mourned the loss of an exceptionally gifted writer. In 1599 Shakespeare alluded to Marlowe in *As You Like It,* when the character Phoebe addresses the "dead shepherd." Later in the play, the character Touchstone alludes to the quarrel in the small room in Deptford when he says that "When a man's verses cannot be understood … it strikes a man more dead than a great reckoning in a little room."

Though Marlowe's artistic career was tragically brief, he gave the English language poems and plays that profoundly influenced the development of literature. As Ruoff concluded, "Marlowe's language towers above any life we have ever known or guessed. . . . [His] golden declamations were shouted across the narrow streets of London by young apprentices for twenty years after his death. It was perhaps their way of paying tribute to the 'dead shepherd' who had given them during his 'two hours' traffic of the stage' a rare glimpse of life as it is seen from the heady mountaintops of the world."

For More Information

BOOKS

Kuriyama, Constance Brown. *Christopher Marlowe: A Renaissance Life.* Ithaca, NY and London: Cornell University Press, 2002.

Riggs, David. *The World of Christopher Marlowe.* New York: Henry Holt and Company, 2004.

Ruoff, James E. *Major Elizabethan Poetry & Prose.* New York: Thomas Y. Crowell Company, 1972.

WEB SITES

"Christopher Marlowe." *In Search of Shakespeare.* http://www.pbs.org/shakespeare/players/player24.html (accessed on July 11, 2006).

"Christopher Marlowe: 16th Century British Literature." *Classic Literature Library: British Authors.* http://www.classic-literature.co.uk/british-authors/16th-century/christopher-marlowe/ (accessed on July 11, 2006).

The Marlowe Society. http://www.marlowe-society.org/ (accessed on July 11, 2006).

"The Nymph's Reply to the Shepherd." *Luminarium.org.* http://www.luminarium.org/renlit/nymphsreply.htm (accessed on July 11, 2006).

"The Passionate Shepherd to His Love." *Bartleby.com.* http://www.bartleby.com/106/5.html (accessed on July 11, 2006).

Walton, Brenda. "Christopher Marlowe and the Creation of Dr. Faustus." http://www.teachersfirst.com/lessons/marl-1a.htm (accessed on July 11, 2006).

Mary I

BORN: February 18, 1516 • Greenwich, England

DIED: November 17, 1558 • England

English queen

"In life and death I will not forsake the Catholic religion of the church our mother . . . [even if compelled by] threats or violence."

Queen Mary I took power when England faced troubled times. She attempted to restore the Roman Catholic religion, which her father, **Henry VIII** (1491–1547; see entry), had outlawed. She believed that this step would unify the country that had experienced much religious and political turmoil. The English people supported Mary at first, but they soon began to hate her for her harsh policies toward Protestants. Because she ordered many Protestants to be burned to death for heresy (religious opinions that conflict with the church's doctrines, or principles), she became known as "Bloody Mary." She is remembered as a tyrant who oppressed her people and who failed to create the wise governmental policies that England needed in order to become a more powerful and modern nation.

Queen Mary I. TIME LIFE PICTURES/MANSELL/TIME LIFE PICTURES/GETTY IMAGES.

Early life and education

Mary was the only surviving child born to Henry VIII and his first wife, Catherine of Aragon (1485–1536), whose parents were the Spanish

159

monarchs Ferdinand (1452–1516) and Isabella (1451–1504). Henry desperately wanted a male heir and hoped that after Mary's successful birth Catherine would at last give birth to a son. As the years passed, though, Catherine did not become pregnant again.

Henry provided his daughter with a good education. Her Spanish tutor, Luis Vives (1492–1540), taught her Latin, Spanish, Italian, and French. He also emphasized Christian virtue, instructing the young princess on the importance of obedience to God and the church. Though Mary was intelligent, she was taught to believe that, as a woman, she was not capable of making complex decisions. She learned that her role was to allow men—her father, future husband, or male advisors—to make decisions for her and to follow their authority.

Mary's first few years were happy ones, but when she was only ten years old her father began taking steps that changed her life completely. Frustrated that Catherine had not given birth to a son, Henry wanted to dissolve his marriage and take a new wife. He petitioned the pope, the head of the Roman Catholic Church, to allow this. But the pope refused to make a decision. Finally, after six years, the pope informed Henry that he would not declare the marriage invalid. But by then, Henry's mistress, Anne Boleyn (1507–1536), an attendant at the royal court, was pregnant and he wanted to marry her. So Henry declared that his marriage to Catherine had not been legitimate, and he married Anne.

Loses her royal status

The Act of Supremacy, passed in 1534, declared that Henry was the supreme head of the church in England. The Act of Succession, also passed that year, declared that Mary was not his legitimate child and could not inherit the throne. After Boleyn gave birth to a daughter, **Elizabeth I** (1533–1603; see entry) in 1533, Mary was sent to live in her sister's household as one of her attendants. Boleyn resented Mary and treated her unkindly. She forbade her to attend Catholic Mass or even to go outside for exercise and fresh air. Even worse, Mary was not allowed to see her mother. Mary lived almost as a prisoner.

Henry pressured Mary to take an oath promising loyalty to him as supreme head of the church. She refused, as did her mother. Though Henry could have condemned them to death for this, he feared provoking war with Spain by such an action. Instead, he kept them under watch. In 1536 Boleyn was executed for adultery, and Henry married Jane Seymour (1509–1537). A new act of Parliament declared that both Mary and

Elizabeth were illegitimate, making it lawful for the child Seymour bore, Edward VI (1537–1553), to inherit the throne. Mary was placed in isolation and forbidden any contact with friends until she finally agreed, with great reluctance, to sign a document affirming the act.

A time of relative happiness followed. Mary got along well with her new stepmother and was again welcome at court. Henry even changed his final will, making her second in line to inherit the throne after her brother. But when Edward became king after Henry's death in 1547, Mary's position was again threatened. Since Edward was only nine at the time he was crowned, he was guided entirely by his advisors. These men were eager to make further changes in the English church, separating it even more from the Catholic religion. They enacted reforms that required all people in England to attend a new, simple worship service instead of the Catholic Mass. Mary was ordered to conform to this new law, but she refused. Only after Mary's cousin, the Catholic Holy Roman Emperor Charles V (1500–1558), threatened war did Edward's advisors allow Mary to have Mass said in her private chambers.

Fights for her right to the throne

In addition to reforming religious practices, Edward's councilors wanted to strengthen their own political power. Edward was sickly, and they feared that he might die without producing an heir. John Dudley (Earl of Warwick; 1502–1443) convinced Edward to sign a document that removed Mary's claim to the throne and named Lady Jane Grey (1537–1554), Dudley's daughter-in-law, as his successor.

In 1553, at age sixteen, Edward died of tuberculosis. Mary knew her life was now in danger if she refused to support the succession of Grey, who had powerful lords on her side. But many other nobles were loyal to Mary. They believed that, as Henry's daughter, she had a much stronger claim to the throne. So Mary took a chance. Though Grey had already been named queen, Mary issued a proclamation declaring her legal right to the throne.

Mary raised an army of loyal supporters in Suffolk, in southern England. The army gathered near her castle of Framlingham to prepare to meet Dudley and his force of three thousand men. People throughout the region rallied to Mary's side. Armed gentlemen joined her army, which grew to almost twenty thousand men; poorer people sent bread, meat, or beer. Dudley, while camped at Cambridge, begged military help from the French king. But support for Mary continued to grow. While

Dudley awaited word from France, one of Mary's officers went to Yarmouth, where Dudley had stationed seven ships to guard the coast. The officer rowed out to the boats and inspired the two thousand sailors on board to mutiny, or rebel. Shouting "Long live our Queen Mary" they joined her forces and brought one hundred large cannons with them.

Edward's Privy Council, which had the duty of proclaiming the next monarch, had by this time met at the Tower of London to await the results of the expected battle. (The Tower of London is a fortress on the Thames River in London that was used as a royal residence, treasury, and, most famously, as a prison for the upper class.) When the council received news of this mutiny, they decided to take Mary's side. On July 18, 1553, they offered a reward for Dudley's arrest. The next day they publicly proclaimed Mary queen. The people of London were overjoyed with this news. People rushed into the streets, shouting and dancing. When Mary came to London two weeks later to be crowned, according to an account quoted by Carolly Erickson in *Bloody Mary: The Remarkable Life of Mary Tudor,* the streets were "so full of people shouting and crying Jesus save her grace, with weeping tears for joy, that the like was never seen before."

Queen and tyrant

This popularity did not last long. Mary's reign began gently. She arrested the conspirators who had supported Grey, but executed only Dudley and a few others, pardoning the rest. She also told the council that she did not intend to compel her subjects to conform to any religious practice that went against their consciences. But Mary believed that most English people wished to return to Catholicism, and that the leaders who had pushed for religious reforms had done much harm. After Parliament reenacted heresy laws, which stated that convicted heretics should be burned to death at the stake, Mary authorized her government to arrest Protestant leaders and put them on trial.

Mary did not set out to execute heretics out of cruelty. She wanted to put an end to the unrest that had been caused by the conflicts about religion. She believed that the English people would willingly return to Catholicism if they could be made to see that the Protestant faith was heresy. According to Erickson, the queen wrote that "Touching the punishment of heretics, I believe it would be well to inflict punishment at this beginning, without much cruelty or passion, but without however omitting to do such justice on those who choose by their false doctrines to

Bishop John Hooper's Death

The execution of Bishop John Hooper (1495–1555) showed the extreme suffering of death by burning. Not wanting to spend too much money on wood for the fire, the local authorities in charge of his execution bought only a little wood that was still green. When the fire was lit, it burned Hooper's feet but it did not reach higher. Then the wind almost extinguished the flames. Since there was not enough wood to keep a good fire going, the authorities had to send for more. But this was also green, so the slow fire burned just a little and did not kill its victim. By this time Hooper's legs had almost entirely burned, but his upper body had not been touched. He begged for more fire. When the kindling was lit a third time, the flames finally reached the bags of gunpowder he wore near his waist. But the wind blew them away before they could explode and kill him. He remained standing in the flames, and witnesses could hear him praying as his arms, torso, and throat finally started to burn. He beat his arms on his chest, asking God to receive his soul, until one arm fell off. He had been standing conscious in the flames for forty-five minutes before he finally died.

Although condemned heretics knew that their deaths would be terribly painful, many of them welcomed their executions. They believed that, after death, their souls would go immediately to God. When two or more victims were burned together, they often reassured each other that they would soon be feasting together in heaven. They were proud to die in such a horrible way. Some of the victims told their supporters that they would not cry out in pain while being burned in order to demonstrate their unshakable religious faith.

deceive simple persons, that the people may clearly comprehend that they have not been condemned without just cause."

Almost everyone in England considered heresy to be the most horrible type of crime imaginable. For at least 150 years, Protestant and Catholic rulers had ordered heretics to be burned at the stake. In fact, Mary's father had ordered ninety heretics executed during his thirty-seven-year reign. Even **John Knox** (1505–1572; see entry), a Protestant reformer and one of Mary's most extreme critics, approved of this punishment for heretics. "It is not only lawful to punish to the death such as labor to subvert the true religion," he wrote in a passage quoted by Erickson, "but the magistrates and people are bound to do so."

What was different about Mary's policy, however, was the scale of persecution. So many Protestants were burned at the stake during her reign that the English people grew disgusted by the suffering. About three hundred people—powerful individuals who preached against Catholicism, uneducated people, and even teenagers—were burned to death as heretics while Mary was queen. Because the executions were public, many people witnessed the agonies of those who were burned. Sometimes the flames moved swiftly and the victim died in a relatively short time. Some condemned persons were able to wear a little pouch of gunpowder around their necks or waists, hoping that the flames would ignite it and the explosion would kill them quickly. But in many cases—for example, if the wood did not burn well or if the wind blew the flames away from the stake—the victim took a long time to die. John Foxe (1516–1587), who wrote accounts of these deaths in his *Book of Martyrs,* described executions in which the flames burned the victims' legs or arms completely off while the person was still conscious.

Marriage to the king of Spain

Mary further angered her subjects by arranging a marriage with **Philip II** (1527–1598; see entry), who became the king of Spain in 1556. Everyone agreed that the queen should have a husband, not only to father an heir to the throne but also to help the queen rule. But the English resented the idea of Spanish control. Mary's advisors urged her to marry an English nobleman instead, but Mary accepted Philip's proposal soon after she was crowned. Deeply disappointed in this decision, the council and Parliament forced Mary to accept strict limits on Philip's power as her husband. Parliament refused to let Philip be publicly crowned king of England or to enjoy the usual rights of a king. Furthermore, if Mary died without giving birth to a child, Philip would have no right to the English crown.

When the marriage took place in July 1554, Mary was already thirty-eight years old, and she was not in good health. Philip was only twenty-seven. The marriage was not a happy one. Philip remained in England for only ten months after the wedding. During this time Mary announced that she was pregnant. She experienced the usual symptoms of pregnancy and awaited the birth of a child. But after more than nine months, no child came; she had only imagined that she had conceived. The queen urged her husband to return to England, but Philip was busy conducting a war against France. In 1557 he finally returned, but only to seek Mary's support for the Spanish military campaign. England had suffered two years of bad harvests and was facing financial problems. But Mary agreed to give Philip money and troops, a move that increased resentment against her. The situation grew even worse when the town of Calais, England's last possession in Europe, fell to the French. Mary's subjects blamed Philip for this disaster.

In late 1557 Mary again believed herself to be pregnant. But as before, the queen had not in fact conceived. In worsening health, Mary prepared to die. She changed her will to name her sister, Elizabeth, as her successor.

Mary I and her husband, Spanish king Philip II. BRIAN SEED/TIME LIFE PICTURES/ GETTY IMAGES.

Death and legacy

After Mary's death on November 17, Elizabeth became queen. Mary's attempts to return the country to Catholicism had failed, and England's alliance with Spain quickly ended. Elizabeth and her advisors steered the country back to the course that Henry and Edward had begun, confirming England's break with Catholic influences.

Though Mary had hoped to eliminate anti-Catholic feeling in England, her policies had the opposite effect. During Elizabeth's reign and afterward, the country became more strongly Protestant. It became illegal for an English monarch to be a Catholic or to marry a Catholic. Once loved by her subjects, Mary ended her reign as a despised tyrant. The day of Mary's death was a national holiday in England for two hundred years.

Historians consider Mary a ruler who did not understand that times were changing. She held fast to a belief that religion and obedience to the Catholic Church were the most important principles in life. She did not realize that her subjects were beginning to question this view and to demand changes in their type of government. She ruled as earlier monarchs had done, believing themselves to be immune from criticism because their religion gave them supreme authority. Though Mary, as queen, demonstrated the strength of her convictions, she failed to create policies that would strengthen England.

For More Information

BOOKS

Erickson, Carolly. *Bloody Mary: The Remarkable Life of Mary Tudor.* Garden City, NY: Doubleday, 1978.

Ridley, Jasper. *Bloody Mary's Martyrs: The Story of England's Terror.* New York: Carroll & Graf Publishers, 2001.

WEB SITES

Forbush, William Byron, ed. *Foxe's Book of Martyrs.* http://www.ccel.org/f/foxe/martyrs/home.html (accessed on July 11, 2006).

"Mary I: Queen of England." *Tudor Place.* http://www.tudorplace.com.ar/aboutMary.htm (accessed on July 11, 2006).

"Queen Mary I." *Tudor Monarchs.* http://englishhistory.net/tudor/monarchs/mary1.html (accessed on July 11, 2006).

Grace O'Malley

BORN: 1530 • County Mayo, Ireland
DIED: 1603 • County Mayo, Ireland

Irish pirate

> "This was a notorious woman in all the costes [coasts] of Ireland."
>
> — Sir Philip Sidney. Quoted by Anne Chambers in *Granuaile: Ireland's Pirate Queen.*

Grace O'Malley, known as the "Pirate Queen," led a clan of seafarers and pirates on the west coast of Ireland. Her ships, including swift-moving galleys that were propelled by oars, controlled access to ports near Galway and Clew Bay, demanding payment from merchant ships or even seizing their cargoes. When **Elizabeth I** (1533–1603; see entry) sent officials to Ireland to force chieftains there to accept English political authority, Grace defied them. She sailed to London, demanded an audience with the queen, and obtained royal permission to live freely in Ireland. Some considered Grace a brave and daring heroine; others considered her a ruthless thief. Whatever the case, Grace chose a life of power and control rare for a woman in her time. The O'Malley clan's motto, "Powerful by land and sea," was an accurate description of Grace herself.

Childhood and early life

Little is known about Grace O'Malley's childhood. She was the only daughter of Owen and Margaret O'Malley, and she had a brother, who some historians believe was not Margaret's child. Grace's father, who was known as "Black Oak," was chieftain of a powerful clan in western Ireland. Unlike most other clans, the O'Malleys made their living by the sea. They controlled Clew Bay and surrounding areas, where the clan

The Gallowglass

The term "gallowglass" comes from the Irish word for foreign soldiers, "gallóglaigh." The gallowglass were fierce warriors from the clans who lived in the northern mountains and western isles of Scotland. These Scottish clans were related to the Irish, but also had Viking heritage. They served chieftains in Scotland and Ireland, who hired the gallowglass to fight their clan battles. From about the mid–1200s to the late 1500s the gallowglass played a major role in clan warfare and in Irish resistance to English control.

The gallowglass fought with broadswords and a type of two-handed axe, six feet in length, that the Vikings had been noted for using. They wore chain-mail armor and iron helmets. They were paid in cattle, with each warrior receiving three cattle per quarter-year and all the grain and butter he could eat. Officers were paid even more, often buying land which enabled them to settle comfortably in Ireland. So fiercely did the gallowglass fight in rebellions against the English that, in 1573, the English governor in Ireland ordered some seven hundred of these foreign fighters to be executed. After guns became a more common weapon of war in the late 1500s, the role of the gallowglass began to weaken. But they continued to participate in Irish wars until around 1640.

fished, traded, and sold licenses to others who wished to fish in that area. As was customary in coastal Ireland at the time, the clan demanded payment from ships entering waters under its control. This meant that trading vessels were forced to pay a percentage of the value of their cargoes before they were allowed to pass through or anchor. Sometimes the clan seized everything a ship carried and stole the ship as well. The O'Malleys also raided along the Irish coast, and they transported fighters known as "gallowglasses" from Scotland to Ireland, where they were hired to fight in battles between clans.

Piracy—the raiding of ships at sea—was very common in the Elizabethan Era, the period associated with the reign of Queen Elizabeth I (1558–1603) that is often considered to be a golden age in English history. Nevertheless, pirates were outlaws. They kept their stolen property by force, not by legal right. Pirates risked attacks from rival ships as well as arrest by government authorities; the punishment for piracy was death by hanging. In order to protect themselves the O'Malleys had built strong castles at strategic points along the western shore of Ireland and on Clare Island. These sites were well guarded by forests and water. It was almost impossible for the clan's enemies to attack them in these strongholds.

Grace grew up in her family's castles and on her father's ships. Although she may not have been formally educated, she could read and write, and she knew several languages. Historians believe that she probably spent much of her childhood learning the complex skills of seafaring from her father. According to legend Grace was a fearless girl who loved the sea. When her father told her that she could no longer sail with him because she was a girl, she chopped off her long hair in order to look like a boy. She also climbed into the rigging (the ropes around the sails) of her father's ship, pulled down her trousers, and defiantly exposed her backside to the rival pirates that were chasing them. Grace once saved her father from assault when sailors from an English warship boarded O'Malley's ship. Shrieking as loudly as she could to alert her father to the danger, she jumped onto the back of a sailor who had drawn a knife.

Makes herself an independent chieftain

When Grace was sixteen she married Donal O'Flaherty, a chieftain's son from a neighboring clan. She moved south to Connemara, where she lived with her husband in Bunowen Castle. They had three children: Owen, Murrough, and Margaret. "Donal of the Battles," as her husband became known, was a reckless man who paid little attention to leading the O'Flaherty clan. Grace herself began to take over this role. She started to raid ships bound for the port of Galway, demanding payment for safe passage through O'Flaherty waters.

When O'Flaherty was murdered in his fortress, Grace defended it from the rival clan from which Donal had originally stolen it. When English soldiers were called in to force her to surrender, she ordered her men to strip the lead from the castle's roof and melt it down. She then ordered the molten lead poured on her enemies' heads. However, Grace was finally forced to surrender because laws in that part of Ireland did not allow her to inherit her husband's property. She returned to O'Malley lands and settled in their castle on Clare Island, taking with her several O'Flaherty fighters who had shifted their allegiance to her.

Grace now began to assemble her own forces. After her father's death she inherited all the O'Malley ships. She was able to gather two hundred sailing and fighting men under her command, and began raiding ships—mostly merchant vessels from France, Portugal, or Spain—that sailed near Clew Bay. Life at sea was difficult. Ships provided little privacy or physical comfort, and bad weather and storms created dangers. In addition, as Anne Chambers describes in *Granuaile: Ireland's Pirate Queen,* there was "swearing, disregard for hygiene, carousing, violence, as well as the sexual difficulty posed by the presence of a female among an all-male crew." To command the respect of her followers, Grace had to be an exceptionally strong leader. She could never show weakness, and she had to demonstrate greater physical strength and bravery than the men under her command.

Power and wealth

Grace's exploits soon made her famous. She attacked castles all along the coast and raided fishing ports. She was known to be ruthless in avenging what she considered to be wrongs against herself. According to one traditional story cited by Chambers, Grace seized Doona Castle on the coast of Erris because it belonged to the MacMahon clan, who had killed her lover, Hugh de Lacy. In another story, Grace and her crew had anchored in Dublin to take on supplies. She rode north to nearby Howth Castle to seek shelter for the night, which, according to Irish custom, was her right. But she was turned away. Furious, she retaliated by kidnapping the Lord of Howth's grandson, whom she met on the neighboring beach. She took the boy back to Clare Island. When Lord Howth offered a ransom, Grace refused. Her only demand for the boy's release was that Howth Castle should never again refuse hospitality to anyone. That tradition has been honored to this day.

Rich and powerful, Grace owned several castles and more than one thousand head of cattle—the symbol of Irish chieftains' wealth. Through her second husband, Richard Bourke (known as Iron Dick), she obtained his clan's castle at Rockfleet in the northern region of Clew Bay. Legends claim that Grace proposed the marriage, telling Richard that she wanted both him and his castle. Legends also claim that the marriage soon ended in divorce. Even so, Grace bore Richard a child, Tibbot-ne-Long ("Toby of the Ships"). According to legend Grace gave birth to this fourth child while she was at sea. When she went into labor she decided there was no need to go ashore; she went below deck and delivered the baby. The next day, while she was recovering from childbirth, Algerian pirates attacked her ship. Grace's first mate came below and begged her to lead the crew in defense. Angry that her men could not cope without her, she charged onto the deck half-dressed and swearing. She fired her musket at the pirates and screamed at them. They were so shocked at the sight of her that they fled.

Despite stories that Grace was not happy in her second marriage, she and Bourke worked well together as business partners. After Bourke died in 1583 Grace was able to claim a third of his property. She also ensured that their son received his proper inheritance.

Trouble with England

By the 1570s the government in England was growing impatient to bring Ireland under its control. Though the English had conquered Ireland in the twelfth century, the ruling lords in Ireland had intermarried with local nobles over the years and had become more Gaelic than English. Ireland remained a country ruled by rival clans and Gaelic customs. King Henry VII (1457–1509) of England had imposed new policies to subdue the Irish and force the chieftains to accept the authority of English governors. His son and successor, **Henry VIII** (1491–1547; see entry), declared himself king of Ireland as well as England. But it was Elizabeth I who set out systematically to make Ireland conform to English laws. She offered the chieftains a bargain: if they agreed to submit to the authority of the English monarch, they would be "regranted" their rights to their ancestral lands and given titles. But the chieftains had to agree to accept English law. They would have to pay rent and taxes to the English government on lands that they had owned for centuries.

This scheme caused much resentment. Some chieftains battled with English troops to retain their ancestral freedoms; others chose to submit, though many of these did so without really intending to obey the terms of the agreement. In 1577 Grace went to Galway to appear before the English authority there, Lord Deputy Henry Sidney (1529–1586). She offered her services to Sidney and told him she accepted the queen's authority. But soon afterward she defied English law by raiding the estates of the Earl of Desmond, one of the Irish chieftains who had submitted to the government and received an English title. The earl captured Grace, however, and turned her over to the English authorities. She spent eighteen months in prison at Limerick and in the dungeons of Dublin castle.

Soon after Grace's release from prison Rockfleet Castle was attacked. Realizing the danger that they faced from the English, as well as from rival clans, Grace and Richard Bourke submitted to the government and received titles in 1581. But in 1584 northwestern Ireland was assigned a new governor, Sir Richard Bingham. He disapproved of how the clans promised obedience to the queen while, at the same time, they continued to resist English authority. He set out to force them into submission by military might. And he made Grace one of his primary targets.

Bingham declared that Grace, now a widow, had no right to inherit Bourke's property. He also blamed her for encouraging rebellions among the clans. Intent on destroying her power, he executed two of her stepsons and, evidence shows, may have ordered the murder of her oldest son, Owen O'Flaherty. He also kidnapped her youngest son, Tibbot, and kept him as a hostage. Bingham sent Grace to prison and began arrangements to have her executed. He agreed to release her, however, after her daughter's husband offered himself as a prisoner in her place.

Petitions Queen Elizabeth

Grace returned to her stronghold in Clew Bay, where she resumed raiding. Bingham responded by killing her cattle, burning her crops, and finally sailing into Clew Bay and capturing her ships. With no way to make a living Grace decided to contact the queen herself. She sent a polite letter to Elizabeth in 1593, making the case that she and her clan should be allowed to resume their seafaring activities without interference. Grace also asked Elizabeth to order Bingham to release her son from captivity.

After sending the letter Grace set sail for London. This was a daunting journey for a woman already in her sixties. Not only was there the danger of storms and treacherous waters, but there was also the risk of chase and capture by rival pirates known to sail these seas. Grace took the chance, however, navigating around southern England and up the Thames River to London. There she waited for an audience with the queen. She also managed to impress Elizabeth's most influential advisor, **William Cecil** (Lord Burghley; 1520–1598; see entry). He knew of her reputation and demanded that she fill out a questionnaire about her background and her motives for coming to England. In this document, reproduced in Chambers's book, Grace stated that she lived a farmer's life in the county of Connaught, and "utterly did she give over her former trade of maintenance by sea and land." She presented herself as a harmless woman who was only trying to earn a living, and she minimized her role in stirring up rebellion against the English in Ireland.

Cecil's support helped Grace obtain an interview with the queen. Earlier chieftains who had attempted to argue their cases before the royal court had been imprisoned, but Elizabeth listened

Grace O'Malley meets Queen Elizabeth I. © THE BRITISH LIBRARY/TOPHAM-HIP/THE IMAGE WORKS.

to Grace and agreed to everything she asked for. According to Barbara Sjoholm in *The Pirate Queen: In Search of Grace O'Malley and Other Legendary Women of the Sea,* Elizabeth wrote to Bingham ordering him to "have pity for the poor aged woman," which is how Grace evidently presented herself to the queen. Elizabeth told Bingham to release Grace's son and to allow Grace to live undisturbed. The queen also gave the O'Malleys her permission to raid ships from France and Spain, which were then enemy countries of England.

Grace took this royal command to mean that she could return to her life of piracy. She built three large galleys, each big enough to hold three hundred men, and resumed her raids along the Irish coast. When Bingham continued trying to punish her, Grace made a second trip to London two years after her first. She asked Cecil to help her, saying that Bingham's actions were making it impossible for her to claim her property and conduct her legitimate business. She returned to Ireland with Cecil's support.

Final years

In 1595 Bingham fled to England after his own followers turned against him. Without this enemy, Grace was now free to go back to the business of piracy. One of the last written references to her, from an English captain who was able to capture one of her ships, was dated 1601. Grace was seventy-one years old that year, and she was still a pirate.

Grace died in Rockfleet Castle in 1603. Her son, Tibbot-ne-Long, realized that times were changing. He took the side of the English in the Battle of Kinsale in 1601, where the Irish were finally defeated. For this he was made a knight and given title to extensive lands. (A knight is a man granted a rank of honor by the monarch for his personal merit or service to the country.)

Though Grace O'Malley has received relatively little attention in history texts, her story has lived on in legends and songs. Grace refused to accept a passive or minor role in the affairs of her family or her country. She is remembered today as a woman who challenged assumptions about women's traditional place in society, and who acted as she thought necessary to increase the wealth, power, and influence of her clan.

For More Information

BOOKS

Chambers, Anne. *Granuaile: Ireland's Pirate Queen.* Wolfhound Press, 1979; reprinted 2003.

Sjoholm, Barbara. *The Pirate Queen: In Search of Grace O'Malley and Other Legendary Women of the Sea.* Emeryville, CA: Seal Press, 2004.

WEB SITES

Colombraro, Rosemarie. "Grace O'Malley." *Renaissance Central.* http://www. rencentral.com/oct_nov_vol1/graceomalley.shtml (accessed on July 11, 2006).

"Royal Galloglas." http://home.earthlink.net/~rggsibiba/html/galloglas/ gallohist.html (accessed on July 11, 2006).

Staley, Judy. "Grace O'Malley." *Adventurers.* http://www.rootsweb.com/~nwa/ grace.html (accessed on July 11, 2006).

Workman, Brian. "Grace O'Malley." *Irish Clans.* http://www.irishclans.com/ articles/famirish/omalleyg.html (accessed on July 11, 2006).

Philip II

BORN: May 21, 1527 • Valladolid, Spain

DIED: September 13, 1598 • El Escorial, Spain

Spanish king

Spanish king Philip II. PUBLIC DOMAIN.

"You may assure His Holiness [the pope] that rather than suffer the least damage to religion and the service of God, I would lose all my states and a hundred lives, if I had them; for I do not propose nor desire to be the ruler of heretics."

Ruler of the most formidable power in Europe during the 1500s, King Philip II of Spain played a major role in world affairs and in the development of England's foreign policy during the Elizabethan Era, the period associated with the reign of Queen Elizabeth I (1558–1603) that is often considered to be a golden age in English history. His empire included not only large territories in Europe, but also rich colonies in Mexico, the Caribbean, Central America, and much of South America. Wealth from these possessions filled Spain's treasury and gave Philip control of the strongest army and navy of the time. Strongly devoted to the Roman Catholic Church, Philip acted to strengthen the power of Catholic rulers at a time of increasing dissent from Protestant factions in Europe. He faced increasing religious conflicts in Protestant parts of his empire, as well as challenges by England to Spain's dominance of the transatlantic sea trade, or trade with the Western Hemisphere across the Atlantic Ocean. During the reign of **Elizabeth I** (1533–1603; see entry), Philip was drawn into open conflict with England. He became involved in several plots to assassinate the queen, and he made Spain England's most formidable enemy.

Though Spain was stronger and wealthier than England, Philip did not succeed in crushing English power. His attempted naval invasion of England in 1588—which failed as the result of bad planning, superior English technology, and disastrous weather—destroyed his mighty naval fleet and led to a prolonged war. By the time of Philip's death in 1598, England had emerged as a significant rival to Spanish dominance in Europe and in the Western Hemisphere.

Early life and education

Son of Holy Roman Emperor Charles V (1500–1558) and Isabella of Portugal, Philip II inherited an extensive and powerful realm that included Spain, the Low Countries (Belgium and the Netherlands), Sicily and southern Italy, the duchy of Milan, and Franche-Comte, as well as Spain's colonies in the Americas. As heir to this empire he received a good private education that was closely monitored by his father. Philip learned to read several languages in addition to Spanish, including French, Italian, and Portuguese. The young prince also learned Latin, Greek, mathematics, history, geography, science, and architecture. He enjoyed books, music, and art, and eventually owned a library of more than fourteen thousand volumes. He also loved the outdoors, and he became such an avid fan of hunting that his father worried that he would kill all the animals in the royal game preserve. Charles had to limit Philip's hunting to once a week.

Philip's mother, in whose household he lived as a young boy, died when he was twelve. Thereafter he lived in his own household, which included eight chaplains (priests), more than fifty pages (noble attendants), and hundreds of servants. An introspective person, Philip enjoyed privacy and sometimes commented in later life that he craved solitude. He spent time each day in prayer, and he also enjoyed weaving tapestries (large wall hangings) and jousting.

Charles V prepared his son carefully for the responsibility of ruling an empire. From 1543 on, Charles gave Philip the task of governing Spain whenever Charles himself had to be absent from the country. From 1548 to 1551 Philip traveled throughout his father's empire to learn about affairs of state. Charles emphasized to his son that ruling was a duty given them by God, and that they should take this role seriously. He advised Philip to make wise decisions and to guard against becoming too influenced by any one advisor. A dutiful and respectful son, Philip took this advice, eventually becoming known by his people as the "Prudent King."

Marries queen of England

In 1543 Philip married his cousin, Maria of Portugal, who died two years later, leaving him a son, Don Carlos. His second marriage, to **Mary I** (1516–1558; see entry), queen of England, took place in 1554. The match, which Charles V had proposed, was meant to strengthen ties between England and Spain, thus weakening the power of France and providing Mary with a powerful Catholic ally. Mary was the Catholic ruler of a predominantly Protestant country. Her father, **Henry VIII** (1491–1547; see entry), had severed ties to the Roman Catholic Church in the 1530s, and for decades the English had lived under Protestant rule. Mary's efforts to force England back to Catholicism met with great resentment. Though Mary's advisors urged her to marry an English nobleman, she felt more comfortable choosing a Catholic prince.

Philip was twenty-seven at the time of the wedding; Mary was thirty-eight. The marriage was not a happy one and produced no children. Philip hated England, and resented the hostility with which Mary's advisors treated him. Deeply suspicious that a foreigner had designs on the English crown, they insisted that Mary agree to severe restrictions on Philip's power. He would be king in name only; he would not enjoy any of the traditional powers of an English ruler. None of the courtiers (people who serve or participate in the royal court or household as the king's advisor, officer, or attendant) he brought with him from Spain could hold office, and if Mary died without producing a child, Philip would have no claim whatsoever on the English crown.

Though Philip was unhappy in England, after Mary's death he proposed marriage to Queen Elizabeth. He had defended Elizabeth, a Protestant, when Mary had suspected her loyalty and considered executing her for treason. Elizabeth, however, was wary of any marriage alliance and turned Philip down. The bond between England and Spain, which had never been a strong one, broke down soon after this and conflict between the two countries arose once more.

Philip married twice more. In 1559 he married Elisabeth of Valois (1548–1568), daughter of King Henry II of France. Elisabeth bore Philip two daughters and died in 1568. Philip then married Anna of Austria (d. 1580), daughter of Emperor Maximilian II, in 1570. She had one surviving son, Philip III.

Philip took the throne in 1558. At the time Spain held extensive possessions and military power, but decades of war with France had exhausted its economy. The Spanish government faced challenges in administering territories that were quite distant from the capital in Madrid. And the Ottoman Turks, who had been at war with Spain since 1551, threatened valuable Spanish territories in Italy and the Mediterranean Sea. Ever cautious, Philip did not let any of his ministers or advisors make government decisions. He insisted on researching every issue himself in painstaking detail before he came to any decision. According to one report he read through four hundred separate documents in one day, making careful notes in the margins before putting his signature on them.

Dutch revolt

The war with the Ottomans dominated foreign policy during the first twenty years of Philip's reign. But in 1566 a rebellion broke out in the Netherlands, where the Protestant population resented Philip's imposition of new taxes and other administrative policies that restricted their rights. This conflict, which developed into an outright war that was not finally resolved until 1648, became a central problem of Philip's reign and drew him into an increasingly hostile relationship with England, which supported the Dutch Protestants.

In 1567 Philip ordered his general, the duke of Alva (also spelled Alba; 1507–1582), to crush the rebellion. Alva used brutal tactics, in one instance executing twelve thousand rebels and their leaders. However, the Dutch grew even more determined to resist. Elizabeth and her advisors watched the situation with great interest. It would work to England's advantage to see Spain's power weakened in the Netherlands, and some of Elizabeth's councilors advised her to aid the rebels. But the queen, reluctant to intervene, waited. She did not authorize open support of the Protestant rebels until 1585, after their leader, William of Orange (1533–1584), was assassinated by a Spanish agent. Though England did not succeed in damaging Spanish interests in the Netherlands, its intervention placed it openly at war with Spain.

Meanwhile, England had also begun to challenge Spain's dominance of the sea trade, especially with the Americas. Since 1494 Spain and Portugal had enjoyed the exclusive right to exploit the riches of the Western Hemisphere, including its vast wealth in gold and silver. English merchant ships wishing to trade in the Americas risked having their goods confiscated by the Spanish unless they agreed to pay steep bribes. In order to weaken Spanish control in the Caribbean and other parts of the Western Hemisphere, the queen had, since the 1570s, given English seafarers such as **Francis Drake** (1540–1596; see entry) secret permission to raid Spanish treasure ships and attack Spanish colonies. Despite the fact that England and Spain were technically at peace, the queen wished to damage Spain as much as possible. As these attacks increased after 1585, Philip became convinced that it was essential to Spain's interests that he invade England and remove the queen from power.

Plots to assassinate Elizabeth

Though Philip had territorial motives for planning an invasion, he also acted on the belief that God wished him to free England from Protestant heresy. He came to believe that this goal was justified by any means, no matter how brutal. As early as 1570 he began to consider joining conspiracies to assassinate Elizabeth and replace her with her Catholic cousin, **Mary Stuart** (Queen of Scots; 1542–1587; see entry). Mary, the queen of Scotland, had been forced out of power there by Protestant lords and had sought refuge in England in 1568. Elizabeth allowed her cousin to remain in England, but suspected her of conspiring to seize power and kept her under close guard. Desperate to regain her freedom and convinced that, as a great-granddaughter of Henry VII (1457–1509), she had a more legitimate claim to rule England than Elizabeth did, Mary sought Catholic support for her cause. Philip did not at first approve of Mary or her schemes. If she became queen of England, the French, who strongly supported her, would gain considerable influence in England, which would work to Spain's disadvantage. But by the 1570s Philip was willing to consider any means of removing Elizabeth from power.

In 1570 Spain agreed to join a plot led by Roberto di Ridolfi (1531–1612), an Italian banker who conspired with nobles in northern England to overthrow Elizabeth and make Mary queen. Mary would then marry one of the chief conspirators, Thomas Howard

(Duke of Norfolk; 1536–572). This plot, however, was discovered and Howard was executed for treason in 1572.

Another plot in the early 1580s involved Spain's ambassador to England, who agreed to assist in a conspiracy headed by Francis Throckmorton (1554–1584). This young English Catholic nobleman had, through Mary, convinced the Spanish ambassador in England to join a plot to assassinate Elizabeth and launch a French invasion that would place Mary on the throne. Elizabeth's councilors discovered the plot and tortured Throckmorton to obtain a confession. He revealed details that implicated Spain. Throckmorton was executed for treason, and the Spanish ambassador, one of his chief contacts, was expelled from England.

The most serious of the conspiracies that Philip supported, the Babington plot, resulted in Mary Stuart's execution for treason in 1587. Sir Anthony Babington (1561–1586) obtained Philip's promise to send troops to England to support a planned Catholic rebellion that would assassinate Elizabeth and give the crown to Mary. Again, Elizabeth's agents discovered the scheme and executed the leaders. Finally realizing the seriousness of Mary's designs against her, Elizabeth was forced to sign Mary's death warrant, and the queen of Scots was beheaded.

Spanish Armada defeated

With no hope that any further conspiracies could succeed, Philip went ahead with plans to launch a full invasion of England. He took many years to draw up careful military plans. He would use his mighty navy, the Armada, to launch a naval attack in the English Channel, the body of water separating England from France. The ships would carry about eight thousand sailors as well as nineteen thousand troops. Philip had every reason to believe that his plan would succeed. His Armada was the most powerful navy in the world; indeed, many believed it to be incapable of defeat. But England's many spies kept Elizabeth's government well informed regarding Spain's preparations for war, and Elizabeth was able to plan a good defense. She appointed Charles Howard (1536–1624) to head the English fleet, with Francis Drake as his second-in command.

The Armada sailed from Lisbon, Portugal—by that time part of Philip's empire—in May 1588 with about 130 ships. But heavy winds forced it back to Spain for repairs. It sailed again in July, and it reached

The Invincible Armada

Philip II had every reason to believe that his naval assault on England would succeed. His fleet, which his subjects called "the Invincible Armada," was the largest and mightiest in the world. An inventory that Philip requested while he was drawing up battle plans listed 130 ships that could carry 30,000 men, including about 19,000 soldiers and 8,500 sailors. About 3,000 others—noblemen, volunteers, priests, surgeons, and officials, as well as all their servants—were also part of the Armada. Spain's ships had 2,830 cannons, 123,700 cannonballs, 22,000 pounds of shot, and 2,000 pounds of gunpowder. There were also more than 2,000 galley slaves, some of whom were English prisoners taken during raids between English and Spanish ships. These galley slaves, who propelled the ships with oars when sails alone provided insufficient speed, were chained to their seats and were often compelled to sleep and eat there. If a ship was sunk or wrecked, galley slaves drowned unless someone on board thought to unlock their chains.

Despite all this, the English navy possessed several unexpected advantages. England's navy, by contrast, was lighter and more streamlined than the Armada. According to Neil Hanson's *The Confident Hope of a Miracle,* its commander's flagship, for example, weighed 800 tons and carried 300 sailors and 125 soldiers. The Spanish flagship, weighing 1,000 tons, carried 300 soldiers but only 177 seamen. The superior maneuverability of the English ships played a large part in the Armada's defeat.

England also had an advantage in seamanship. While Spanish captains had gained most of their experience in the relatively calm Mediterranean Sea or in the transatlantic trade, where trade winds eased navigation, England was surrounded by treacherous rocky shores and violent storms. By necessity, English sailors developed exceptional seafaring skills and were used to difficult conditions. When the Armada was chased out of the English Channel into the northern waters near Scotland and Ireland, it encountered daunting weather for which it was not well prepared.

All these factors contributed to the Armada's defeat. Though Spain rebuilt its navy, it never recovered the absolute dominance it had once enjoyed at sea.

the southwest coast of England on July 29 and the Strait of Dover, near France, on August 6. There the Armada waited for land troops from the Netherlands to join the battle. This, however, took several days, and in the meantime England was able to launch its defense. At midnight on August 7 the English set fire to eight ships and aimed them at the Spanish fleet. The Armada was forced to cut its anchor cables in order to escape quickly, thus breaking formation. The English fleet, with lighter and more maneuverable ships, then inflicted serious damage on the Armada. The English drove the Spanish out of the Channel and northward, and then the English ships retreated to guard the southern coast. The Armada was forced to sail around the northern coast of Scotland to return to

Spain. However, it encountered devastating storms that wrecked more than half of the fleet. Only sixty ships returned to Spain, and many of these were too badly damaged to repair. As many as fifteen thousand Spanish died. Though England lost between several hundred and a few thousand men to disease, it sustained relatively little damage to its fleet. Spain's defeat greatly boosted English morale, and gave Elizabeth's government cause to authorize continued raids against Spanish ships and possessions.

The defeat of the Armada was a shattering blow to Philip. He rebuilt his fleet as best he could, but from then on his efforts to conquer England failed. War dragged on for fifteen years with neither side able to win a clear advantage. Philip sent a larger Armada to the English Channel in 1596 and 1597, but bad weather once again forced the ships to scatter. War with England remained essentially at a stalemate, and neither Philip nor Elizabeth lived to see peace, which was finally declared in 1604 under Elizabeth's successor, **James I** (1566–1625; see entry).

From 1589 to 1598 Philip involved Spain openly in France's wars of religion. He gave financial and military support to the Catholic League, which fought against the French Protestants called Huguenots under Henry of Navarre (1553–1610). The conflict, which drew Spanish troops away from the Netherlands and thus indirectly helped the Dutch rebel cause, ended with Philip's adversary, Henry of Navarre, becoming king of France. Philip died of cancer that same year at his palace, El Escorial. Though he had preserved much of his realm from attacks on many fronts, Spain at the time of Philip's death had entered a period of decline.

For More Information

BOOKS

Hanson, Neil. *The Confident Hope of a Miracle: The True History of the Spanish Armada.* New York: Knopf, 2005.

Hilliam, David. *Philip II: King of Spain and Leader of the Counter-Reformation.* New York: Rosen Publishing Group, 2005.

Kamen, Henry. *Philip of Spain.* New Haven, CT: Yale University Press, 1999.

PERIODICALS

Wernick, Robert. "Philip II's Grand Design for the Glory of God and Empire." *Smithsonian,* December, 1987.

WEB SITES

"Elizabethan Propaganda: How Did the English Government Try to Show that the Spanish Were Threatening to Invade England in 1588?" http://

www.learningcurve.gov.uk/snapshots/snapshot45/snapshot45.htm (accessed on July 11, 2006).

"King Philip II." *History Mole.* http://www.historymole.com/cgi-bin/main/results.pl?type=theme&theme=SpainPhilipII (accessed on July 11, 2006).

"Philip II." *NNDB.* http://www.nndb.com/people/229/000092950/ (accessed on July 11, 2006).

"The Revolt of the Netherlands." *Spain from Ferdinand and Isabella to Philip: Chapter 18.* http://vlib.iue.it/carrie/texts/carrie_books/gilbert/18.html (accessed on July 11, 2006).

Walter Raleigh

BORN: 1552 • Devonshire, England

DIED: October 29, 1618 • London, England

English statesman; explorer; poet

"No one is wise or safe, but they that are honest."

An influential statesman in the court of **Elizabeth I** (1533–1603; see entry), Walter Raleigh (also spelled Ralegh) played a major part in advancing English colonization, or settlement, of North America. He was also a soldier, explorer, poet, and historian. Though he achieved great success with the queen's early support, he later fell out of her favor and had to struggle to regain his status and power. After Elizabeth's death Raleigh's political enemies conspired to turn the new king, **James I** (1566–1625; see entry), against him. Raleigh spent thirteen years in prison, and he was executed for treason in 1618.

An adventurous youth

Walter Raleigh, born in 1552, was the youngest child of parents with important connections in Devon, a county in southwestern England. His father, also named Walter, was related by his first marriage to the explorer **Francis Drake** (1540–1596; see entry). Twice widowed, the elder Raleigh married Katherine Champernowne in 1548 or 1549. Katherine had three sons by an earlier marriage to Otho Gilbert, and three children by Raleigh: a son, Carew; a daughter, Margaret; and another son, Walter.

Few details are known about young Walter's childhood. He grew up in the country, and historians believe it is likely that he learned about seafaring from his father and half-brothers. It is also likely that he enjoyed hearing about the adventures of local pirates and adventurers such as **John Hawkins** (1532–1595; see entry). Another important influence was his half brother, Humphrey Gilbert (1539–1583), who was seventeen years older than Raleigh and had served with honor in English military campaigns in France and Ireland.

In 1568 Raleigh registered at Oriel College, Oxford University, but he did not remain there long. In 1568 or 1569 he went to France to help fight on behalf of the Huguenots, French Protestants whose challenge of Roman Catholic political power led to the French Wars of Religion (1562–1598). Raleigh participated in two major battles, as well as the St. Bartholomew's Day massacre in which Catholic mobs slaughtered Huguenots.

Raleigh returned to England around 1572 and resumed his studies at Oxford. He left the university in 1574 without completing a degree. He then entered Lyon's Inn, a law school in London, and later studied at another law school, the Middle Temple. Though Raleigh did not become a lawyer, he made important political and social contacts at these schools. In 1576 his earliest known poem was published in the preface to friend George Gascoigne's (1539–1578) book, *The Steel Glass.*

Raleigh's early attempts to build fame and fortune did not meet with success. In 1577 and 1579 Raleigh joined his half-brother, Humphrey Gilbert, on an expedition to search for the Northwest Passage, a route through northern seas that the English hoped would provide a shortcut to Asia. They did not find this passage, but they did raid Spanish ships. This action earned Raleigh the displeasure of the queen's advisors. During a six-month period after his return from sea in 1579, Raleigh was imprisoned twice for disturbing the peace.

In 1580 he headed a company of soldiers that was sent to Ireland. Irish rebels there, with help from Spanish and Italian troops, were fighting against English control of the region of Munster, in southern Ireland. Obeying the orders of his commanding officer, Raleigh led the massacre of captured Spanish and Italian troops at Smerwick, Kerry. This action, which some historians consider disgraceful, earned him honor as a military hero. He was later appointed a temporary administrator of Munster.

Gains the queen's favor

Soon after Raleigh's return to England in 1581, the queen made him her advisor on Irish affairs. Raleigh was intelligent, witty, and handsome. He dressed in extravagant fashions and demonstrated self-confidence and good manners. In fact Raleigh's manners were so polished that he is said to have once draped his own beautiful cloak over a mud puddle so that the queen could step on it and avoid dirtying her shoes. The queen greatly enjoyed the company of men with Raleigh's qualities, and she grew particularly fond of him. She gave him many favors, including a house in London and two country estates in Oxford. She also helped him financially by granting him the exclusive right to sell wine licenses and to export broadcloth, a cloth that was commonly used for making shirts. He also became warden, or overseer, of stannaries (mines) in the counties of Devon and Cornwall. Raleigh reformed the mining codes there, which increased his popularity in the region. In 1585 he was appointed lord lieutenant of Cornwall and vice admiral of the West (Devon and Cornwall).

The queen made Raleigh a knight in 1584. (A knight is a man granted a rank of honor by the monarch for his personal merit or service to the country.) He continued to serve the government in several powerful positions. He was elected to Parliament, England's legislative body, in 1584 and again in 1586 as a representative from Devonshire. Raleigh received his highest office at the royal court in 1586, when he was made captain of the queen's personal guard.

During the 1580s Raleigh joined his half-brother in organizing a project to establish an English colony in North America. Raleigh did not obtain the queen's permission to accompany his half-brother on the voyage, but he was able to invest money in the project. He also contributed a ship that he had designed himself. After Gilbert's death on the return voyage, the queen granted Raleigh a charter to occupy new lands. Though he was still forced to remain at court, he immediately sent an expedition that landed in the region near North and South Carolina and claimed the territory for himself. He called this land Virginia in honor of the queen.

Plantations in Virginia

Raleigh was eager to obtain the queen's permission for a new idea: the establishment of plantations, or colonies, in Virginia. Rather than exploiting the area for its natural resources, Raleigh wanted to establish a permanent settlement for English families. The plantation would

Tobacco

Though it is not certain that Raleigh was the individual who first brought tobacco to England, he was the person who made smoking fashionable there. At first tobacco was considered a type of medicine that was good for headaches, toothaches, cancer, and even bad breath. It was usually smoked in pipes. The most common type of pipe was a walnut shell with a straw for a stem, but Raleigh had a silver pipe that, reportedly, he once persuaded the queen to try. She disliked smoking and said it made her feel sick to her stomach.

Tobacco quickly became very popular in England. By 1614 approximately seven thousand shops in London sold it. Though doctors, by this time, were beginning to warn that tobacco was addictive and caused major health problems, its popularity continued to grow. In 1624 England established a royal monopoly, or exclusive trading rights, on tobacco. In the mid-1660s, when the Great Plague struck London, people believed that smoking tobacco could protect them from infection. (The Great Plague was an outbreak of the bubonic plague that killed more than one-fifth of London's population.) Eton, a school near the city, even made smoking a requirement in hopes of keeping the plague away.

By the 1700s snuff became a more popular way to enjoy tobacco. (Snuff is powdered tobacco inhaled through the nose.) Cigars became fashionable in the 1800s, and by the 1900s cigarettes were the most popular tobacco product.

Walter Raleigh sits smoking tobacco from a pipe. His servant, unfamiliar with the new practice of smoking, thinks Raleigh is on fire and rushes toward him with a jug of water. HULTON ARCHIVE/GETTY IMAGES.

include a school for seafarers and teach settlers the language of the native people. To help convince the queen to support this plan, Raleigh enlisted the help of writer **Richard Hakluyt** (1552–1616; see entry). Hakluyt's *Discourse of Western Planting* explained the benefits of such a project and argued in its favor. Though the queen was not entirely convinced, she provided Raleigh with a ship and some money. But she would not let him make the voyage himself. She insisted that he remain in England where he could be close by if she wished to consult him.

Raleigh's cousin, Richard Grenville (1542–1591), brought the first colonists to Virginia. But the project did not go well. The settlers argued among themselves and refused to work or obey orders. They also encountered hostile native people. Discouraged, they returned to England in 1586 with a fleet under the command of Francis Drake. They brought back two crops that had never before been seen in England: potatoes and tobacco.

The next year Raleigh launched a second expedition, under the command of John White. The colonists settled on Roanoke Island, off the coast of North Carolina. But a political emergency diverted Raleigh's attention from this new project. Spain, hoping to overthrow Elizabeth and make England a Catholic country, launched a massive naval attack against the English fleet in 1588. Raleigh was called to Devon to help organize a militia. He also served on the queen's war council, though he did not take part in the actual battle. The Spanish Armada (navy) was defeated, but the crisis had prevented Raleigh from organizing a voyage to bring new supplies to the colonists. By the time supply ships finally reached North America in 1591, the Roanoke colony had disappeared. Though Raleigh sent other expeditions to Virginia, none of them succeeded.

Provokes the queen's displeasure

After the defeat of the Armada, politics at court shifted. The queen's new favorite advisor, **Robert Devereux** (Earl of Essex; 1566–1601; see entry), was jealous of the influence Raleigh had on Elizabeth. In fact Raleigh and Devereux almost fought a duel once after they had quarreled. Even more troublesome, however, was the fact that Raleigh had secretly married one of the queen's maids of honor, Elizabeth Throgmorton (d. 1647). When the queen found out about this, she was furious.

Elizabeth had decided that her favorite servants should not marry because she wanted to keep all their attention for herself. When she discovered that Raleigh and her serving maid had married, she sent them both to prison in the Tower of London. (The Tower of London was a fortress on the Thames River in London that was used as a royal residence, treasury, and, most famously, as a prison for the upper class.) She released Raleigh after two months. A ship had docked in England to unload captured Spanish goods, but the crew would not obey its commanding officers. Elizabeth needed Raleigh to supervise this unruly crew, but she removed him as captain of her guard. She also, in effect, exiled him from court. In addition, she never allowed Lady Raleigh into her presence again.

The Raleighs had three sons. The first died in infancy. Two others, Carew and Walter (known as Wat), survived.

Raleigh retired to his estate in Dorset, in southern England, and he devoted his time to study and writing. He joined the Society of Antiquaries, a historical association, and he also helped Hakluyt prepare his writings about English voyages of exploration.

By late 1594 Raleigh had begun to gain back the queen's favor, and she allowed him to make a voyage to Guiana (now Venezuela). Finding gold ore there, he became convinced that the region would be a rich source of this precious metal. His written account of this expedition, *The Discoverie of the Large, Rich and Bewtiful Empire of Guiana,* showed his belief in the natural wealth of this region. He hoped one day to return there to establish mining operations, but he had to wait many years to receive permission.

In 1596 the queen sent Raleigh and his rival, Devereux, on a naval raid against the Spanish city of Cadiz. The year before Spain had attacked Penzance, a port city on the remote southwestern coast of England, and now England hoped to retaliate. In the battle to capture the city, Raleigh received a serious leg wound; he walked with a limp for the rest of his life. As the English occupied Cadiz and stole its riches, its governor approached Devereux and Raleigh with a deal: he would pay them two million ducats if they allowed the merchant ships in the harbor—loaded with rich cargoes—to escape. They refused, demanding to be paid twice as much. The governor then ordered all the Spanish ships burned.

When news of this waste reached London, the queen was outraged. She blamed Devereux for making bad decisions on this campaign, but she did not criticize Raleigh's conduct. She allowed Raleigh back into her court, and she gave him more naval commands. He was also appointed governor of the island of Jersey, in the English Channel. When Devereux was executed on a treason charge in 1601, Raleigh did not come to his defense. But Raleigh's new success did not last long. When the queen died in 1603, Raleigh's political rivals saw their chance to act against him.

Prison years

On the advice of Lord Henry Howard (1540–1614) and secretary of state Robert Cecil (1563–1605; see entry), who had greatly resented Raleigh's influence over the queen, King James I dismissed Raleigh as captain of the guard, warden of stanneries, and governor of Jersey. He also took away Raleigh's exclusive trading rights and forced him to move out of his London house. When Raleigh's enemies reported, falsely, that he had plotted against the king, he was arrested and imprisoned in the Tower of London. Near despair, Raleigh tried to take his own life. He was put on trial in Winchester in late 1603, found guilty, and sentenced to death. The king, however, allowed the sentence to be postponed. Raleigh remained in prison for thirteen years.

As a wealthy and influential man, Raleigh was treated well during his imprisonment. He lived in a large apartment at the Tower, which contained not only dungeons and prison cells but also royal apartments, the royal mint (where the country's money was made), and even a zoo. Raleigh's wife and family were able to join him at the Tower; in fact, his second son was conceived there. Raleigh was allowed to have his library with him, and he spent his time studying and writing. He developed his interest in science; his experiments with chemistry resulted in a substance he called "Balsam of Guiana," which he sold as a popular medicine. Also during this time he began writing *The History of the World,* which he dedicated to James's son, Prince Henry (1594–1612). Henry liked Raleigh and considered him a father figure, but he was not able to convince the king to pardon Raleigh. (A royal pardon would release Raleigh from punishment for his convicted crime.) After Henry died of typhoid fever in 1612, Raleigh abandoned his plan to finish *The History of the World,* and published it in incomplete form. Though it is only a fragment of the book he had intended to write, it is considered one of his most impressive prose (non-poetry) works.

In 1616 Raleigh was released from prison but not pardoned. The king allowed him, finally, to send an expedition to Venezuela to look for gold. Raleigh led the expedition himself, but when he reached the Venezuelan coast, he developed a serious fever. This illness forced him to stay aboard the ship and he could not lead his men upriver to explore. Against the king's strict orders, Raleigh's men fought with Spanish

Raleigh says goodbye to his wife on the morning of his execution. © BETTMANN/ CORBIS.

colonists in the area and burned a Spanish settlement. Raleigh's son, Wat, died during the fighting. Finding no gold, the failed expedition returned to England.

Death and legacy

Angry that his orders had been disobeyed on this expedition, the king immediately had Raleigh arrested again. Spain urged the king to execute him as a pirate. But because Raleigh was still under a death sentence for treason, he could not be tried on this new charge. The king ordered him to be executed for the treason charge that had been brought in 1603. He was beheaded on October 29, 1618.

Those who witnessed his execution said that Raleigh behaved with outstanding dignity and bravery. Dr. Robert Tounson, a priest who ministered to him in his last hours, later wrote in a letter, quoted by Raleigh Trevelyan in *Sir Walter Raleigh*, stating that Raleigh was "the most fearless of death that ever was known; and the most resolute and confident, yet with reverence and conscience." On the morning of his execution Raleigh enjoyed a good breakfast, smoked a pipe, dressed carefully, and walked to the scaffold. There he spoke to the crowd who had come to watch him die. He repeated that he had always been loyal to the king, and he defended himself against various lies that his enemies had told about him. Then he knelt and prayed. He refused a blindfold. When the executioner held up Raleigh's severed head, according to Trevelyan, he could not bring himself to say the usual words, "Behold the head of a traitor."

In addition to the major role he played in politics and exploration, Raleigh also made significant contributions to English literature. He was a friend of the poet **Edmund Spenser** (1552–1599; see entry), author of the epic poem *The Faerie Queene,* and helped promote Spenser's career. Raleigh's many prose works attracted attention during his own life and remained popular into the 1800s. His poems, which employed a simpler and more direct style than was typical in his day, contained elements that later poets such as John Donne (1572–1631) would also use.

Though his life contained many failures, Raleigh played a major role in Elizabethan England's policy of exploration. He served England successfully as a military leader and as an administrator. Though he failed to establish a permanent colony in North America, he is still remembered for this effort. The capital of North Carolina, Raleigh, is named for him.

For More Information

BOOKS

Fecher, Constance. *The Last Elizabethan: A Portrait of Sir Walter Ralegh.* New York: Farrar, Straus & Giroux, 1972.

Trevelyan, Raleigh. *Sir Walter Raleigh.* New York: Henry Holt and Company, 2002.

WEB SITES

"Factsheet 1: Smoking Statistics: Who Smokes and How Much." *Action on Smoking and Health.* http://www.ash.org.uk/html/factsheets/html/fact01.html (accessed on July 11, 2006).

"Sir Walter Raleigh." *BBC: Historic Figures.* http://www.bbc.co.uk/history/historic_figures/raleigh_walter.shtml (accessed on July 11, 2006).

"Sir Walter Raleigh." *British Explorers.* http://www.britishexplorers.com/woodbury/raleigh.html (accessed on July 11, 2006).

"Sir Walter Raleigh." *Schools History.* http://www.schoolshistory.org.uk/walterraleigh.htm (accessed on July 11, 2006).

"Tobacco Timeline." *Tobacco History Links.* http://www.tobacco.org/History/history.html (accesssed on July 11, 2006).

"Walter Raleigh." *u-s-history.com.* http://www.u-s-history.com/pages/h1138.html (accessed on July 11, 2006).

William Shakespeare

BORN: April 23, 1564 • Stratford-upon-Avon, England

DIED: April 23, 1616 • Stratford-upon-Avon, England

English playwright; poet

"Men at some time are masters of their fates: The fault ... is not in our stars, but in ourselves, that we are underlings."

Considered the greatest playwright in the English language and one of the greatest writers in the world, William Shakespeare created a body of work that has remained unparalleled for its poetic brilliance and its depth of understanding. His long poems and sonnets are among the best in the English language. But his masterpieces are his plays, which communicated the vast complexity of human experience through characters that were more real than literature had ever known.

More than any writer before him, Shakespeare created individual characters with deep and conflicted inner lives, who recognized their capacities to act and to change. As poet Percy Bysshe Shelley (1792–1822), quoted by Harold Bloom in *Shakespeare: The Invention of the Human*, wrote, Shakespeare created "forms more real than living men." Audiences from Shakespeare's time onward have related to the psychological and emotional issues explored in his work, which continues to be read and performed throughout the world more than four centuries later.

William Shakespeare.
COURTESY OF THE LIBRARY
OF CONGRESS.

Early life and family

Born in the small but prosperous town of Stratford-upon-Avon in 1564, William Shakespeare was the son of glovemaker John Shakespeare and his wife, Mary Arden. John Shakespeare, a farmer's son, had earned success in his trade and held various government positions in the town. Mary Shakespeare, of a slightly higher social class, was the daughter of a local landowner. William was the oldest of six children. He had three younger brothers and two younger sisters; one sister died in childhood.

Few facts are available about Shakespeare's early life. It is most likely that he, like other Stratford children, attended the local grammar school, the King's New School. Here students learned Latin, logic, and rhetoric (the art of constructing formal arguments). It was a rigorous course of study that familiarized students with the works of ancient Roman writers such as Ovid (43 BCE–17 CE) and Virgil (70–19 BCE).

Though many of the most outstanding Elizabethan poets and play-wrights studied at university, there is no record of Shakespeare having done so. In 1582, at age eighteen, he married a slightly older local woman, Ann Hathaway (c. 1556–1623). She gave birth to a daughter, Susanna, six months later. The couple had twins—a boy, Hamnet, and a girl, Judith—in 1585. Hamnet died at age eleven, but his sister survived. Judith had one daughter, Elizabeth, who was Shakespeare's last descendant; she died in 1670. Though Shakespeare lived most of his adult life in London, he maintained close ties to Stratford and returned to live there after retiring from writing plays.

Joins London theater world

Nothing is known about Shakespeare's activities between 1585 and 1592. By 1592, however, he was known in London; playwright and critic Robert Green (c. 1560–1592) wrote a jealous attack that year dismissing him as an upstart. This suggests that Shakespeare had already begun to establish a literary reputation. By 1594 he was acting with and writing plays for the Lord Chamberlain's Men, a theater company for which he was also a managing partner. Their playhouse, The Theater, was located in Shoreditch, just north of London. Most of the city's local leaders were Puritans, or strict Protestants. Because the Puritan leaders disapproved of many popular entertainments such as plays and gambling, they banned theaters from operating within the city proper. Thus, theaters were built outside the city walls. Despite the fact that they were not considered entirely respectable, theaters were extremely popular. Plays drew large audiences and often attracted disreputable characters such as pickpockets. The Theater was the most popular playhouse in London. Its principal actor, Richard Burbage (c. 1567–1619), is credited with doing more than any of his contemporaries to increase respect for the theater profession.

Shakespeare began writing for the stage at a time when English theater was entering an exciting new era. Playwrights were experimenting with new forms, incorporating elements of classical (ancient Greek and Roman) and Renaissance literature into their work. (The Renaissance was the era beginning around 1350 in Europe, in which scholars turned their attention to classical Greek and Latin learning and shifted to a more rational [based on reason rather than spiritual belief or church authority] approach to philosophy, religion, and science.) Earlier plays were generally unsophisticated pieces; they dramatized moral issues or religious stories or presented bawdy (sexually suggestive) comedy. But Elizabethan plays emphasized tragedy, and featured tragic heroes as serious, complex figures. Elizabethan playwrights were also exploring the possibilities of dramatic verse. **Christopher Marlowe** (1564–1593; see entry), for example, was the first to demonstrate the power of blank verse, a type of poetry with regular meter (the pattern of stressed and unstressed syllables) but no rhyme, in stage dialogue. Shakespeare went on to take dramatic blank verse to brilliant new heights, with language filled with puns, complex metaphors, and rich imagery. (Puns are a deliberate confusion of similar-sounding words usually for humorous effect; metaphors are comparisons made between two seemingly unrelated subjects.)

Scholars disagree as to the exact dating of Shakespeare's thirty-seven plays, many of which were not published until after his death. According to a chronology accepted by many historians, Shakespeare's first plays were his history cycle, *Henry VI, Part One, Henry VI, Part Two, Henry VI, Part Three,* and *Richard III,* which date from 1589 to 1593. These works conformed to the traditional genre of chronicle, or history, plays that were quite popular in Elizabethan times. (History plays are plays about historical figures and events.) But Shakespeare's works far surpassed previous examples of this type of play, which merely presented a sequence of events. Shakespeare provided a larger shape for his cycle of plays. Together, they made the story the Tudor dynasty, or period of reign by a particular ruling family, from which **Elizabeth I** (1533–1603; see entry)

Elizabethan Theaters

Plays in Shakespeare's time were performed outdoors and attracted large audiences. Public theaters, like the Theater or the Globe, were large wooden structures that were roughly circular. The galleries along the sides were covered, but most of the structure, including the large raised stage which projected about halfway into the theater, was unroofed. All of the actors were males; younger men or boys played the roles of women characters. No scenery was used. This allowed for unhindered movement on stage, with plenty of room for the battle scenes and swordfights that were an exciting part of many plays.

Among the leading theaters in Elizabethan London were the Swan, the Rose, and the Globe. The Globe was built in 1599 after its owners, the Lord Chamberlain's Men, were forced to find a new location for their popular theater in north London, the Theater. They had the Theater dismantled and reassembled on the south bank of the River Thames in Southwark, and named the new building the Globe Theater. Shakespeare, a member of the Lord Chamberlain's Men, wrote exclusively for them and most of his greatest plays were performed at the Globe.

The Globe, which opened with a performance of Shakespeare's *Henry V,* could accommodate an audience of about three thousand people, and individuals from all walks of life attended plays there. The least expensive ticket allowed people to stand in the yard, at the base of the stage. These spectators, called "groundlings," were often uneducated or even illiterate, but they enjoyed Shakespeare's plays as much as the more educated theatergoers did. It was not uncommon for audiences to bring food and drink into the theater, and even throw food at the stage when they disliked a performance.

A replica of the original Globe Theater now stands near its original location in London. © PAWEL LIBERA/CORBIS.

The Globe burned down in 1613, after material from a cannon that was shot off during a performance of *Henry VIII* set fire to the gallery roof, which was made of thatch (thick straw). Its owners rebuilt it and it reopened later that year. By the 1640s, however, the Puritan faction had succeeded in shutting down theaters in London. The Globe was torn down in 1644 and housing was built on its site. A replica of the famous theater now stands on or near its location in south London.

was descended, into an epic story. Each of the four plays in this cycle was an integral part of the whole.

Henry IV, Part One, generally considered Shakespeare's finest history play, was probably written around 1596. It takes as its subject the Scottish rebellion against Henry IV (1366–1413), who had earlier usurped the English throne from Richard II (1367–1400). To many scholars, the most interesting dynamics in the play occur between the king's son, Prince Hal, and his comrade, Sir John Falstaff. Indeed, Falstaff—who exudes intense joy—is generally considered to be Shakespeare's finest comic character.

Shakespeare's earliest comedies, *The Two Gentlemen of Verona, The Comedy of Errors,* and *The Taming of the Shrew,* also date from around 1592 to 1593. *Titus Andronicus,* his first tragedy, was written around 1593. The playwright used an extensive range of influences in these works, from English folklore to classical plays and Italian Renaissance literature.

Shakespeare's more mature plays from the 1590s include the comedies *A Midsummer Night's Dream, The Merchant of Venice, Much Ado About Nothing, The Merry Wives of Windsor,* and *As You Like It.* In these works Shakespeare demonstrated increasing stylistic sophistication. His use of blank verse became more complex, and his dialogue became more rich, dynamic, and effective.

The middle period: 1594–1600

In 1599 the Lord Chamberlain's Men built the Globe Theater on the south bank of the Thames River. Many of Shakespeare's greatest plays were written in the first ten years of the company's residence at the Globe, and they were first performed there. Examples include the tragedies *Julius Caesar, Macbeth, Hamlet, Othello,* and *King Lear;* and the comedies *Twelfth Night, All's Well That Ends Well,* and *Measure for Measure.* These later comedies, noted for their darker tone, are sometimes called the "problem plays." Less reliant on elements of traditional comedy, they explore serious themes and are far less cheerful than the earlier comedies.

In Macbeth *three witches tell Macbeth that he is destined to become king.* WILLIAM SUMITS/TIME LIFE PICTURES/ GETTY IMAGES.

Among Shakespeare's major tragedies, scholars often cite *Hamlet* as the greatest. Based on a legend from Denmark, it follows some conventions of the genre known as revenge tragedy, which was immensely popular. As the term suggests, revenge tragedies concerned the theme of vengeance for a past wrong—usually murder. Like typical revenge tragedies, *Hamlet* ended with a stage scattered with bloody corpses. But Shakespeare's work rose far above the standard plays of this genre, largely because he invested the character of Hamlet, a young man who seeks to avenge his father's death, with such complex human feeling.

When Hamlet learns that his father had been killed by Hamlet's uncle, now married to Hamlet's mother, the young prince is tormented by intense and contradictory emotions. He struggles with his conscience and his personality about what action to take. Indeed, in his famous soliloquy (a speech intended only for the audience to hear, as if the character is speaking aloud to himself), he wonders whether to commit suicide, endure his sorrows, or fight them: "To be, or not to be, that is the question— / Whether 'tis nobler in the mind to suffer / The slings and arrows of outrageous fortune, / Or to take arms against a sea of troubles, / And by opposing end them." According to Bloom, Hamlet is the most fully human of Shakespeare's characters and is, except for Jesus Christ, the most-referenced figure in Western culture.

Macbeth, based on the history of an ancient Scottish king, Duncan, is Shakespeare's shortest tragedy. Its theme is the danger of unrestrained ambition. Macbeth, a Scottish noble, meets three witches who predict that he will become king. Though he had been King Duncan's loyal general, Macbeth now wishes to fulfill the prophecy. His wife urges him to go along with her plan to murder the king while he is staying in their castle. Though at first he worries about committing such an immoral act, Macbeth stabs the king to death and seizes the throne. Increasingly concerned that his enemies will rise against him, Macbeth slaughters many innocents before he is killed in battle. One of the most notable features of the play is the character of Lady Macbeth, who is more bloodthirsty and cold-hearted than her husband.

Shakespeare based *King Lear* on an old English legend. In Shakespeare's version, Lear, an old man, needs to decide how to divide up his kingdom among his daughters. He demands that they demonstrate their love for him. He fails to recognize that his two older daughters, who pretend affection, care only about getting the inheritance. By contrast, his youngest daughter, Cordelia, refuses to play her sisters' game because she recognizes it is insincere. Lear, however, is blind to the truth and banishes her. He realizes his mistake too late, after Cordelia dies. In the play's most powerful scene, the man who was once a great king is now ragged and in despair, wandering over the moors carrying Cordelia's lifeless body.

In *Othello* a jealous husband is driven to murder when his trusted general, Iago, suggests that Othello's wife, Desdemona, has been unfaithful. Othello cannot see that Iago hates him and wishes to destroy him. He goes along with Iago's scheme to demonstrate proof of Desdemona's betrayal, and finally kills her. The play's subtitle, "The Moor of Venice," refers to the fact that Othello is a

Scenes from Shakespeare's plays. MARY EVANS PICTURE LIBRARY. REPRODUCED BY PERMISSION.

black African; his wife is white. Shakespeare uses black-white imagery throughout the play, especially in Iago's speeches, which demonstrate the villain's crude racism and contempt for women.

In 1603 **James I** (1566–1625; see entry) granted the Lord Chamberlain's Men a royal patent, and the company changed its name to the King's Men. This royal support helped to increase the status of theater professionals. James enjoyed plays, and the company performed at court several times a year. The King's Men also performed at an indoor private venue in London, the Blackfriars Theater.

The later period: 1600–1608

The plays that Shakespeare wrote in the final years of his career are sometimes classified as romances. They conform less closely to conventional genres of comedy or tragedy, mixing elements from several genres within one work. The major plays from this period date from between about 1607 and 1613, and they include *Coriolanus, Timon of Athens, Pericles, Cymbeline, The Winter's Tale,* and *The Tempest.*

The Winter's Tale is considered one of Shakespeare's finest plays. It begins as a tragedy but then shifts to pastoral comedy, or a comedy about country life. Leontes, king of Bohemia, irrationally suspects his friend, Polixenes, of having an affair with Leontes's wife. He orders Polixenes killed and orders the wife, Hermione, thrown into prison where she gives birth to a daughter. Leontes orders this child to be killed as well, but instead she is adopted by shepherds. Polixines, too, escapes. Sixteen years later the action shifts and the tragic actions are resolved, often through wondrous events.

The Tempest is Shakespeare's best-known play from this late period, and some scholars consider it his farewell to the theater, since he retired soon after producing it. Magic plays a prominent part in the play, which concerns a powerful sorcerer, Prospero, whose brother stole his kingdom and set him adrift at sea with his baby daughter. They are saved by an enchantress, and live on a remote island for several years. Discovering that this untrustworthy brother will be passing near the island on a ship, Prospero conjures a storm that makes his brother a castaway on the island. After much romantic plotting and scheming with his servant, the strange and demonic creature Ariel, Prospero sees to it that kingdoms and relationships are restored to their proper order.

Poetry

From 1593 to 1594 London theaters were closed because of plague in the city. (The plague was a disease that killed nearly one-fourth of the city's population.) Needing income, Shakespeare wrote two long poems, *Venus and Adonis* and *The Rape of Lucrece,* for his patron, or financial supporter, the earl of Southampton. These works are considered masterpieces of Elizabethan narrative poetry. (A narrative poem is a poem that tells a story.)

Shakespeare's best-known poems, however, are his sonnet sequence, probably also composed around this time but not published until 1609. Sonnets are fourteen-line poems written in iambic pentameter—ten syllables in each line, with the emphasis on the second syllable in each word or phrase. The sonnet sequence, in which individual poems are arranged to develop a particular theme or argument, had been made popular by **Philip Sidney** (1554–1586; see entry). Shakespeare's contribution to the genre established him as one of the finest poets in the English language.

Was Someone Else Shakespeare?

While most critics and historians believe that William Shakespeare of Stratford-upon-Avon was the writer of the plays now credited to him, many others over the years have doubted it. Most point to the limited education Shakespeare received in Stratford and note the vast knowledge displayed by the author of the plays. Some find evidence that the plays were written from the perspective of a member of the aristocracy, not the son of a glove maker. Others point to the lack of any reference to a playwright from Stratford in the documents of the era. These skeptics have suggested other authors for the plays, primarily the scientist and writer **Francis Bacon** (1561–1626; see entry), Christopher Marlowe, William Stanley (Earl of Derby; 1561–1642), and Edward de Vere (Earl of Oxford; 1550–1604). Most such claims have been discredited, however.

The 154 poems of Shakespeare's sonnet sequence form an extended dialogue between the poet or speaker and two mysterious characters: a "friend" who appears to be a young man, and a "dark lady." The poems consider themes of beauty, friendship, love, and death, often expressing conflicting feelings within a single poem. They are considered masterpieces that, alone, would have established Shakespeare's reputation as a poetic genius.

Last years: 1608–1616

Shakespeare's career was quite successful. He earned a comfortable income from his plays and from his share in the profits of the theater company. In 1596 his father had obtained the right to have a coat-of-arms (a symbol representing a family), and Shakespeare inherited this after his father's death in 1601. The playwright was also granted the right to call himself a gentleman—a distinguished achievement in an age that often considered actors to be disreputable.

In 1597 Shakespeare purchased a large house, New Place, in Stratford. This became his family home. Over the years he invested in additional property in Stratford. He retired there around 1611, and lived quietly with his family. He died there on his birthday, April 23, 1616, at age 52. He was buried at Holy Trinity Church.

Shakespeare's work was so admired in his own time that, in 1623, two actors compiled his plays and published them in the *First*

Folio. This volume contained thirty-six plays, including *Henry VIII,* on which he collaborated with playwright John Fletcher (1579–1625). The *First Folio* did not contain *Pericles,* which is not accepted by most scholars as Shakespeare's work.

Actors, audiences, and readers through the centuries have continued to find new excitement in Shakespeare's work. As his contemporary Ben Jonson (1572–1637) wrote in a preface to the *First Folio,* Shakespeare "was not of an age, but for all time!"

For More Information

BOOKS

Ackroyd, Peter. *Shakespeare: The Biography.* New York: Nan A. Talese, 2005.

Bloom, Harold. *Shakespeare: The Invention of the Human.* New York: Riverhead Books, 1998.

Braunmuller, A. R. and Stephen Orgel, eds. *The Complete Pelican Shakespeare.* New York: Penguin Classics, 2002.

Charney, Maurice. *All of Shakespeare.* New York: Columbia University Press, 1993.

Fraser, Russell. *Shakespeare: The Later Years.* New York: Columbia University Press, 1992.

———. *Young Shakespeare.* New York: Columbia University Press, 1988.

Greenblatt, Stephen. *Will in the World: How Shakespeare Became Shakespeare.* New York: W. W. Norton, 2004.

WEB SITES

Prefatory Material to the First Folio, 1623. http://shakespeare.palomar.edu/ Folio1.htm#Beloved (accessed on July 11, 2006).

Shakespeare Homepage. http://www.shakespeare.org.uk/content/view/10/10/ (accessed on July 11, 2006).

Shakespeare Online. http://www.shakespeare-online.com/index.html (accessed on July 11, 2006).

Shakespeare Resource Center. http://www.bardweb.net/ (accessed on July 11, 2006).

"William Shakespeare." *Classic Literature Library.* http://william-shakespeare.classic-literature.co.uk/ (accessed on July 11, 2006).

"William Shakespeare." *Poets.org.* http://www.poets.org/poet.php/prmPID/122 (accessed on July 11, 2006).

Philip Sidney

BORN: November 30, 1554 • Kent, England

DIED: October 17, 1586 • Arnheim, Netherlands

English poet; courtier

"But the poet is the food for the tenderest stomachs; the poet is, indeed, the right popular philosopher."

Widely admired for his intelligence, courtesy, and bravery, Philip Sidney was considered by his contemporaries to be the ideal Elizabethan gentleman. He passionately supported the Protestant cause and fought with valor on the battlefield, where he was mortally wounded during a campaign to aid Dutch Protestants who had rebelled against Spanish rule. He also wrote poetry and prose that advanced the development of English literature. His *Astrophel and Stella* was the first sonnet sequence in English, and his *Apology for Poetry* was the first literary essay in English. His prose writings and his poetry profoundly influenced his contemporaries and continue to inspire new generations of writers.

Born into prestigious family

Philip Sidney.
© HULTON-DEUTSCH
COLLECTION/CORBIS.

Philip Sidney was born into a prosperous family with aristocratic connections. His mother, Lady Mary Sidney, was the daughter of John

Dudley (Earl of Northumberland; 1501–1553), whose oldest son was married to Lady Jane Grey (1537–1554), a descendant of the royal family. Sidney's father, Sir Henry Sidney (1529–1586), was a favored advisor of Edward VI (1537–1553), and held several important government positions during the reign of **Elizabeth I** (1533–1603; see entry). Sidney's uncles, **Robert Dudley** (Earl of Leicester; 1532–1588; see entry) and Ambrose Dudley (Earl of Warwick; c. 1528–1589), were among England's most wealthy and powerful men. In fact, Robert Dudley was one of the queen's closest personal friends.

Sidney grew up expecting to enjoy a life of influence, wealth, and fame. In 1564 he began his formal education at the Shrewsbury School, and two years later he entered Christ Church, Oxford University. Though he demonstrated exceptional intelligence, he left Oxford without completing his degree. From 1572 to 1575 he toured Europe. He was living at the English embassy in Paris at the time of the St. Bartholomew's Day massacre in 1572, when Catholic mobs killed thousands of French Protestants called Huguenots. Leaving France immediately after that traumatic event, which contributed to his hostility toward Catholicism, he visited Austria, Germany, Poland, Italy, and France. He studied languages, music, and astronomy, or the study of the sun, moon, and other celestial bodies. He impressed those he met with his extraordinary graciousness and intelligence.

When he returned to England, Sidney spent much time with his uncle, Robert Dudley, who helped him maintain influential connections that would advance his career. In 1576 Sidney traveled to Ireland, where his father was serving as lord deputy. Ireland had been under English rule since the twelfth century, but over the years English administrators there had gradually reverted to Irish customs. Rival chieftains competed for power, and English laws were not effectively enforced. After Elizabeth became queen, she began taking steps to bring Ireland under control. But the Irish were not easily subdued; the chieftains waged war against English troops sent to maintain order. Sir Henry Sidney, who was named lord deputy in 1565, governed the country with skill, but he employed ruthless measures to subdue rebellions. Many of the queen's advisors criticized his policies. Seeing conditions in Ireland for himself, Philip Sidney wrote *Discourse on Irish Affairs,* which he presented to the queen in defense of his father's administration.

Begins writing poetry

In 1577 Sidney undertook a diplomatic assignment to Germany. His task was to try to organize Protestants there against Catholic rule. Little came of this effort, however, and he returned to England soon afterward. During this period he began to cultivate several literary friendships. He met poets such as Fulke Greville (1554–1628), Edward Dyer (d. 1607), and **Edmund Spenser** (1552–1599; see entry), whose efforts to create a new kind of English poetry inspired him to attempt writing as well. He wrote several experimental poems during the late 1570s. He also wrote *Lady of May,* an entertainment performed in 1578 in honor of the queen.

Around this time Sidney began work on his *Arcadia,* most of which he wrote while living with his sister, the countess of Pembroke, to whom he dedicated the work. *Arcadia* mixed prose and poetry in a wide-ranging discussion of large themes such as justice, virtue, honor, friendship, love, and morality. Scholars believe Sidney wrote most of this work around 1580, but it was not published until 1590, after his death. *Arcadia* was immensely popular in the 1590s and the early 1600s.

During the 1580s Sidney was also working on his *Apology for Poetry.* This work, the first literary essay in English, was also the most important essay of its era. At the time many writers and thinkers argued that imaginative literature (such as lyric poetry and prose romances) was a waste of time because it did not tell the truth and was not serious. They believed that such literature encouraged people to believe in silly things and even to behave in immoral ways. In their view, only such subjects as history, philosophy, ethics, and religion were suitable for study. In contrast, Sidney presented a defense of imaginative literature. He argued that poetry—a term he used to encompass all imaginative literature—was a better way to approach the truth than the study of either philosophy or history. He stated further that poetry could inspire people to be virtuous, because it could describe ideal ways of living; history, on the other hand, could only describe events that had really occurred and was therefore more limited.

Sidney also criticized earlier English love poetry, saying that it lacked energy and passion. "Many of such writings as come under the banner of unresistible love," he wrote, "if I were a mistress, would never persuade me they were in love; so coldly they apply fiery speeches." Sidney argued that the English language was perfectly suited to express passion and that writers should devote their energies to developing lyric poetry in English.

The Sonnet

Sonnets are short lyric poems, often about romantic love, that contain fourteen lines and follow a regular meter (the pattern of stressed and unstressed syllables) and rhyming pattern. English poets of this time admired sonnets by Italian writers such as Petrarch and began experimenting with the form. The Petrarchan sonnet consists of eight lines (called an octave) followed by six lines (called a sestet). Though English poets imitated this type of sonnet, they began creating sonnets that consisted of three groups of four lines each (quatrains), followed by a concluding rhymed couplet of two lines. Though **William Shakespeare** (1564–1616; see entry) was not the first to write this type of poem, it became known as the Shakespearean sonnet.

Though sonnets can employ various rhyme schemes, or the pattern of rhymes in a poem, they traditionally use a rhythm known as iambic pentameter. This is one of the most commonly used rhythms in English poetry because it follows the natural rhythms of the English language. In iambic rhythms, the second syllable of a word or phrase is stressed. Many kinds of poems in English use iambic meter, as can be seen in the first lines from a modern poem by Robert Frost, "Stopping by Woods on a Snowy Evening":

"Whose woods these are I think I know, / His house is in the village, though." In this case, there are four stressed syllables in each line. Sonnets, however, contain five stressed syllables in each line. Iambic rhythms, as the passage from Frost shows, allow poets to use speech patterns that sound natural and relaxed instead of stiff and artificial.

In a sonnet sequence individual sonnets about a general subject are arranged in order, each poem expanding in a particular way on the sequence's general theme. Sidney's *Astrophel and Stella,* the first sonnet sequence in English, inspired leading poets such as Shakespeare and Edmund Spenser to compose sonnet sequences of their own. In the seventeenth century John Donne (1572–1631) and John Milton (1608–1674) expanded the sonnet's thematic range from romantic love to religious feelings and other serious philosophical issues. The sonnet remained a popular form through the nineteenth century; poets such as John Keats (1795–1821) and William Wordsworth (1770–1850) frequently wrote sonnets. Though less common in modern literature, sonnets can convey complex feelings within the strict boundaries of a concise form.

He concluded that poets "are so beloved of the gods that whatsoever they write proceeds of a divine fury," and added that if anyone had "so earth-creeping a mind that it cannot lift itself up to look at the sky of poetry," then that person deserved to fail in love and to die forgotten.

Like *Arcadia, Apology for Poetry* circulated among Sidney's friends in manuscript form. It was extremely influential, contributing to a renewed interest in exploring the poetic possibilities of the English language. *Apology for Poetry* was not published until 1595, after the poet's death.

Astrophel and Stella

Sidney had meanwhile fallen in love with Penelope Devereux, daughter of the earl of Essex. He longed to marry her, but in 1581 she married Lord Rich. She became the inspiration for the figure of Stella in Sidney's sonnet sequence, *Astrophel and Stella*. In these poems, a young man, Astrophel (from the Greek words for star and lover) addresses his love, Stella (from the Latin word for star). Astrophel expresses the various feelings associated with romantic love, including the struggle in his heart between reason and passion, ideal love and physical desire. These poems, which Sidney's friends read in manuscript form, were greatly admired. The sequence was first published in 1591 and inspired numerous imitations.

Though *Astrophel and Stella* was modeled to some extent on the sonnets of the Italian writer Petrarch (1304–1374), Sidney claimed that his poems sprang freely out of his own heart without any careful attention to formal rules. Therefore, he felt his poems were much more than a rehashing of older literary conventions. He aimed to infuse a more personal and dramatic energy into his sonnets than could be found in earlier models. By using more natural language and by writing about his emotions in the present time—not as if he were remembering them much later—Sidney succeeded in making the Elizabethan sonnet a more natural and energetic type of love poem than earlier lyric forms had been.

Death on the battlefield

In 1583 Sidney married Frances Walsingham (1569–1631), daughter of the queen's secretary of state, **Francis Walsingham** (1530–1590; see entry). That year Sidney was also made a knight. (A knight is a man granted a rank of honor by the monarch for his personal merit or service to the country.) He was a passionate supporter of the Protestant cause in England, and he advocated policies that would strengthen the development of a reformed Protestant church. With other committed Protestant leaders such as his uncle, Robert Dudley, he urged the queen to send military aid to Protestants in Europe who were rebelling against their Catholic monarchs. Sidney believed that it was not only England's duty to help fellow Protestants, but also that England's security was at stake. Catholic power in Europe threatened Elizabeth's authority; in fact, **Philip II** (1527–1598; see entry) of Spain had been associated with conspiracies to overthrow Elizabeth and replace her with her Catholic cousin, **Mary Stuart** (Queen of Scots; 1542–1587; see entry). Many in

Elizabeth's government recommended an aggressive foreign policy that included direct aid to Protestant revolutionaries in Europe.

Though the queen was reluctant to commit England to costly and controversial wars, the threat from Spain intensified during the late 1580s. In 1585 she finally agreed to send troops to the Netherlands. Sidney accompanied his uncle, Dudley, who had been given command of the expedition. Several months after arriving in Europe Sidney received a leg wound at the battle of Zutphen on September 22, 1586. The wound did not heal, and Sidney died three weeks later at the age of thirty-one.

Sidney's death prompted a huge outpouring of grief. The Dutch proclaimed him a national hero. More than one thousand English troops in the Netherlands gathered at the docks to pay their respects as his coffin was loaded onto a ship to be taken back to England. In London the streets were crowded with people who reportedly cried "Farewell, the worthiest knight that lived!" as his coffin passed them. Tributes to Sidney from more than 140 writers were collected and published in three volumes, while dozens of his friends wrote independent tributes.

Sidney died in debt, without ever having published any of his writings. His father-in-law, Walsingham, took on the responsibility for his debts. Sidney's family saw to it that all of his works were published, though it took almost a decade. Immensely popular in England, Sidney's works also attracted interest in Europe. In the early 1600s they were translated into Dutch, Spanish, Italian, German, and French.

Writers of Sidney's and later generations were profoundly influenced by his writings. Many of his contemporaries dedicated poems or books to him. Edmund Spenser, for example, paid tribute to Sidney in his poem "Astrophel." Modern poet William Butler Yeats (1865–1939) mentioned Sidney in "In Memory of Major Robert Gregory," describing the poet as "our perfect man."

For More Information

BOOKS

Duncan-Jones, Katherine. *Sir Philip Sidney, Courtier Poet.* New Haven, CT: Yale University Press, 1991.

Hamilton, A. C. *Sir Philip Sidney: A Study of His Life and Works.* Cambridge, UK and New York: Cambridge University Press, 1977.

Ousby, Ian, ed. *The Cambridge Guide to Literature in English.* Cambridge, UK: Cambridge University Press, 1993.

Ruoff, James E., ed. *Major Elizabethan Poetry and Prose.* New York: Thomas Y. Crowell Company, 1972.

WEB SITES

"Sir Philip Sidney." *Renaissance English Literature.* http://www.luminarium.org/renlit/sidney.htm (accessed on July 11, 2006).

"Sir Philip Sidney World Bibliography." *Resources in Renaissance Literature at St. Louis University.* http://bibs.slu.edu/ (accessed on July 11, 2006).

Stump, Donald. "Sidney as a 'Renaissance Man.'" *Sir Philip Sidney Online.* http://bibs.slu.edu/sidney/history.html (accessed on July 11, 2006).

Edmund Spenser

BORN: 1552 • London, England

DIED: January 16, 1599 • London, England

English poet

"So much more profitable and gratious is doctrine by ensample [example], then by rule."

Known to his contemporaries as the "prince of poets," Edmund Spenser was widely admired for both his writing and his actions. Courteous, devout, and loyal to the Protestant cause and to **Elizabeth I** (1533–1603; see entry), he served the English government in several administrative jobs. He read extensively and wrote some of the most important poems in the English language. He is best known for his epic, *The Faerie Queene.* (An epic is a long poem telling the story of a hero's deeds.) This rich and complex work is an allegory, or symbolic representation, of both the eternal struggle between good and evil and the more specific struggle between Protestantism in England and the threats it endured from rival Catholic nations.

Humble beginnings

Edmund Spenser. ARCHIVE PHOTOS/GETTY IMAGES.

Edmund Spenser was born into a London family of modest means. Few facts about his early life are available, but historians believe it is likely that

217

his father worked as a cloth maker. There were several children in the family and money was scarce, but because Spenser showed exceptional intelligence his parents arranged for him to receive a good education. At age nine he began attending the Merchant Taylor's School in London on scholarship. He studied Latin, Greek, and possibly Hebrew, as well as music and drama.

In 1569 Spenser enrolled at Pembroke College, Cambridge University. He paid his tuition by working as a sizar—a student who was paid to wait on wealthier students. Though he was often ill, Spenser was known as an excellent student. He mastered Italian, French, Latin, and Greek; studied classical literature, or the literature of ancient Greece and Rome; and extensively read the poetry of modern languages. He even wrote his own poems in Latin. He received his bachelor of arts degree in 1572 and his master of arts degree in 1576.

After leaving Cambridge Spenser visited relatives who lived in Lancashire, in northern England. He became particularly interested in the region's unique dialect of English. (Dialect is the language used by people of a particular region.) His dialect studies influenced his use of language in his later poem, *The Shepheard's Calendar*. Around this time Spenser also served **Robert Dudley** (Earl of Leicester; 1532–1588; see entry), one of the England's most powerful leaders and the queen's closest friend. There is some evidence to suggest that Dudley sent Spenser on diplomatic errands to Ireland, Spain, France, and Italy. In 1578 Spenser became secretary to the bishop of Rochester, John Young, who had been master (headmaster; presiding officer) at Pembroke College. Historians believe that Spenser composed most of *The Shepheard's Calendar* while at Rochester.

Begins publishing his poetry

In early 1579 Spenser returned to London, where he spent much time with literary friends including Gabriel Harvey, Edward Kirke, and **Philip Sidney** (1554–1586; see entry). These friends encouraged Spenser to begin publishing his poetry. That year he published *The Shepheard's Calendar,* a work containing twelve poems in the pastoral tradition. Pastoral poetry idealized country life, especially the lives of shepherds and shepherdesses. *The Shepheard's Calendar,* which Spenser dedicated to Sidney, became the most important example of the pastoral poem in English. Spenser published *The Shepheard's Calendar* under the pseudonym Immerito, which means "unworthy." The work was extremely popular and influential; it went into four new editions from 1581 to 1597.

The twelve poems in *The Shepheard's Calendar* corresponded to the twelve months of the year, and expressed the typical themes of pastoral works: regret for a lost golden age of pure love, art, and morality, and sadness that the poet's own time fell short of these ideals. *The Shepheard's Calendar* employed a wide variety of poetic forms, including songs of praise, laments (which express grief), and complaints (which express the poet's sadness, often about unreturned love). It also showed Spenser's love of the English language, with its fascinating dialects and its ability to absorb foreign terms. As James E. Ruoff noted in *Major Elizabethan Poetry & Prose, The Shepheard's Calendar* "heralded a new era of poetry, a genuine new voice of sure rhythmic … that made the courtly verses of [previous poets] seem old-fashioned, stilted, and drab."

The Faerie Queene

Despite his success with publication of *The Shepheard's Calendar,* Spenser realized he could not support himself solely by writing. In London he lived in Dudley's house and studied law. With Dudley's help, Spenser received a diplomatic job in 1580 as secretary to Lord Grey, the lord deputy of Ireland. He moved to Dublin that year, and Ireland remained his home for the rest of his life.

After Lord Grey was called back to England in 1582, Spenser held various government jobs in Ireland. In 1586 he rented Kilcolman Castle in County Cork, on Ireland's southern coast, where he lived from 1588 on. During the 1580s Spenser worked on what would become his most famous piece of poetry, *The Faerie Queene.* He intended this work to consist of twelve books, and he had finished the first three by 1589. When **Walter Raleigh** (1552–1618; see entry) visited Spenser that fall, he was so impressed by this portion of *The Faerie Queene* that he brought Spenser with him when he returned to London. There the work was published in early 1590, with an elaborate dedication to Queen Elizabeth.

The Faerie Queene was like nothing else in English literature. Spenser intended it to be a great English epic poem, with each of its books centered on one of Greek philosopher Aristotle's (384–322 BCE) moral virtues, which include courage, self-discipline, modesty, generosity, friendliness, humility, truthfulness, and justice. In each book Spenser used the figure of a knight to personify each virtue. This approach

Edmund Spenser reading an excerpt of The Faerie Queene *to Walter Raleigh.* HULTON ARCHIVE/GETTY IMAGES.

combined elements of two popular literary forms, the chivalric romance (a form that originated in twelfth-century France and described the adventures of a single ideal knight) and the handbook of manners, which advised readers on correct attitudes and behavior. At the same time Spenser incorporated a wide range of other influences, including the epic poetry of Greek writer Homer (eighth-century BCE) and Roman author Virgil (70–19 BCE), as well as the writings of Italian poets Ariosto (1474–1533) and Tasso (1544–1595).

Literary critics have admired *The Faerie Queene* on many levels. It succeeds as an allegory of the struggle between good and evil. It also serves as an allegory of the struggle in England between what Spenser saw as the pure goodness of Protestantism and the corrupt influence of Roman Catholicism. It refers as well to the particular issues of its day, including England's war with Spain and support of Protestant rebels in the Netherlands. *The Faerie Queene* also introduced a new type of poetic stanza, or a group of lines that form a section of a poem. This Spenserian stanza consisted of nine lines, with the first eight in traditional iambic pentameter (ten syllables in each line, with the second syllable receiving the stress) and the ninth using iambic hexameter (six stresses). The rhymes followed an a-b-a-b-b-c-b-c-c rhyme scheme, or pattern.

Other works

Publication of *The Faerie Queene* brought Spenser considerable fame. He remained in London for over a year, renewing his literary contacts and hoping to obtain a new government job in England. Failing in this effort, he returned to Ireland in 1591. Before leaving London he arranged for *Complaints,* a collection of minor poems, to be published. One of these, "Mother Hubberd's Tale," satirized Elizabeth's consideration of a marriage to the French Catholic Françis (Duke of Alençon; 1555–1584). The poem was notable not only for its political content but also because of Spenser's creative use of medieval English sources, particularly from Geoffrey Chaucer (c. 1346–1400).

After returning to Ireland Spenser resumed work on *The Faerie Queene.* He also wrote "Colin Clout's Come Home Again," a pastoral poem dedicated to Raleigh. He compiled a collection of poems honoring the memory of Sidney, who had died of wounds he received in battle in the Netherlands; Spenser's "Astrophel" was the first elegy (lyric meditation on death) in the book.

In 1594 Spenser married Elizabeth Boyle, daughter of a prominent Anglo-Irish family. His sonnet sequence "Amoretti" represented the development of his love for his wife. "Epithalamion," which also dated from this period, combined themes of romantic love and religious devotion. It is considered one of the greatest love poems in English.

Final years

Spenser returned to London in 1595, staying for more than a year. During this time he published three more books of *The Faerie Queene.* He also worked on *View of the Present State of Ireland,* a prose piece that defended the policies in Ireland of Lord Arthur Grey. Spenser argued that England should use military force to conquer the Irish, who staged repeated rebellions against English control. Though Elizabeth's government basically agreed with such a policy, Spenser was not allowed to publish this pamphlet. It was not published until 1633, several decades after the poet's death.

Spenser's *View of the Present State of Ireland*

Edmund Spenser recommended a harsh policy toward the Irish, who by the late 1570s had obtained support from Catholic Spain to plan an uprising against English rule in Ireland. In 1579 James Fitzmaurice Fitzgerald took control of southern Ireland, with the help of another Irish chieftain, John of Desmond, and seven hundred Spanish and Italian troops. Queen Elizabeth had much to fear from these events. Spain, the largest and wealthiest state in Europe, was fiercely anti-Protestant, and its king, **Philip II** (1527–1598; see entry), had already pledged support to other Catholic conspiracies against Elizabeth. His alliance with the Irish chieftains, therefore, was a significant threat to England's national security. The queen sent Lord Grey to stop this rebellion, and Spenser accompanied him there in 1580.

Grey's first battle against the Irish at Glenmalure was a disaster; more than eight hundred English soldiers died. But Grey was able to regain control of the south coast, and then launched a relentless offensive campaign. The English captured lands, burned crops, and slaughtered the local people. When six hundred of the pope's troops arrived to support the Irish, Grey's men massacred them. By 1581 most of the rebels had surrendered. But Grey refused to offer terms of surrender to John of Desmond, who fled with his men to the mountains in the west of Ireland. Fighting continued until November 1583, when Desmond was finally killed by the local O'Moriarty clan, who received a reward from the English government.

Though Grey's strategy had been effective in weakening the rebels, it caused immense suffering for civilians. With crops and fields destroyed, the region experienced extensive famine. By April 1582, approximately thirty thousand people had starved to death. Desperate to avoid the fighting in the countryside, peasant families fled to the city of Cork, where disease broke out. The devastation from hunger and disease continued for years after the fighting had ended. By 1589 as much as one-third of Munster's population had died.

Furious at the excessive brutality of his campaign, Queen Elizabeth called Grey back to England in 1582. Spenser remained in Ireland, becoming a government administrator. He defended Grey's conduct, and argued that Grey should have been allowed to remain in Ireland to carry out his initial plans to subdue the country. Spenser believed that English policy had been dangerously indecisive; for years, troops had been sent to Ireland but had failed to defeat the rebels. In Spenser's view, nothing short of an all-out campaign could succeed. He supported Grey's policy, admitting that it would cause famine and suffering but insisting that these conditions were necessary in order to bring a swift end to the fighting.

When Spenser put these opinions into writing in his *View of the Present State of Ireland,* he created significant controversy. The English government agreed that the Irish rebel chieftains must be defeated, but could not approve of such brutal methods and refused to allow Spenser to publish his pamphlet.

In 1597 Spenser returned to Ireland, once more resuming work on *The Faerie Queene.* Two portions of Book VII of *The Faerie Queene* were published in 1609, but most of Spenser's writings from this period were destroyed when his castle was burned down by Irish rebels in 1598. Spenser escaped with his wife and four young children, but almost all of his manuscripts were lost.

Spenser died before completing his masterpiece, *The Faerie Queene.* In December 1598 he was sent to London on a diplomatic mission for Sir Thomas Norris. After briefing Queen Elizabeth and her advisors on the state of affairs in Ireland, Spenser, exhausted by the stress of the previous few months, fell ill. He died in London on January 16, 1599, reportedly from lack of food. He was buried at Westminster Abbey in London, with the leading poets in the city carrying his coffin. To demonstrate their esteem for Spenser and their sorrow at his death, they threw verses and quill pens into his grave.

Greatly respected in his time, Spenser also influenced later generations of poets. Though writers in the later 1600s considered his work obscure and difficult, the Romantic poets from the mid-1700s admired his passion, his startling imagery, and his inspired imagination. More recent critics have appreciated Spenser's work for its sophisticated poetic technique and its understanding of the complexities of human experience.

For More Information

BOOKS

Bernard, John D. *Ceremonies of Innocence: Pastoralism in the Poetry of Edmund Spenser.* Cambridge, UK: Cambridge University Press, 1989.

King, John. *Spenser's Poetry and the Reformation Tradition.* Princeton, NJ: Princeton University Press, 1990.

Maclean, Hugh and Anne Lake Prescott, eds. *Edmund Spenser's Poetry: Authoritative Texts, Criticism.* New York: W. W. Norton & Company, 1993.

Ousby, Ian, ed. *The Cambridge Guide to Literature in English.* Cambridge, UK: Cambridge University Press, 1993.

Ruoff, James E., ed. *Major Elizabethan Poetry & Prose.* New York: Thomas Y. Crowell Company, 1972.

PERIODICALS

Dolven, Jeff. "Spenser's Sense of Poetic Justice." *Raritan: A Quarterly Review,* Summer 2001, pp. 127–141.

Hunt, Maurice. "Hellish Work in *The Faerie Queene.*" *Studies in English Literature, 1500–1900,* Winter 2001, p. 91.

WEB SITES

The Edmund Spenser Home Page. http://www.english.cam.ac.uk/spenser/ main.htm (accessed on July 11, 2006).

"Edmund Spenser." *Renaissance English Literature.* http://www.luminarium.org/ renlit/spenser.htm (accessed on July 11, 2006).

Mary Stuart

BORN: December 7, 1542 • Scotland

DIED: February 8, 1587 • Northamptonshire, England

Scottish queen

Mary Stuart, Queen of Scots.
ARCHIVE PHOTOS.
REPRODUCED BY
PERMISSION.

"Tell my friends that I die a true woman to my religion, and like a true Scottish woman and a true French woman."

The most famous queen in Scottish history, Mary Stuart was also queen of France and tried to claim the throne of England. The cousin of **Queen Elizabeth I** (1533–1603; see entry) and a Roman Catholic, Mary became Elizabeth's primary rival for power. Associated with several plots to remove Elizabeth from the throne and to make herself queen of England, Mary was found guilty of treason in 1587 and was beheaded.

Early life

Mary Stuart was the only surviving child of King James V (1512–1542) of Scotland and his wife, Mary of Guise (1515–1560). Her two older brothers died before she was born, placing her in line to inherit James's throne. The king, bitterly disappointed at the birth of a daughter, died before the baby was a week old. Mary became queen of Scotland at the age of six days.

Mary, Mary, Quite Contrary

Many children know something of Mary, Queen of Scots without even realizing it. A well-known nursery rhyme is about her:

> Mary, Mary, quite contrary
> How does your garden grow?
> With silver bells and cockleshells
> And pretty maids all in a row

As John Guy explains in *The True Life of Mary Stuart, Queen of Scots*, the garden refers to the one at Holyroodhouse, the most magnificent of the Scottish royal estates. Mary lived there when she first returned to Scotland. The silver bells were used in Mary's private chamber when Mass was said. Cockleshells were symbols that Catholic pilgrims wore on badges when they visited major shrines. The pretty maids refer to Mary's childhood playmates, four girls all named Mary.

Mary also had a claim by birth to the throne of England. James's mother, Margaret Tudor (1489–1541), was the sister of **King Henry VIII** (1491–1547; see entry), making Mary a great-granddaughter of King Henry VII (1457–1509). From her Roman Catholic mother, daughter of one of the most powerful noble families in France, Mary also inherited strong ties to the French royal court.

Mary became queen at a troubled time for Scotland. In order to protect itself from a political takeover by England, Scotland had established an alliance with France, a Catholic country and one of Protestant England's most powerful rivals. James V's marriage to Mary of Guise had strengthened this bond. In 1548, after an English invasion of Scotland, the Scottish government decided that Mary should marry the heir to the French throne, the future Francis II (1544–1560). This marriage would make France an even stronger ally of Scotland.

Education in France

When Mary was only five-and-a-half years old, she was sent to France. Her mother remained in Scotland to rule the country until Mary was old enough to assume power. Mary grew up at the French court and was educated with the king's children, who became her playmates. She learned Latin, French, and the art of persuasive writing and speaking, as well as history. Though she was a good student, Mary preferred outdoor activities. She rode her ponies every day, and loved pets, especially dogs. She also loved to dance.

The members of the French court were thrilled by Mary's beauty, charm, and grace. They welcomed her as a future queen and rejoiced when she married Francis in 1558. Mary was fifteen at the time of this marriage; Francis was only fourteen. The ceremony, held at Notre Dame Cathedral in Paris on April 24, was a spectacle of luxury and happiness. Mary wore her favorite rich fabrics and jewels and danced for hours. She wrote to her mother that she was one of the happiest women in the world.

But this happiness was soon complicated by political change. In November the English queen, **Mary I** (1516–1558; see entry), died and her sister, Elizabeth, took the throne. But Catholic rulers in Europe, especially in Spain and France, considered Elizabeth's claim to power illegitimate. Her father, Henry VIII, had dissolved his marriage to Mary I's mother, Catherine of Aragon (1485–1536), without permission from the pope. Henry then married his mistress, Anne Boleyn (1507–1536), who gave birth to Elizabeth. Since the Catholic Church did not consider this second marriage legal, Catholic rulers and nobles said that Elizabeth should not be able to inherit the English throne. They felt that Mary Stuart was the rightful heir to the English crown.

In July 1559 the French king died and Francis II took the throne, making Mary Stuart queen of France. She was also proclaimed queen of England and Ireland—much to the displeasure of Queen Elizabeth. Less than six months later Mary of Guise died. Then, after only a year as king, Francis II died on December 5, 1560. Mary Stuart was now both an orphan and a widow.

Return to Scotland

Mary decided to return to Scotland. She had been away from the country for thirteen years, and the political situation had changed significantly. Catholics had been in power when Mary was a young child; now, however, with help from Queen Elizabeth, Scottish Protestants had gained control. Under the terms of the Treaty of Edinburgh in 1560, French troops were forced to leave Scotland. The alliance between the Scots and the French ended, and the Scottish government declared Scotland a Protestant country.

When Mary arrived at Leith, Scotland, on April 19, 1561, Queen Elizabeth regarded this as a threat to her own power. She feared that Mary would try to reestablish ties with Catholic countries. If this happened Mary might receive enough support to try to overthrow Elizabeth and make herself queen of England.

Though Protestant nobles in Scotland did not approve of a Catholic monarch, Mary ruled for seven years without an outright opposition to her authority. Realizing that any actions to challenge Protestant authority might jeopardize her rule, she declared that she would not demand any changes to the new Protestant religion, but she insisted on having Catholic Mass said in her own private chapel. To further satisfy the Protestant lords, she approved of an arrangement in 1562 to divide the property of the Catholic Church among those in the new government. On her government's advice she also led a military action against George Gordon (Earl of Huntly; 1514–1562), the most prominent Catholic rebel in Scotland. According to many historians, her warm and lively personality played a large role in her ability to maintain power.

Marriages and murders

In 1565 Mary married her first cousin, Henry Stewart (Lord Darnley; 1545–1567), also a grandson of Margaret Tudor. Since Henry was next in line after Mary to the English throne, this marriage increased fears that Elizabeth's rule was in danger. It also caused concern among Scottish Protestants, who worried that it would inspire a revival of Catholic sympathy since the marriage made Mary's claim to the English throne even stronger. Led by James Stewart (Earl of Moray; 1531–1570), the Protestant lords in Scotland rebelled. Mary was able to defeat them with military force, but it was clear that her rule was growing increasingly unpopular.

Mary quickly grew unhappy with her husband, who was immature and stubborn. She refused to grant him the crown matrimonial, which would have allowed him to rule Scotland. It was also said that she was having a romantic affair with her secretary, David Rizzio (1533–1566). On March 19, 1566, Henry Stewart and a group of others dragged Rizzio from Mary's room and murdered him. Some historians believe that Mary herself may also have been a target.

Mary gave birth to a son, the future **James I** (1566–1625; see entry), on June 19, 1566. But this event did not improve relations with her husband. Soon the queen had befriended James Hepburn (Earl of Bothwell; 1535–1578), whose powerful family was extremely loyal to the crown. Mary wanted to end her marriage to Henry Stewart but she feared that her son's right to inherit the throne would be jeopardized if she obtained an annulment.

Mary Stuart with David Rizzio. TIME LIFE PICTURES/MANSELL/TIME LIFE PICTURES/GETTY IMAGES.

When Stewart was killed after an explosion at his lodging on February 10, 1567, suspicions were immediately aroused. His body, which was found in an adjoining building, revealed that he had been strangled or smothered. Most people suspected Hepburn of the murder. They also assumed that Mary had been part of the conspiracy. Hepburn was arrested and tried for murder, but he was acquitted. He immediately divorced his wife and married Mary. This action so infuriated the Scottish nobles that even the queen's previous supporters now turned against her.

Civil war broke out, and the Scottish lords captured Mary at Carberry Hill on June 15, 1567. They brought her back to Edinburgh, where crowds, insulting her as a whore, called for her death. On July 24 the lords forced Mary to give up her throne in favor of her infant son.

Exile in England

After six months in captivity Mary managed to escape to England in 1568. There she begged her cousin, Elizabeth, to allow her to live in safety. Elizabeth's advisors, particularly **William Cecil** (Lord Burghley; 1520–1598; see entry) warned against this, arguing that Mary could not be trusted. They worried that she would seek support from Catholics to remove Elizabeth from the English throne and make herself queen. But after an investigation into her husband's death showed no actual proof of Mary's involvement, Elizabeth permitted Mary to remain in England.

For the next eighteen years Mary lived almost as a prisoner. She was given comfortable rooms at various estates, but she was always kept under close guard. For much of this period she lived with George Talbot, Earl of Shrewsbury, and his wife, **Bess of Hardwick** (1527–1608; see entry). Mary was rarely allowed to go outside for fresh air and exercise. When she was permitted to ride her horse in the nearby park, she was accompanied by several armed guards. Guards also kept watch over her indoor activities. Fearing that her food might be poisoned, she insisted on hiring her own kitchen staff. Her health began to suffer. She gained weight and developed various ailments, including gout, a painful inflammation of the joints. She felt she was growing old before her time.

During her exile in England Mary was not allowed to contact her son, a condition that caused her great sorrow and bitterness. She spent much of her time doing fine embroidery with Bess of Hardwick. In fact needlework allowed Mary to express her political frustrations. She embroidered one piece that showed a grapevine with one fruitful branch and one barren one. A large hand with a pruning hook threatened the barren half. The piece also featured a motto, "Virescit Vulnere Virtus" (Virtue flourishes by wounding), that was thought to be an encouragement to a nobleman who was plotting against the queen of England.

The Ridolfi plot

Elizabeth's advisors had been right to worry about the threat posed by Mary. In 1571 Cecil found out about a conspiracy to assassinate Elizabeth and make Mary queen. It was led by an Italian merchant, Roberto Ridolfi (1531–1612). Ridolfi conspired with rebels in northern England, who launched an unsuccessful rebellion in 1569 and 1570 that became known as the Northern Rising. These rebels were also allied with Thomas Howard (Duke of Norfolk; 1536–1572), who had proposed marriage to Mary.

When the uprising failed, Ridolfi went to Europe to seek support from Catholic leaders there.

King Philip II (1527–1598; see entry) of Spain and the Duke of Alva, the Spanish governor-general of the Netherlands, gave their support to Ridolfi and planned to send Spanish troops to help overthrow Elizabeth. But Cecil's agents discovered the plot when they intercepted letters that identified Howard as the leader and incriminated Spain.

Parliament, England's legislative body, denounced Mary and urged the queen to punish her. Her embroidery of the grapevine, which she had sent to Howard, was seen as Mary's approval of the plot. But Elizabeth was reluctant to take any action against Mary. Proof against her was not absolute, and Elizabeth had no wish to stir up more anger among Mary's supporters by executing her. Howard was executed in 1572 as a traitor, but Mary remained a prisoner.

The Throckmorton plot

Another conspiracy was uncovered in 1583 by agents working for Elizabeth's spymaster, **Francis Walsingham** (1532–1590; see entry). Francis Throckmorton (1554–1584), an English Catholic, had conspired with Catholics in France in a plan that called for French troops to invade England and assassinate the queen. They would then free Mary, place her on the throne, and restore the Catholic religion in England.

There was good reason to believe that Mary supported this plot. When Walsingham had Throckmorton arrested, he was using a secret code to write a letter to Mary. To obtain even stronger evidence against her, Walsingham placed a spy in Mary's household. The spy read Mary's letters, which showed that she had indeed encouraged the conspirators. This information so infuriated the queen that she refused to consider any reconciliation with Mary. Throckmorton was executed for treason in July 1584.

In 1585 Parliament passed the Act for the Queen's Safety. This law stated that any claimant to the throne found guilty of involvement in an invasion, rebellion, or plot, would be permanently barred from inheriting the throne. If Elizabeth were assassinated, the guilty parties would be caught and put to death. This, in effect, established the legal basis to execute Mary if she were found guilty of plotting Elizabeth's death.

The Babington plot

In 1586 Walsingham discovered a conspiracy led by Anthony Babington (1561–1586). Again, Walsingham suspected Mary of involvement. To obtain proof, he used an undercover agent, Gilbert Gifford, who was able to intercept Mary's letters. Finally Gifford discovered a letter from Mary to Babington that confirmed her support for his plot to assassinate Elizabeth.

Babington and the other conspirators were executed for treason in September 1586, and Mary was taken to Fotheringhay Castle in Northamptonshire. In October she was put on trial for treason. Though she presented a skillfully argued defense, she was found guilty and condemned to death.

Elizabeth's advisors urged her to sign Mary's execution warrant, but she hesitated for several months. The execution of a queen would cause intense political controversy, and Elizabeth wished to avoid such an extreme action. Finally, after demands from Parliament and persistent urgings from Cecil and Walsingham, Elizabeth reluctantly signed the warrant.

Execution

Cecil and Walsingham acted immediately and, without Elizabeth's knowledge, ordered the execution to take place. Mary was beheaded on February 8, 1587, at Fotheringhay Castle. Three hundred spectators, as well as her weeping attendants, witnessed the execution. Carefully dressed in a blood-red bodice with a crucifix around her neck, Mary knelt and prayed before the executioner struck. The first blow struck the back of her head where her blindfold was fastened. A second blow almost severed her neck, but a third blow of the axe was necessary to behead the queen of Scots.

After Mary was beheaded, the witnesses were horrified as her body appeared to move. But it was only her pet dog, which had been hidden in the folds of her dress during the entire proceedings. The animal reportedly refused to eat or rest after his mistress's execution and died soon afterward.

To eliminate the risk that her Catholic sympathizers might somehow get pieces of Mary's clothing or possessions and use them to create an image of her as a martyr (someone who dies for their faith), Walsingham ordered all of her possessions destroyed. The clothes from her dead body were removed and burned, as were her prayerbook and crucifix. Her body was sealed in a lead coffin and buried at Peterborough Cathedral. In 1612,

The beheading of Mary Stuart, Queen of Scots. © BETTMANN/CORBIS.

however, her son, James I, ordered her body removed from its original tomb and placed in the vault of King Henry VII's chapel in Westminster Abbey, London.

A symbol of the Catholic cause during her own life, Mary has continued to inspire admiration for several centuries after her death. Her story has inspired numerous books, films, and even an opera by Gaetano Donizetti (1797–1848). Many historians consider her a tragic figure who acted nobly, if sometimes unwisely.

For More Information

BOOKS

Dunn, Jane. *Elizabeth and Mary: Cousins, Rivals, Queens.* New York: Alfred A. Knopf, 2004.

Guy, John. *The True Life of Mary Stuart, Queen of Scots.* Boston and New York: Houghton Mifflin, 2004.

PERIODICALS

Wilkinson, Alexander. "Mary Queen of Scots and the French Connection." *History Today,* July 1, 2004.

WEB SITES

"Mary, Queen of Scots." *English History Net.* http://englishhistory.net/tudor/relative/maryqos.html (accessed on July 11, 2006).

"Mary, Queen of Scots." *Kings and Queens of Scotland.* http://www.royal.gov.uk/OutPut/Page134.asp (accessed on July 11, 2006).

Francis Walsingham

BORN: 1532 • Kent, England

DIED: September 6, 1590 • London, England

English statesman; spy

"There is less danger in fearing too much than too little."

Francis Walsingham, who served as secretary of state to **Queen Elizabeth I** (1533–1603; see entry), organized and ran a vast spy network that kept the English informed about the potentially dangerous activities of rival powers, especially France and Spain. He also oversaw spy operations within England itself. He uncovered several plots against the queen, including one supported by **Mary Stuart** (Queen of Scots; 1542–1590; see entry). The fact that Elizabeth lived to enjoy a long and prosperous reign was due in large part to the work Walsingham did to keep her safe from her many enemies.

Early life and education

Francis Walsingham was the only son of William Walsingham, a lawyer, and his wife, Joyce Denny. The family lived at Footscray in Kent, where Francis's birth most likely took place. William died when Francis was an infant, and Joyce Walsingham then married Sir John Carey, who was related by marriage to the family of Queen Elizabeth's mother, Anne Boleyn (1507–1536).

Francis Walsingham.
© BETTMANN/CORBIS.

235

Walsingham attended King's College at Cambridge University from 1548 to 1550, but he left without obtaining a degree. He spent the next two years traveling in Europe, where he learned Italian and French. When he returned to England he enrolled at Gray's Inn in London to prepare for a career in law and government. Soon after this, however, **Mary I** (1516–1558; see entry) became queen and began taking steps to restore the Roman Catholic religion in England.

Mary's father, **Henry VIII** (1491–1547; see entry), had rejected the authority of the Catholic pope and made himself the supreme head of the church in England. He took away property from Catholic monasteries and churches, and he outlawed the practice of the Catholic religion. He even executed Catholic leaders, including Sir Thomas More (1478–1535), who refused to accept his religious authority. Mary, however, had remained a Catholic, and she was determined to bring her religion back into power. To reduce Protestant power, she took away the Protestants' land and money. In many cases Protestants were convicted of heresy, or opinions that oppose established church doctrines (principles), and burned at the stake. England under Mary's rule was not a safe place for a loyal Protestant such as Walsingham.

The young Walsingham went back to Europe. He continued his study of languages, becoming one of the top linguists of his time. (Linguists study languages.) He also met many kinds of people and learned how to relate to them—a skill that would prove extremely valuable in his later career as a politician and spymaster.

After Elizabeth took the throne in 1558 and reestablished Protestant rule, Walsingham returned to England and began his political career. He was admitted to the bar as a lawyer in 1562 and the following year was elected to Parliament, England's legislative body. He married Ann Carteill, a widow with a son, in 1562. She died two years later, and in 1566 he married Ursula St. Barbe Worseley, the widow of Sir Richard Worseley. Ursula had two young sons from her first marriage, making Walsingham stepfather to three boys. But Ursula's sons were killed soon after the marriage; the boys had been playing with gunpowder when they died in an accidental explosion. Walsingham and his second wife had one daughter, Frances.

Diplomacy and espionage

The queen's secretary of state **William Cecil** (Lord Burghley; 1520–1598; see entry), soon discovered that Walsingham possessed great political talent. He employed Walsingham to find out whatever he could about foreign spies in London. Tensions were high at this time between England and its primary rivals, France and Spain, and Cecil needed to know in advance about any plots against England. Walsingham performed this job well, and Cecil recommended that the queen send him to France as her ambassador.

In France, which was still strongly Catholic, Walsingham tried to negotiate a marriage between Elizabeth and Henry (1551–1589), the brother of King Charles IX (1550–1574) of France. (Henry later became King Henry III.) This marriage would make France a strong ally of England and would help England overcome threats from Spain. But Elizabeth had no intention of marrying anyone, and Walsingham eventually abandoned this attempt. He went on to negotiate a defensive alliance between England and France, the Treaty of Blos, in 1572.

Later that year, when an uprising broke out against Spanish rule in the Netherlands, Walsingham convinced Charles IX to support the French Huguenots, Protestants who challenged Roman Catholic political power, who were aiding the rebels. After the rebels were defeated, though, the Huguenots faced increasing hostility in France. On August 24, 1572, rioting began in Paris as Catholic mobs raided Protestant districts of the city. The riots, which soon spread to other parts of the country, lasted for several days and resulted in the deaths of an estimated three thousand people in Paris alone. With anti-Protestant feeling at such an extreme, Walsingham felt it was dangerous for him to remain in Paris. He begged the queen to recall him to London, but she kept him at his ambassadorial post until 1573. By acting with great caution and diplomatic skill, Walsingham was able to establish friendly relations again with Charles's court before he finally left France. Even so, the traumatic experience of the St. Bartholomew's Day Massacre, as the event became known, hardened Walsingham's negative view of Catholics and made him even more determined to resist their cause in England.

After returning to London in December 1573, Walsingham was admitted to the queen's Privy Council, the board of advisors that carried out the administrative function of the government in matters of economy, defense, foreign policy, and law and order, and its members served as the queen's chief advisors. He also became secretary of state, a position he kept until his death. He was elected to Parliament again in 1576, and was knighted in 1577. (A knight is a man granted a rank of honor by the monarch for his personal merit or service to the country.) In 1578 he was named chancellor of the Order of the Garter, the most distinguished order of English knighthood. Though Walsingham was not wealthy, he supported artistic and scientific ventures, including voyages of exploration, when he could afford to do so. The writer **Richard Hakluyt** (1552–1616; see entry) dedicated the first edition of his tales of exploration to Walsingham in thanks for his support.

Organized spy network

By the late 1560s Cecil had grown more worried about Catholic plots against Elizabeth. Mary Stuart, a cousin of the queen and a Catholic, had been forced to step down as queen of Scotland, and she had fled to England in 1568 in hopes that Elizabeth would protect her. Though Elizabeth agreed to this, allowing Mary to live in England under guard, Cecil was extremely suspicious of Mary. He feared that she would inspire Catholics to overthrow Elizabeth and make Mary queen instead. Although he kept a close watch on Mary, Cecil soon realized that he needed a whole organization of spies to keep him adequately informed about possible conspiracies. He knew just the man to create and run such a network: Walsingham.

Walsingham excelled at this new job. He hired many new undercover agents, increasing the number of English spies to more than fifty. He recruited many spies at Oxford and Cambridge universities. Without sufficient funding from the government, he paid many of his agents from his own income. Walsingham established a spy school to give agents the professional training they needed. In addition to traveling and seeking information, for example, they needed to know how to decipher coded messages. Some codes simply replaced regular letters of the alphabet with a set of shuffled letters or symbols. In other cases conspirators used invisible ink, made of onion or lemon juice, to write secret messages that could not be seen under normal conditions. When the paper was held near a candle, the invisible words appeared. In another method of secret communication, conspirators would write out a message that seemed innocent. But when it was covered with another paper that had a series of holes punched in it, the letters and words that showed through the holes conveyed the secret message.

The queen trusted Walsingham, though she did not make him one of her favorites. She often said that he knew her mind well. Sometimes, as a joke, she called him her "Moor," a term that referred to dark-skinned people from North Africa, because he always dressed in dark clothing and had a dark complexion. More often, however, she called him her "Spirit," because he guided her government so well. Walsingham seemed to be everywhere and to know everything that was happening, not only in London but in foreign nations as well. He became known, and often feared, as a man who could discover any secret.

The Throckmorton plot

In 1583 Walsingham uncovered a plot involving Francis Throckmorton (1554–1584), an English Catholic. Throckmorton had traveled to Europe and had befriended English Catholics there who were devising a plan to remove Elizabeth from power. According to this plan, French troops would invade England, free Mary Stuart, and restore Catholicism. Throckmorton returned to London to organize communications.

Walsingham learned of the plan and had Throckmorton arrested. At the time of his arrest Throckmorton was encoding a letter to Mary Stuart. He also had a list with the names of his co-conspirators and papers that identified locations that would be poorly protected against invasion. Throckmorton denied everything at first, saying that the men who arrested him had planted the papers on him. But Walsingham refused to believe this. Throckmorton was tortured on the rack to make him confess. His wrists and ankles were tied to a frame that was then stretched to cause intense pain. Throckmorton refused to confess after his first day on the rack. Walsingham ordered another day of torture, after which Throckmorton gave a full confession.

Throckmorton was executed for treason in July 1584. As was the custom for those found guilty of serious crimes, he was hanged, drawn, and quartered. In this especially cruel type of execution, the condemned man was first hanged, then cut down while still alive, disemboweled, hacked into pieces, and finally beheaded. The Spanish ambassador to England, who had been one of Throckmorton's chief contacts, was expelled from London.

The Babington conspiracy

In 1586 Walsingham discovered that Mary Stuart was communicating with Anthony Babington (1561–1586), the leader of a group of English Catholics. Walsingham suspected that she was part of a conspiracy to assassinate Elizabeth, but he had no real proof. So he used an undercover agent, Gilbert Gifford, to help get evidence that would convict Mary of treason.

Political Assassinations

Francis Walsingham's secret service operated at a time when the threat of political assassinations was very real. Attempts to murder kings and nobles often succeeded. William the Silent (1533–1581), leader of the Netherlands, survived an assassination attempt in 1582 but was killed by an assassin two years later. Henry III (1551–1589) of France died in 1589 after being stabbed with a poison dagger. Poison was so feared as a political weapon that people sometimes blamed it for deaths that probably had resulted from natural causes. For example, people believed a rumor that an uncle of Mary Stuart had died after handling coins that had been dipped in poison. In fact historians believe it is more likely that he died from a disease. In later times a story arose concerning a plot to kill Elizabeth with a poison dress. There is no evidence, though, of any poisonous clothing ever being sent to her court.

An actual plot to poison Queen Elizabeth was discovered in 1594. Roderigo Lopez, a Jewish physician who had moved to London from Portugal, was found guilty of this crime and executed. Evidence at the time seemed to show that he had been hired by the king of Spain to assassinate Elizabeth. Some modern historians, however, have questioned whether Lopez was actually the guilty party.

Walsingham arranged for Gifford to act as a double agent. Pretending to sympathize with Mary, Gifford offered to carry letters between Mary and her supporters. He arranged for the letters that she sent and received to be placed in a beer barrel that was delivered to her residence, which was always under guard. Mary agreed to this plan, thinking that her communications would be hidden. But all of her messages were intercepted. Walsingham's agents deciphered the letters, reported their contents, resealed the letters, and sent them on to Mary as if nothing had happened. The correspondence continued without Mary suspecting that the government was aware of her secrets. Meanwhile, Walsingham ordered Gifford to befriend the English Catholics who were part of this plot. Gifford encouraged them to continue with their plans. Eventually he obtained what Walsingham needed: a letter from Mary to Babington that confirmed her support of the plot to assassinate the queen.

Walsingham had Babington and the other plotters arrested immediately. On September 13, 1586, they were tried and found guilty of treason. One week later they were hanged, drawn, and quartered in front of a huge crowd of onlookers.

Though Walsingham urged Queen Elizabeth to execute Mary Stuart, the queen wished to avoid this extreme action. Even after Parliament insisted that Elizabeth sign Mary's death warrant, the queen refused. Finally, after repeated urgings from Cecil and Walsingham, Elizabeth reluctantly signed the warrant. Cecil and Walsingham immediately ordered the execution to take place. Mary was beheaded on February 8, 1587. Walsingham also had Mary's dead body stripped, her clothes burned, and her corpse sealed in a lead case.

The queen regretted Mary's execution and was so angry that Walsingham at first feared for his own safety. But Elizabeth eventually realized that he had acted in her best interests. Meanwhile, Walsingham was receiving extensive reports about Spanish preparations to launch an invasion of England. He tried to convince the queen to prepare for war, but she was slow in taking his advice. Walsingham's agents in Spain continued to intercept letters and orders that detailed Spanish war plans. This intelligence helped England plan a strong defense when the Spanish Armada, or navy, sailed against England in 1588. After several inconclusive battles in the English Channel, the Armada was blown off course by tremendous winds. England chased the Spanish ships north. As the Armada attempted to return to Spain, it encountered a severe storm that destroyed most of its ships. With the Armada defeated, England was safe.

During the last few years of his life Walsingham suffered ill health and heartbreak. His daughter's husband, **Philip Sidney** (1554–1586; see entry), who had been Walsingham's close friend, died of an infected wound received during a military campaign against the Spanish in the Netherlands. Not only did Walsingham lose his good friend and son-in-law, but he also inherited Sidney's debts and faced significant financial hardship in paying them off. Though Walsingham hoped that the queen would grant him some financial favors, she declined. He lived in relative poverty after that, and died in debt on April 6, 1590. He was buried, as he had requested, at St. Paul's Church in London.

In creating the most modern and efficient secret service of his time, Walsingham did more than any other person to protect the queen's personal safety. His espionage system became a model for later government agencies such as the Secret Intelligence Service (MI6) in England and the Central Intelligence Agency (CIA) in the United States.

For More Information

BOOKS

Budiansky, Stephen. *Her Majesty's Spymaster: Elizabeth I, Sir Francis Walsingham, and the Birth of Modern Espionage.* New York: Viking, 2005.

PERIODICALS

Morris, Holly J. "Be Afraid, Be Very Afraid," *U.S. News & World Report,* January 27, 2003, p. 50.

WEB SITES

Briscoe, Alexandra. "Elizabeth's Spy Network." *BBC: Church and State: Monarchs and Leaders.* http://www.bbc.co.uk/history/state/monarchs_leaders/ spying_01.shtml (accessed on July 11, 2006).

"Conspiring Against the Queen." *Renaissance Secrets.* http://www.open2.net/ home/view?entityID=15184&jsp=themed_learning%2Fexpanding_viewer &sessionID=-1152639025080&Name=object (accessed on July 11, 2006).

Freer, Alan. "Francis Walsingham: Elizabethan Spymaster." *British Heritage.* http://www.historynet.com/bh/blelizabethanspymaster/index.html (accessed on July 11, 2006).

"Sir Francis Walsingham, Knight." *Tudor Place.* http://www.tudorplace.com.ar/ Bios/FrancisWalsingham.htm (accessed on July 11, 2006).

Where to Learn More

Books

Bernard, G. W. *The King's Reformation: Henry VIII and the Remaking of the English Church.* New Haven, CT and London: Yale University Press, 2005.

Brigden, Susan. *New Worlds, Lost Worlds: The Rule of the Tudors, 1485–1603.* New York: Penguin Books, 2000.

Brimacombe, Peter. *All the Queen's Men: The World of Elizabeth I.* New York: St. Martin's Press, 2000.

Bryant, Arthur. *The Elizabethan Deliverance.* New York: St. Martin's Press, 1981.

Dersin, Denise, ed. *What Life Was Like in the Realm of Elizabeth: England A.D. 1533–1603.* Alexandria, VA: Time-Warner Books, 1998.

Doran, Susan. *Queen Elizabeth I.* New York: New York University Press, 2003.

Dunn, Jane. *Elizabeth and Mary: Cousins, Rivals, Queens.* New York: Alfred A. Knopf, 2004.

Greenblatt, Stephen. *Will in the World: How Shakespeare Became Shakespeare.* New York: Norton, 2004.

Gregory, Brad S. *Salvation at Stake: Christian Martyrdom in Early Modern Europe.* Cambridge, MA and London, UK: Harvard University Press, 1999.

Hanson, Neil. *The Confident Hope of a Miracle: The True History of the Spanish Armada.* New York: Knopf, 2005.

Kirkpatrick, Robin. *The European Renaissance, 1400–1600.* Harlow, England: Pearson Education, 2002.

Martin, Colin and Geoffrey Parker. *The Spanish Armada.* New York: Norton, 1988.

Miller, Helen Hill. *Captains from Devon: The Great Elizabethan Seafarers Who Won the Oceans for England.* Chapel Hill, NC: Algonquin Books, 1985.

Morrill, John, ed. *The Oxford Illustrated History of Tudor & Stuart Britain.* Oxford, England and New York: Oxford University Press, 1996.

Orme, Nicholas. *Medieval Schools: From Roman Britain to Tudor England.* New Haven, CT and London, England: Yale University Press, 2006.

Palliser, D. M. *The Age of Elizabeth: England Under the Later Tudors, 1547–1603,* 2d ed. London and New York: Longman, 1992.

Picard, Liza. *Elizabeth's London: Everyday Life in Elizabethan London.* New York: St. Martin's Press, 2003.

Powicke, Sir Maurice. *The Reformation in England.* London: Oxford University Press, 1941.

Ridley, Jasper. *Bloody Mary's Martyrs: The Story of England's Terror.* New York: Carroll & Graf Publishers, 2001.

Rollins, Hyder E. and Herschel Baker, eds. *The Renaissance in England.* Boston: D. C. Heath and Company, 1954.

Rowse, A. L. *Eminent Elizabethans.* Athens: University of Georgia Press, 1983.

———. *The England of Elizabeth: The Structure of Society.* New York: Macmillan, 1961.

Ruoff, James E. *Major Elizabethan Poetry & Prose.* New York: Thomas Y. Crowell Company, 1972.

Schama, Simon. *A History of Britain: At the Edge of the World? 3500 BC–1603 AD.* New York: Hyperion, 2000.

Singman, Jeffrey L. *Daily Life in Elizabethan England.* Westport, CT and London, England: Greenwood Press, 1995.

Starkey, David. *Elizabeth: The Struggle for the Throne.* New York: Perennial, 2001.

Strachey, Lytton. *Elizabeth and Essex: A Tragic History.* Harvest Books, 2002.

Thomas, Jane Resh. *Behind the Mask: The Life of Queen Elizabeth I.* Boston, MA: Clarion Books, Houghton Mifflin, 1998.

Tillyard, E. M. W. *The Elizabethan World Picture.* New York: Vintage Books, 1942.

Watkins, Susan, with photographs by Mark Fiennes. *In Public and in Private: Elizabeth I and Her World.* London: Thames and Hudson, 1998.

Weir, Alison *The Life of Elizabeth I.* New York: Ballantine Books, 1998.

Wells, Stanley. *Shakespeare for All Time.* Oxford, England and New York: Oxford University Press, 2003.

Wightman, W. P. D. *Science in a Renaissance Society.* London: Hutchinson University Library, 1972.

Wood, Michael. *Shakespeare.* New York: Basic Books, 2003.

Web Sites

BBC: Historic Figures. http://www.bbc.co.uk/history/historic_figures/ (accessed July 11, 2006).

BBC History. http://www.bbc.co.uk/history/ (accessed on July 11, 2006).

Catholic Encyclopedia, http://www.newadvent.org/cathen/index.html (accessed on July 11, 2006).

Classic Literature Library: British Authors. http://www.classic-literature.co.uk/british-authors/ (accessed on July 11, 2006).

Educating Shakespeare. http://www.likesnail.org.uk/welcome-es.htm (accessed on July 24, 2006).

Elizabeth I. http://www.elizabethi.org/ (accessed on July 24, 2006).

Elizabeth's Pirates. http://www.channel4.com/history/microsites/H/history/pirates/ (accessed on July 11, 2006).

Elizabethan Authors. http://www.elizabethanauthors.com (accessed on July 11, 2006).

Elizabethan Costume Page. http://www.elizabethancostume.net (accessed on July 24, 2006).

Elizabethan Era. http://www.elizabethan-era.org.uk/ (accessed on July 11, 2006).

Elizabethan Holiday Customs. http://guildofstgeorge.com/holiday.htm (accessed on July 11, 2006).

Elizabethan Law Overview. http://www.twingroves.district96.k12.il.us/Renaissance/Courthouse/ElizaLaw.html (accessed on July 24, 2006).

English Bible History. http://www.greatsite.com/timeline-english-bible-history/ (accessed on July 11, 2006).

History of the British Monarchy. http://www.royal.gov.uk/output/Page1.asp (accessed on July 24, 2006).

In Search of Shakespeare. http://www.pbs.org/shakespeare/ (accessed on July 11, 2006).

The Marlowe Society. http://www.marlowe-society.org/ (accessed on July 11, 2006).

Mary, Queen of Scots. http://www.marie-stuart.co.uk/ (accessed on July 11, 2006).

Medieval History. http://www.medievalhistory.net (accessed on July 11, 2006).

Renaissance Central. http://www.rencentral.com (accessed on July 11, 2006).

Sir Francis Drake: A Pictorial Biography. Published in Amsterdam by N. Israel, 1970. Copyright © 1970 by H. P. Kraus. Library of Congress: Rare Books and Special Collections Reading Room. http://www.loc.gov/rr/rarebook/catalog/drake/ (accessed on July 11, 2006).

16th Century Renaissance English Literature. http://www.luminarium.org/renlit/ (accessed on July 11, 2006).

Shakespeare Homepage. http://www.shakespeare.org.uk/content/view/10/10/ (accessed on July 11, 2006).

Shakespeare's Life and Times. Internet Shakespeare Editions, University of Victoria: Victoria, BC, 2001–2005. http://ise.uvic.ca/Library/SLT/intro/introcite.html (accessed on July 11, 2006).

Shakespeare Online. http://www.shakespeare-online.com/index.html (accessed on July 11, 2006).

Shakespeare Resource Center. http://www.bardweb.net/ (accessed on July 11, 2006).

Sonnet Central. http://www.sonnets.org/eliz.htm (accessed on July 11, 2006).

Tudor England: 1485 to 1603. http://englishhistory.net/tudor.html (accessed on July 11, 2006).

Tudor History. http://tudorhistory.org (accessed on July 24, 2006).

Tudor Place. http://www.tudorplace.com.ar/ (accessed on July 11, 2006).

Index

Bold type indicates major entries. Illustrations are marked by (ill.).

E

East India Company, 100
Edict of Beaulieu (1567), 52
Edinburgh, Treaty of (1560), 144, 227
Edward II of England (1284–1327), 154
Edward II (Marlowe), 154
Edward IV (1442–1483), 119–20
Edward VI (1537–1553), 10, 26, 104, 210
    birth of, 82, 124
    death of, 38, 74, 85, 126, 143, 161
    education of, 83
    government of, 74, 84, 162
    Privy Council of, 162
    Protestant Church and, 84
    right to throne, 161
    Stuart, Mary and, 126, 141

Eliot, George, 22
Elizabeth, daughter of James I, 137
Elizabeth I (1533–1603), 81–93, 81 (ill.), 114, 210
    appearance of, 87
    Bacon and, 9
    birth and early childhood, 82, 122, 160
    Campion and, 19–20
    Catholics under rule of, 1
    Cecil as secretary of state, 27–30
    court of, 89–90, 187
    death of, 11, 93
    Dee and, 35, 39–41
    Devereux and, 92–93
    Dudley and, 19, 73–80, 87, 88
    education of, 83–84
    establishment of Church of England by, 2, 18–19
    foreign policy of, 25
    Bess of Harwick and, 105–6
    imprisonment of, during Mary I's rule, 85–86, 85 (ill.)
    knighting of Drake, 69, 69 (ill.)
    knighting of Hawkins, 117
    Knox and, 139
    last years of, 92–93
    Parr, Katherine and, 84
    Philip II and, 178, 179
    plots against, 45, 90–91, 150, 181–82
    privateers and, 64–65
    Privy Council of, 33
    question of succession and, 88–89, 126
    Raleigh and, 92–93, 189, 191–93
    religious settlement of 1559 and, 87–88
    Stuart, Mary and, 90–91, 240–41
    succession to throne, 81, 86–87
    theater and, 199
    Walsingham and, 235
    war with Spain and, 91–92
Elizabeth (ship), 67
Elisabeth of Valois (1548–1568), 180
Elizabeth of York, 119
Elizabethan theaters, 200–1, 200 (ill.)
Endymion, the Man in the Moon (Lyly), 76
England
    missionaries in, 4–5, 7, 21
    Protestant Reformation in, 84, 123
    relations between Spain and, 5, 31, 70–71, 91–92, 179